# The
# Potter's
## Professional Handbook

## Steven Branfman

Published by

**krause publications**

700 E. State Street • Iola, WI 54990-0001
Telephone: 715/445-2214

www.krause.com

Please call or write for our free catalog of publications. Our toll-free number to place an order or obtain a free catalog is 800-258-0929 or please use our regular telephone 715-445-2214 for editorial comment and further information.

Manufactured in the United States of America

Library of Congress Cataloging in Publication Data

Branfman, Steven
The Potter's Professional Handbook

ISBN 0-87341-678-3

1. pottery    2. business    3. title

98-84101
CIP

# Dedication

In our lives we encounter individuals who we see as being somehow "more" than us. Teachers, mentors, and friends who we have the opportunity to learn from. Celebrities we admire and perhaps envy. Some of these personalities make their marks in our lives in quiet ways that encourage us to reach to their level, while others remain forever distant and fantasy-like, giving us no inspiration to pursue a similar direction. If you are lucky, you might have an encounter with a person of greatness who appears distant, yet after time seems near. You're not a peer, though you are made to feel equal. You know you're not quite equal, yet you are made to feel important. Sidney Abend was such a man.

He was a man for all seasons—a sort of renaissance man with interests in music, theater, science, art, and sports. He was able to communicate without speaking, hear without listening, and see without looking. An Eastern philosopher? No, but Sidney was always—and in all ways—gentle, careful in his expression, and above all, humble. Most noble was his consistent desire to be out of the spotlight, shying away from accolades and appreciative gestures. What he did for family and friends was done for them entirely, providing for others without expectation of recompense.

I met, no encountered, Sidney almost 30 years ago. I was a long-haired just-back-from-Woodstock artist-to-be—not exactly Sidney's idea of a model citizen with proper aspirations. He was rigid, and in my 16-year-old eyes, close minded and ignorant. We battled (I lost). We discussed (I was wrong). We both stood up for what we believed in and I was not disparaged.

A potter? He was skeptical and his restrained praise for my studies and my work was evident. Did he disapprove? No. By watching me, monitoring my work, and recognizing my passion, he was learning what he didn't understand. It took a while (I think he was testing my perseverance) but I did begin to sense a respect and appreciation ultimately growing to love and understanding. Much to the surprise of his peers, he became my greatest advocate. When my first book was published, he embraced it, showed it to all who came into his house, and cherished it. His pride in me and my accomplishment was electric. He would have been even more delighted to have seen this manuscript reach fruition.

Sidney was my father-in-law. He was wise beyond comprehension. Memories are inadequate, and that's the way it should be. This book is for Sidney. I miss him every day.

# Table of Contents

# Foreword

When Steven Branfman first told me he was going to write a book about what it meant to embark on a pottery career my first thought was, "Oh no, not another one." In fact, I guess I told him as much. He then sent me the typescript of the first part of the book and I realized that this just might be a different approach to the problems of becoming a serious potter. I have to say that I have never met Steven, yet we have talked on the phone many times. Reading this book is like sitting across a table from him while the two of us explore his knowledge of ceramics, which is extremely broad, and he carefully opens my eyes to the problems, the technical questions, and the joys of jumping in with both feet.

Branfman has extensive experience in running a ceramic business that includes a school, a pottery supply business, open studio spaces, rental firing space, a gallery, a mail order book and video business, and his own studio space. The story of how he got into it is engaging and I will not spoil it for you, since he will take you through all of the intricacies during the course of this book. What is important is that he uses his experience to introduce you to the entire situation, beginning with the differences between machine and handmade objects and the reasons for each. After all, one has to be a little crazy to buy a bowl to eat cereal out of for $30 when the machine made one available at the local discount store for $3.95 does almost the same thing.

Starting from this essay, Branfman leads you through his lifetime of experiences. If this sounds dull, I want to disabuse you of that thought. It is a roller coaster of ideas and answers that are always interesting and also challenging. There are no easy answers or quick fixes. Instead he tries to challenge the reader to find solutions after giving the facts and suggesting directions.

Steven Branfman draws on his own life to point ways and suggest choices, but in the end he expects every person to do it their own way. In this, he is what we all aspire to be, a good teacher. This is an incredibly rich book and I hope you enjoy it.

Warren MacKenzie
Stillwater, Minnesota
June, 1998

# Acknowledgments

I could not have done this alone and I would like to acknowledge some special people who have helped me along the way; not only in the concept and completion of this book but in the unfolding of my career as a potter, teacher, writer, and business owner.

My parents, Dorrise and Irwin, gave me a strong sense of the value of art and the power of dedication, concentration, and focus, and I will forever be grateful for that. My teachers and mentors at Cortland State College; the late Gerry Diguisto (to whom I dedicated my first book), Steven Barbash, George Dugan, John Jessiman, and others, provided a rigorous program, giving me a sound foundation of art and craft studies. Norm Shulman, my teacher at Rhode Island School of Design, took a chance with a young student who wanted to be a potter and changed his life.

Once again, thanks go out to Carol Temkin and Jodine Kuhlman, my right and left hands at The Potters Shop and School, for taking up the slack and giving me time off to finish this work.

My good friend Dan Levinson gets my thanks for his friendship and support and for taking the time to read over the manuscript. His critical clarity and suggestions were very helpful. Thanks to my friend David Mason for his review and helpful suggestions of portions of my work. Never a conversation went by without Ruth Abend, my mother-in-law, asking me how the book was coming. If it wasn't for you, I might have forgotten I was working on one!

My career would not be where it is today if not for a number of people at Thayer Academy. Former headmaster Peter Benelli had the courage to allow a creative scheduling idea, paving the way for my professional future. Thanks go to current headmaster Eric Swain and principal Michael Clarke for their continued support for what I do both in and out of the classroom; Donna Milani Luther, former Head of Fine Arts, and Jeff Browne, current Department Head, for their unyielding appreciation and encouragement; and my close colleague and teaching mentor William Ross Searle, with whom I have worked side by side for the past 21 years. We have seen each other's art (and families) grow, mature, and flourish and his honest insights have become essential elements in my pots. Bill has always had an open mind and an eye towards balance while he championed my endeavors and accepted my sometimes unorthodox methods of doing things. I owe a debt to my students as well, who always keep me alert, fresh, and primed for new perspectives.

My appreciation goes out to Barbara Case, my editor at Krause, who inherited this project and worked with me to see it through, and to Don Gulbrandsen, managing editor, who had the confidence in me that was so critical.

Richard Aerni, Jackie Allen, Steven Barisof, Barbara Brown, Tom Buck, Bill Capshaw, George Dymesich, Dan Finch, Bill Geisinger, Sandy and Bob Kinzie, Catherine Merrill, Bryan McGrath, Neil Moss, and others, invited me into their studios and homes and shared their stories and experiences with great honesty and candor. Those visits were of immense help. Thank you. Vincente Clemente loaned me some treasures from his library that were a treat to read and helpful to my writing. Thank you. And to those individuals whose photos, drawings, or comments appear directly in the text, I say a hearty thank you. The generosity that craftspeople extend to each other is one of the most wonderful things about being a potter and goes to our common interest in sharing knowledge and passing on information.

Hal Reigger, potter emeritus, and I began a respectful correspondence in 1988 that quickly grew into a meaningful friendship. His keenness of perception, aesthetic convictions, and personal integrity have profoundly influenced my work. Thank you Hal.

My wife and children all had to endure my sometimes solitary and short tempered behavior, especially while I worked on the final stages of the manuscript. Ellen's pride in me is always evident and her support and understanding for what I do is extraordinary. Eight years ago, while I was writing *Raku*, Jared and Adam had to relinquish their computer time, doing without the games Brickles and Tetris. Now they are older, with the stakes more serious, yet they still sacrificed important Internet access, research time, and school work to their dad's computer use. Ellen, Jared, and Adam, you are the most important, everything else is second. Thanks and I love you!

# Introduction

Here I go again. My second full length literary effort. My first book, *Raku: A Practical Approach* specifically addressed the raku process with all its intricacies, variables, and methods. While writing a book is never a simple task (as I naively discovered), in many ways that project was about as easy as a book writing project could have been. Being a teacher and raku potter, the areas to cover, the information to include, and the way to address it all came quite naturally to me. Having taught the raku technique for quite some time, I guess I had been writing the book all those years without realizing it. Furthermore, the subject of raku—while grand in its possibilities and aesthetic, and of course deeply rooted in history and culture—is limited in its focus. *The Potter's Professional Handbook,* however, is another story. Again, I call on my experience as a potter and teacher, but I also summon up my business, philosophical, and practical experience which is not quite as easy to organize and put into words.

In this book, my objective is to address the needs of those individuals who wish to take the next step in their involvement with clay. This next step may involve arranging and outfitting your first studio space or building one from scratch. It may mean your first attempts at marketing your wares or trying to figure out how you can extract hidden hours from your weekly schedule to devote more time to your clay work. You may have just graduated from college or art school and are looking for some guidance in getting your career off the ground. You may have spent your entire life to date in a more conventional career while harboring a passion for clay and now you'd like to bring pottery to the forefront of your life. But whatever your particular situation is, you all share in the goal of making the transition from what has been either a limited, incomplete, part-time (either emotionally or actually), or student affair with clay, to one that is more engrossing, more serious, more time consuming, independent, and more professional, if you will.

Many of you are, by facts of circumstance, very part-time potters. No value judgment is being made regarding the earnestness of your current approach to clay. However, when you are engaged in an activity, your degree of involvement intellectually, physically, and emotionally, as well as your eventual expertise in that discipline, is directly affected by the amount of time you can spend doing it. While you can certainly learn to use your available time more efficiently, thereby increasing your involvement, your goal may be to decrease the amount of time you spend in your current job (or eliminate it altogether) in order to be a more full-time craftsperson.

When I finished art school and began my career as a potter, I had little—as a matter of fact, I had no—formal education in the areas of career planning, business, studio design, establishing myself as a professional, or any of the themes I discuss in this book. Too bad. However, I did have two important bits of experience—one that I realized I had and knew how to use, and another that I had no idea how to utilize or even the realization that it was an asset. What I knew was that I was the owner of a first rate education in the historical, cultural, technical, and aesthetic aspects of my craft. This I knew how to begin to use. I had made so much mud (as my son Jared calls it) as a student that I was prepared and ready to hit the real world and make more mud. My teachers—who were all practicing, professional potters and artists—were the asset I didn't know I had. Oh, I knew that while I was a student they were valuable to me, and of course, they had taught me all I knew about clay. However, while my experience with them was instrumental in establishing my knowledge of clay and my ultimate move towards a career in pottery, they hadn't taught me squat about the nitty gritty information necessary to successfully practice a craft away from the safe, nurturing haven of school. Mind you, it's not that they were bad teachers or that they necessarily kept helpful information from me. There are good reasons to limit the focus in school to learning the craft, its aesthetics, intellect, and technical scope (more on that later). Having been taught to

*Figure I-1. **Author**. Covered Jar. 1978. Wheel-thrown porcelain, 10" H, electric fired. (Photo by author)*

look beyond my immediate influences and surroundings, I observed and noted the well known potters (the celebrities, if you will) as well as some local potters with regional followings and reputations. They seemed to be exactly where I wanted to be. Of course, it was all circumstantial and I was young and naive. I didn't really know anything about their lifestyles or professional careers. How could I expect to? Still, I wanted to be like them, so I thought. It wasn't until much later that I realized that I probably had much, if not all, the information and many of the answers I needed to get a professional approach to pottery making off to a high flying start right there locked up for safekeeping in the minds of those teachers I mentioned before. At the time, I couldn't unlock it.

I was ready, but how to know the questions? As you might surmise, there was no literature that offered an insightful, logical guide through the maze of how to go about seriously pursuing a career in clay. Just like today, there were many books that contained a mention of, or perhaps even a longer section on pottery as a profession, but they were all so incomplete. Only as I began my career did I begin to identify and ask the questions. How do I design a studio? Where do I find a suitable space or location for one? Where do I buy supplies? Can I make money at this? How do I measure my success? Will my mother approve? And on and on and on…

I have learned that being a professional *anything* is much more than simply looking and acting the part. It goes well beyond the elementary interest in selling your work and is much more complex than handing out business cards. In fact, while marketing and selling may be the activities that make it financially possible for many to pursue pottery, you will see that the active pursuit of selling your work is not paramount or even necessary for you to view yourself as a "professional."

You and I have a common bond, a mutual interest that brings us together—a love of clay and handmade objects and the desire to be able to devote as much time, energy, intellect, and overall focus to our craft as possible. Hopefully, we also want to develop and continually deepen our cognizance of what drives this love of craft in ourselves and in others whom we may be drawn to, be interested in, or otherwise admire.

If your present level of experience, expertise, or professionalism is elementary, and labeling yourself professional seems presumptuous, you may question the relevance of this study for you. However, regardless of your preconceptions, there is much to be learned about a professional approach that will have a direct influence on how you pursue your craft. Being professional is as much a state of mind and attitude about yourself and your work as it is a measure of your accomplishments, sales, exhibitions, and degree of recognition. If this concept is a revelation to you or seems like a way to justify labeling anyone's involvement in craft as professional, then this book is absolutely for you!

I have been a studio potter since 1975. During this time I have operated a studio, founded my own pottery school, workspace, and clay-related business, and taught all ages and ability levels in public and private schools, art centers, and college. I have marketed my ceramics through galleries, shops, fairs, and catalogs. I have written books and articles and lectured on various aspects of ceramics. I am successful at what I do, even moderately well known. So in writing this book, what separates me from those late night info-mercial hawkers? (You know, the real estate moguls who make their money from talking instead of doing.) Very significantly, I do all the things I talk about and I wouldn't have it any other way. For me, the desire to be completely immersed in clay activities is what overwhelmingly drives my career interests. And it is a broad range of clay-related activities that helps keep my enthusiasm feverish and fresh and my interest in clay alive and vibrant.

The last thing I want anyone to subscribe to is the belief that your career or other serious professional activity has to occupy all your time and energy. Yes, I do have a life outside of clay! (And so can you.) Do you have to make a living from your craft to be professional? Do you have to be the best potter on your block? Must you have your own studio, furnished with every conceivable piece of equipment? Read on and you will see how being a professional cannot only apply to you, but can be of great benefit and importance in your continued work with clay. You will see that a professional approach can help insure in you a constantly evolving feeling of interest, growth, involvement, and love of your craft. And that's what this is all about!

As a young writer beginning work on *Raku: A Practical Approach*, I was advised not to tell the reader what the book was not about. It seemed to make good sense. Indeed, since I thought I knew everything there was to know about raku, following that advice was a piece of cake. Though that book has been a success and very well received by the clay community, writing it showed me that there was plenty about raku I didn't know. Just as well, I'll have something to add in a revised edition. I have since become much more humble and have recognized from the start that for this book, there are subject areas in which I have no expertise and there are subjects that, while appropriate and appealing to write about, would have extended the book beyond a reasonable length.

*The Potter's Professional Handbook* is not a turnkey operation. You won't find step-by-step instructions on building a studio, getting incorporated, or repairing a wheel. You'll not find "Ten Tips for a Successful Craft Booth" or "Five Steps to Financial Independence Through Clay." I have no interest in presenting an oversimplification of our profession, nor would I ever trivialize your ideals, interests, goals, and expectations. I have patterned my teaching style after the philosophy that a good teacher teaches their students to be thinkers, problem solvers, to show resourcefulness, and to use knowledge and experience as a ticket to the next adventure. Remember the adage, "Give a man a fish and you feed him for a day. Teach a man to fish and you feed him for a lifetime." This book is not about being fed.

In my conversations with craftspeople and through my own experience as a potter, teacher, writer, and business operator, I have become aware of some common themes shared by those who have forged successful craft practices and who appear to lead productive, rewarding, and satisfying lives. Among these are an uncontrollable drive, a sincere interest in always learning and expanding their abilities and experiences, and a desire for something unconventional in their lifestyles. Perhaps the most important is a characteristic and theme that will surface over and over again throughout these pages and one that has guided and directed me more than anything else. That is, a deep emotional passion for their craft.

*The Potter's Professional Handbook* is a practical guide, but make no mistake—it is not a blueprint. More importantly, it is about thinking and learning. It is about confidence and courage. It is about figuring out where you are right now, where you might want to be, and how to begin the journey. This is a book about learning how to fish, so get out the pole and let's go.

*Steven Branfman*

# Chapter 1

## The Professional Potter: Making a Career in Crafts

*Art is not a matter of giving people a little pleasure in their time off. It is, in the long run, a matter of holding together a civilization.*
--David Pye, author of *The Nature and Aesthetics of Design* and *The Nature and Art of Workmanship*

### What is a Professional?

I have already bantered around the term "professional" enough times to make you dizzy. Now I'll try to define the term in some meaningful way. One widely accepted understanding is that a professional is someone who engages in an occupation requiring specialized knowledge and academic training. While the notion of specialized knowledge is absolutely true, not all professional occupations, including pottery, require academic or school training. Furthermore, along with this traditional interpretation usually comes the supposition that a professional derives their income (or a substantial portion of it) from this profession.

Many of you have learned your craft outside a formal educational institution and a great number of successful, even well known craftspeople do not derive the bulk of their income from the practice of their craft. I propose that the making of art craft objects, being an unorthodox occupation in this era and western culture, requires an alternative approach when it comes to defining it as a profession and defining its practitioner as a professional. Remember, we are talking about our approach to pottery, not an IRS-approved definition of a professional career activity!

Being a professional craftsperson involves much more than creating objects. We have certain responsibilities, not only to the integrity of our craft, but to society. Our contemporary western culture has placed a serious burden on those of us who make art craft objects on more than an occasional or hobby basis. This burden is the de facto responsibility placed on us for educating the public about crafts. We may choose to ignore this charge, and many do. But when we do, the audience for our craft efforts is greatly reduced. From my perspective, this mandate to educate people about what we do to attain a degree of respectability and serious presence is unusual, if not unique, to our profession. Understand that I am not referring to a situation where artists and craftspeople explain their work to justify spending public funds or to compete for a grant. These situations are comprehensible, palpable, and a necessary part of the system. I am talking about a potter having to explain their interest in clay to keep people from laughing at what they do!

When I was studying clay and studio art in college (not art school), my non-art friends would refer to me (in a pejorative yet charming sense) as "majoring in hobbies." Unquestionably, this was a burden. On the other hand, having to explain our craft and educate the public forces us into an intellectual confrontation that can serve us well. For integral to the creation of successful craft objects is not only mastery of craft techniques and aesthetics, but a cognitive understanding of what we purport to do. To us, our involvement in clay is elemental—serious, important, and requires no explanation or justification. But to others, it is not so clear. Its significance can be as individual and personal as an indefinable inner drive to make pots and be around clay, to a philosophy that places your efforts in the thick of human endeavors. It is a belief that espouses the making of craft objects as an integral aspect of human existence and that these objects not only better society, but help to define our culture and the human race. We go here from a drive that seems to affect a single individual to one that places the craft creator in the greater context of human emotion and existence.

Why differentiate between "occasional" practitioners and those of us who spend more time in the craft? It seems it is easy for some to dismiss an individual's interest and involvement in a craft as harmless and frivolous if only a limited amount of time is spent at it. It is a diversion, a hobby—unimportant and not too serious. It is done once or twice a week and the objects created are "cute," "lovely," "very nice." However, once the amount of time spent becomes greater than what's considered appropriate for an avocation, those same people become less tolerant. It's not within the realm of their experience or understanding to accept what we do as a crucial or critical behavior. Often, we are put in the position of having to justify our engagement in this hobby exercise.

So for me and many others, a professional is one who engages in their craft with a serious mind towards intellectual, aesthetic, and personal achievements and satisfactions. It is one who maintains the utmost respect and esteem for the craft while continually striving for excellence through increased knowledge and experience. It is one for whom an honest approach and effort is more important than the finished craft object.

## The Living Crafts

*What is a craftsman? He is a person who is impelled by an inner necessity to learn the language of materials and constantly explore their possibilities; to think of new uses for old materials and functional, aesthetic uses for new materials. He is one who must exercise great self discipline and knows that he must be willing to labor long and lovingly before he earns his freedom of expression. He is one who is always making great demands upon his powers of choice and wisdom. He must have a knowledge of tradition in its true perspective and be able to judge the present on the basis of the past. He must have the ability to interpret what he "feel-sees" into a three-dimensional material in a manner suited to its use and aesthetically appealing. He uses his judgment as an instrument, which is sensitized by the conditions of his times and geography as well as by the necessity of his own personal expression and experience. Like the musician who takes a simple little folk tune and makes it pulsate with symphonic flesh and blood, the artist-craftsman is one who, from a humble material such as clay, metal, or yarn, creates an object of beauty to delight the senses of touch and sight as well as give comfort in use.*

*The most direct link to the humanistic is the creative craftsman. Internationally, he is the one whose products speak most directly and constructively to his fellow men and help to bring them into closer communion.*

*Thus, the hunger from the humanistic element in our surroundings is fulfilled. Perhaps technology will someday be able to dispense with the craftsmen who serve science and those who man the machines in industry. But the creative craftsman who searches for his own heart and mind and is dedicated to serve the aesthetic needs of his fellow men will always be necessary to a balanced society.*

*--Just Lunning, vice president of The Artist/Craftsman of New York,* Crafts Horizons Magazine, *May/June 1960*

## The Role of Handmade Objects in Contemporary Society

If you can find it in your heart to excuse the social and political incorrectness of the gender references in Mr. Lunning's remarks, I'm sure you will find them, as I did, to be thought provoking and perhaps even visceral and essential to our own personal connections to craft making and the appreciation and importance of the craft object. It was only through very recent serendipity that I came across this piece and when I did, it was as though an unknown yet familiar voice was talking to me and for me. The words echoed my own feelings and at the same time gave credence and validity to a feeling about crafts that had been fermenting within me for my entire career. I don't

know the writer, his background, or subsequent story, yet I can't help but feel a kinship. Making our feelings about craft and our craft involvement a more integral part of our lives and perhaps to even help elevate crafts to a more prominent place in our society is important to us.

To help us to better identify our own professional direction, goals, our craft raison d'etre if you will, it would be helpful to gain some insight and understanding as to where craft producers and the objects they produce currently fit into our culture and what, if any, relevance handmade objects have in contemporary society.

I am intimately involved with crafts—making them, using them, evaluating them, and teaching about them. Art, and crafts especially, is my heartbeat; its existence in my life is necessary.

*Figure 1-1.* **Jill Gross**. *Mardis Gras Cups. 1998. Wheel-thrown porcelain, 5" H, underglaze decoration. (Photo by Warren Patterson)*

My feelings about the use of handmade objects, though, arise from an even deeper source. It is a desire that seems to be unconscious and involuntary. Just as my desire and drive to make objects is elemental to my personality, lifestyle, and profession, so is my interest, desire, and need to use and surround myself with handmade objects. It is an absolutely difficult conviction to explain. One might think it natural that there would be a relationship between a craftsperson's interest in *making* and *using* handmade objects. Not necessarily! Experience has taught me that just because someone is a craftsperson or artist doesn't necessarily predispose them to a lifestyle surrounded by handmade objects. It may surprise you to know that I have several friends in the crafts and arts, and have come across others in my professional travels, who clearly do not make any effort to utilize handmade objects over machine made ones. Perhaps you share the same attitude or know others who do. I would guess that most of this book's readers are more likely to share convictions similar to mine towards crafts and handmade objects than not.

I have, of course, talked about this subject many times, mostly in the context of a pottery workshop or demonstration I was presenting. When the inevitable questions are asked about my training and how I became involved in pottery, my dialogue almost always includes some mention of my desire to surround myself with handmade objects. So, when we talk about the role of the craftsperson and handcrafted objects in contemporary society, we need to attempt to answer some key questions.

1) What is the significance, if any, of handmade objects as opposed to machine or mass produced ones?

2) Should we make an effort to use handmade objects over their machine made counterparts?

3) Does the handcrafted nature of an object somehow contribute to its enjoyment by the user and to the quality of life?

Take a moment to examine your surroundings—clothes, jewelry, wallet, handbag, briefcase. Your home—furniture, kitchen utensils, dishes, appliances, woodwork, home construction, wallpaper, floor coverings. How many of the objects that surround you on an everyday basis can you identify as handmade? There are probably at least a few, though I'd guess that for most of us, the answer is not many. For some, the answer might even be none! If you can identify some, how many of them have you consciously chosen over their machine made counterparts? This brief assessment might lead you to assume that there is little significance in the use of handmade objects and this notion bothers me. I hope that through this discussion, you will find that there is no need for a sophisticated appreciation of art, craft, and the human creative drive, nor is it necessary to be the maker of objects to appreciate the existence and use of a handmade object over a mass produced one. You may also come to realize (if you don't already) that an increase in the use of handmade objects can be a source of joy and unparalleled pleasure. I will even go so far as to say that the use of handmade objects has a profoundly positive effect on society and our relationships with one another. (I may not have much proof to back that up, but I will say it anyway!) The short answer, therefore, is a resounding yes, handmade objects are absolutely important in our lives!

Of course, the question is not as simple as it may seem and neither is an answer to it. To really understand and discuss the issue intelligently, we must expand its context significantly. For the

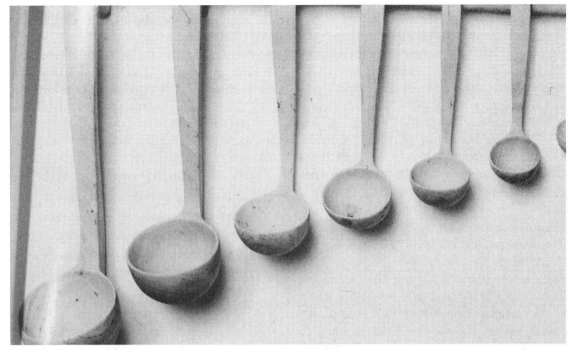

*Figure 1-2.* **Algot Nordstrom**. *Wooden Ladles. From In Praise of Hands, New York Graphic Society, Greenwich. 1974. While these objects may be unremarkable in their design, for many there is comfort and humanity in using them instead of their machine made counterparts.*

making, use, and appreciation of handcrafted objects are obviously no longer the norm and no longer conform to universal cultural standards as we enter the 21st century. Though the focus here is on the relevance of the handmade object and whether there is any special significance to its use over a mass produced counterpart, a discussion of craft objects in any context must also include mention of aesthetics, function verses form, history, and other aspects of the individual creative process.

Much to my disappointment (although not at all to my surprise), I am too often asked why one should bother with handmade craft objects? Why make them, why choose them, why use them at all? This attitude is not new to me. You will recall that I had been labeled as a hobby major in college! Indeed, in the face of popular sensibilities that find it difficult to differentiate between the mass produced mug with the words "I Love You THIS Much" emblazoned across its face at the department store checkout line and its finely handcrafted distant cousin made by an individual's hand, the task does seem daunting. To many, there seems no possible justification for paying $15 for that so-called handmade mug when the one for $1.98 keeps tea just as hot and holds just as much. As a matter of fact, it works better! It is perfectly shaped and smooth as glass with not a single imperfection. Each one is exactly the same (important for matching sets) and if one breaks, it can be replaced with a flawless duplicate.

Today, speed, accuracy, uniformity, and efficiency guide much, if not most of our work ethic, work environments, and for that matter, careers. It's no wonder so many people find it hard to connect with our desire and drive to be craftspeople. Equally understandable is their lack of sensitivity to the handmade object. Many individuals not involved in the arts see these societal objectives as being in conflict with the desire to be a craftsperson. Rather than being in conflict with this desire, these objectives are simply in conflict with the way potters go about their craft involvement. I and others see them as compelling reasons for becoming a craftsperson and for using handmade objects.

To coalesce the entire value of the craft object into a difference of $13 is, of course, ludicrous and trivializes the entire issue. However, we mustn't ignore cost as a factor in the decision to utilize a handmade object over a machine made one. As a craftsperson, I mustn't take my own perception of the value of the object for granted. Worse still would be if I idly sat by while the rest of the world is perfectly satisfied with the $1.98 mug.

The first order of business is to put some parameters on what is considered, for this discussion, a handmade object. A case can be made— since all objects come in contact with human hands during some phase of their manufacture— that all objects can be considered at least partially handmade. No definition or justification like that will hold water in this room tonight! I propose to begin to categorize a handmade object using the following criteria:

1) All the components of the object are hand wrought.
2) All the assembly is performed by human hands.
3) All tools used in making the object are controlled by hand.

While I think these criteria are for the most part valid, we are undoubtedly going to run into some trouble somewhere along the way. There is a clear distinction between the machine made coffee mug at one end of the production spectrum and the mug made in the studio by the stoneware potter. But what about other examples of machine made objects that are more aesthetically pleasing? This brings up some additional important considerations when weighing the importance and relevance of handmade vs. mass produced or machine made objects.

1) Is the handmade object inherently better than one not considered handmade?
2) Can a distinction be made between mass produced and machine made objects?
3) If a series of objects are mass produced, does that characteristic of their production remove them from being considered handmade?
4) What is the connection between the design phase of an object and its actual production?
5) If an object is designed and a prototype made by hand but the production pieces are produced by machine, is it handmade or machine made?

Clearly this issue of definition is a quagmire, but using the before mentioned criteria and agreeing to leave some margin for interpretation, I think we can move on. In the context of this discussion, there's the added feature of function to differentiate between objects that, while produced by hand, are designed to be looked at and appreciated as aesthetic objects only (fine arts, if you will). Critical to my belief that handcrafted objects are important in our lives is that the objects are mostly common and for daily use. The purchase and appreciation of nonfunctional art objects such as paintings, drawings, prints, photos, etc., is unremarkable, not to be extolled, easy. It's a rare household that doesn't have some kind of decorative objects adorning the home. Not that important decisions don't have to be made. Does it fit over the couch? Does the color go with the carpet? What will the neighbors think? It is easy because it can be undertaken and understood in the same context as hanging bath towels or pushing the chair under the table. Decorating with art is a finite activity with clearly defined borders and need not have any emotional ties between the objects and the owner. I'm not suggesting that the act of choosing and displaying art objects is trivial or superficial. Clearly, some individuals are more discriminating than others and for many, choosing art objects is filled with emotion, intellect, and a highly critical aesthetic. The decision to choose a handmade object over a machine made one when the object is a common and functional one is much more extraordinary. This decision requires premeditation, sensitivity, sophistication, deep thinking, and an alternative way of looking at daily existence.

The following anecdote illustrates exactly what I mean. In preparing to deliver a lecture on this very subject, I went on a search for common objects that exist in both machine made and handmade versions that I could show as examples. I had remembered seeing an exhibit of handmade fire fighter helmets at a museum and I recalled that they were, to this day, made by hand. The fact was confirmed by the owner of a fire fighting equipment company in Rhode Island who told me the making of the leather helmets involved many detailed steps that no machine could do as well.

His description was rather excited and I began to get the feeling that even though he was not a helmet user, he did have a certain pride about their manufacture. I pressed further about whether there were also machine made helmets and how they compared to the handmade ones. He went on to tell me that there are plastic helmets made by machine. They are much cheaper ($125 vs. $400), will withstand greater impact, and are lighter in weight. So why do fire departments still choose the leather ones? "Out of tradition and appearance," he answered. "That's wonderful," I said, adding a comment about using a handmade object over a machine made one in an area that is so functional, so industrial, and so removed from art. He then made sure to clarify his position on the subject. "Absolutely foolish," he said.

The moment early man fashioned the first object and became the first craftsman, so began the history of crafts. All people were craftsmen, crafting objects out of necessity and all objects were handcrafted. Craft skills were taught to children as a matter of future survival. All family members contributed to the production of the object, with individual responsibilities delegated according to skill level and physical abilities. As culture and societies developed and community needs expanded, people began to specialize in certain craft skills. Most often, objects were bartered and the craftsperson was at least equal in standing to any other person in the community. As classes of citizens became part of the society's structure, craft objects and craftspersons began to take on different meanings and occupy different positions in the hierarchy. Continuing social evolution, along with advances in technology, particularly in the areas of materials gathering and handling and manufacturing, contributed to somewhat of a craft irony—a decline in the social position of craft makers in the midst of a rise in the attraction of fine handcrafted objects. Citizens with more education, wealth, and discriminating taste demanded higher quality and more artistic interpretations of their daily objects. Individuals of modest means, but no less need for functional items, were provided with cruder versions of the same objects. So began the distinctions made between fine art, art crafts, and crafts.

Despite the continuing gap between so-called "fine crafts" and everyday functional crafts, prior

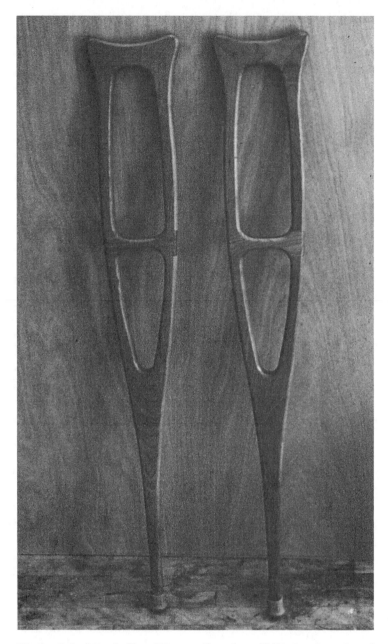

*Figure 1-3.* **Joseph Van Benten**. *Crutches. 1985. Laminated and hand-carved Bubinga wood, 48" L. These were not made as an exhibition piece but rather for an individual whose daily mobility depended on them. Like a shovel or a carpenter's level, not many people would even think of crutches as a potential handcrafted object anymore. (Photo by author)*

to recent technology (within the last 100 years), all functional objects were handmade. Potters, coopers, metalworkers, weavers, and carpenters all handcrafted their products. The citizens and society that used these products did so naturally, without regarding their handcrafted nature. After all, what else was there? There was no choice regarding whether or not to purchase and use a handmade object. But there *were* choices to be made. In the case of kitchenware, there were varying degrees of quality and craftsmanship available. But all the objects—from the least expensive to the most distinctive and extraordinary—shared the commonality of being handmade.

Handmade objects and their use influence our society by affecting (among other things) the interaction between people. Prior to the proliferation of industrial means, through hand production the maker and user shared a common humanistic bond. Unspoken, unrecognized as special, and transparent as it may have been, it existed nevertheless. The craftsperson lived the connection between the materials used in the creation of the product and the creation of the product itself. It was (and continues to be) a connection with nature, with the earth. The user too shared in that connection through the object and through the craftsperson. For barrels, the customer went to the cooper. For crockery, to the potter and so on. Even when these objects were purchased in the general store, their character spoke of handcraftedness; each one was slightly individual because of a minor imperfection or blemish. These everyday objects were not produced by the craftsperson for exhibition or artistic expression. They contained human characteristics, including a dialogue between the maker, the object, and its user. They possessed a human spirit. They were honest efforts. They exuded the knowledge that this jug

(or stool, or boots) were built by the human hand and heart.

Another societal influence of handmade objects was the fact that through handcrafted work, individuals were more physically engaged, much less sedentary, and more right-brain stimulated. Creativity and imagination in everyday life were more commonplace, resulting in strategies of problem solving that were more intuitive, spontaneous, and personal. And because of the direct connection between the maker and the object, there was more personal investment, more pride, and more personality to the work.

As industrial manufacture grew, there came an unavoidable decline in the production and availability of the handmade object. Makers of objects have always looked for ways to increase production, whether through mechanized means of materials preparation, manufacturing, packing and transport to market, or other aids. So it is not the mere embracing of technology that has meant the downfall of craft production, but rather the extent of the use of technology. Technology, mechanization, and machines themselves have, instead of helping the individual produce objects, taken over the production. The hand has become secondary to the machine. Soetsu Yanagi, in his book, *The Unknown Craftsman,* suggests that a more responsible use of machinery and technology would be to use its power in the preparatory or initial stages of work, applying the use of the hand in the finishing stages, thereby utilizing each for its clear strengths.

The greatest disasters of mechanization ironically exist on the flip side of one of its greatest advantages—the ability to quickly produce large quantities of objects at low prices. Certainly this ability has brought much needed items into the hands of people who otherwise might not be able to get them. But in doing so, we have reduced the spiritual connection and appreciation of the object. We have also increased the numbers of un-employed, since one person can now operate a machine that produces the amount of work it pre-viously took ten or more people to do. Yes, tech-nology has also produced new jobs, but at the great cost of human emotion, individuality, and creative expression. Through its desire for speed, uniformity, cost effectiveness, and efficiency, so-ciety has altered an important balance between production of objects and their human connec-tion.

Clearly I am advocating the use of handmade objects over machine made ones, but there are many questions to answer and many issues at hand. By advocating the use of handmade objects are we to assume that the handmade object is in-herently better? This question strikes at the root of any discussion regarding the merits of hand-crafted objects. To begin with, the only character-istic I can think of as common among all handmade objects is that they are handmade! Other attributes that might be associated with the handcrafted object (higher quality, higher level of aesthetics, produced with more care, perform bet-ter, and higher cost) do not necessarily apply. To assume that being handmade is the most impor-tant characteristic of an object is to disregard its other virtues. Is it pleasing to look at? To hold? Does it perform its function? Is it sanitary? Safe to use? And there can be many additional criteria, depending on the object and its intended use. No, a handmade object is not inherently better than a machine made one. However, if we compare two examples of the same object, one being the best a machine could produce and the other the best an individual could handcraft, we would realize some interesting findings. To the trained or sensi-tive eye, the handcrafted object would be more appealing, more inviting to use, more humane in its presentation. In some cases, a musical instru-ment for example, would be superior because it's handmade. Still, this doesn't make a case for handcrafted objects to be considered universally better. In fact, for objects that require uniformity, specifications of precise exactitude, or that must be constructed of materials that can't be hand worked, the machine comes out on top.

Handmade objects that warrant consideration do have common characteristics. They have a soul, a kind of consciousness, spirit, and humani-ty. Just because an object is made by hand doesn't make it a handcrafted object in my book. The ob-ject must be injected with the lifeblood of the maker. Remember the dialogue I mentioned ear-lier between the object, its maker, and its user that completes the process. In this light, an object be-lieved to be handmade can fulfill the same needs and sensitivities as an actual handmade one.

Earlier I mentioned the aspect of function as being integral to the discussion of the handmade object. This demands some elaboration. Success-ful and proper function is critical. "Form follows function" is no cliché. Function is an absolute ne-cessity. The handle on the teapot must be com-fortable to hold. It must strike a balance between the size, shape, and pouring angle of the pot. The spout must pour smoothly without dripping. The lid must fit securely when the pot is tilted. None of these necessary characteristics are easy to achieve, yet they all must be arranged in a well-crafted aesthetically pleasing package. A craftsperson's task is a daunting one indeed; the integration of craftsmanship, aesthetics, function, and use.

Keep in mind that handmade-ness and aesthet-ics are separate concepts, characteristics, and is-sues. Despite their apparent connection, a handmade object isn't necessarily beautiful or well made. Indeed, many machine made objects, furniture for instance, can be beautiful pieces of work. Photographs can really only help to illus-trate the aesthetics, beauty, and form of the objects they represent. They are incapable of illustrating the quality of handmade-ness which can only be experienced through contact with and knowledge of the object. Craftsmanship—how well an object is made—may or may not be important in the appreciation of a handmade object. For me, if an object is not well-crafted it must possess some extraordinary characteristic to cause me to want to use it (made by a significant individual or given to me out of love or appreciation).

With some objects, the craftsmanship is the aesthetic. Take the example of fine plumbing or electrical work where the hardware is neat, level, well-designed and easy to access for repairs. This kind of care and pride on the part of the craftsman may not contribute directly to the function of the system. The house will probably be kept just as warm with a system that looks sloppy. While this isn't about the choice of a handmade object or system over a machine made one, it's still about a clear choice. It takes a discriminating individual to appreciate the aesthetics in a heating system, but the sensibilities at work here are shared with the individual who chooses a handmade mug over a machine made one.

In most objects, though, craftsmanship is not the aesthetics, rather it contributes to the aesthetics. Craftsmanship certainly can be noticed, appreciated, and extolled, but it is most successful when it exists transparently and allows the aesthetics and function of an object to be expressed.

I have bantered around the terms mass produced and machine made perhaps without enough definition. Mass produced refers to the repetitive production of an object—a set of dishes, chairs, or crystal goblets are not necessarily any less handmade than the one-of-a-kind dish, chair, or goblet. Machine made removes the production of the object from the hand and places it in the system of mechanization. Central to production by

hand is the hand! As complex as the inner workings of a machine may be, its control and operation pales to that of the human hand.

Are you closer to understanding and appreciating the essence of the handmade object? There are many items produced for daily use that, due to the nature, complexities, or economics involved in their manufacture, must involve some degree of hand work (textiles, boat construction, assembly line work, interior finish woodwork, baseballs, and baseball gloves to name a few). While these objects must be considered as partially handmade, to me they lack those most important characteristics that set them apart from machine made objects—the quintessential qualities of spirit, love of and deep commitment to the craft and to the integrity of the craft object on the part of the maker. Just because an object was made by hand doesn't set it apart from the masses of objects around us. There is no automatic positive effect brought about by the handmade object. In order to complete the equation, the user must identify with the maker and the object, being open to its influence. He must possess a sensitivity that will accept its spirit and the special qualities of the object.

While the short answer to the question, "Are handmade objects important in our lives?" is a resounding "Yes," the long answer is perhaps, "Not necessarily." The choice to use a handmade object is yours, as is the choice to have the use of that object affect the quality of your life. I think it takes a more sensitive person, a person who is more tuned in to their daily routine, and a person who chooses to be more connected to their humanity to answer yes. I do absolutely believe that society and civilization would benefit from an increased use of handmade objects. It is not going to happen easily though. All of us who make the choice of a handmade object over a machine made one (not just the craftspeople whose lifestyles revolve around that choice) have a responsibility to educate, inform, and influence the less enlightened. By doing so, our awareness and appreciation of each other's efforts and differences will become stronger in some and perhaps miraculously awakened for the first time in others. The world will be a better place.

## Identifying Your Personal Goals

The work an individual chooses is directly related to a variety of life choices and consequences. Professional paths and careers are generally chosen because of an interest or attraction to that profession's guise. The individual goes through the indicated course of study, field work, or apprenticeship thoroughly enjoying the experience. Usually it is the combination of the study and the preconceived notion of what that career or profession is like that sustains interest and attention. Unfortunately, oftentimes the reality of the career isn't really understood and the result is a great disappointment. In addition to not learning enough about the nuts and bolts of the profession, not enough attention is paid to how the involvement in that profession might affect lifestyle and mental well being. Of course, consideration of lifestyle and life philosophy when investigating career choices is more likely to occur to a mature individual who has been involved in one career and is considering a change than to a young person entering the fold for the first time. Someone with limited work experience naturally has limited life experience and may not be able to apply the potential variables to their own situation. Someone might study law, thoroughly enjoying the academics, intellectual challenge, and general practice but find that the amount of time it requires leaves no time for other interests. Another might get involved in a high-powered professional life and discover it leaves no time to have a family. An extreme case would be a concert pianist who, for fear of hurting her hands, gives up woodworking or racquetball.

If you are recently out of school and are contemplating a professional pottery career, learn as much as you can before you jump in. It's true that our interpretation of a professional potter involves more than making a career at it, and many of you haven't the slightest interest in changing careers or doing pottery as a money making venture. Nevertheless, you must realize that any degree of professional involvement in crafts will have a profound effect on your life.

In choosing to move toward spending more time and increasing your involvement with your craft, you may have to face some intimidating questions and formulate some difficult strategies. On the personal side, perhaps the most difficult issue is financial. Will this change in your approach to clay affect your income? Clearly each person's situation is different. For some, a financial concern doesn't exist. Perhaps you are independently wealthy or have free time for pottery without affecting your job and income, or possibly you are looking at this as a way to add to your income. For others, finances may present a significant roadblock to focused attention on your craft. If you currently depend on income from the job you are engaged in, how much reduction are you willing or able to withstand? For most of us, an increased involvement in clay means a negative effect on our bank accounts one way or another. Even if it is not going to reduce your income, how about the additional money you will spend on equipment, space, increased electrical use firing your kiln, clay, raw materials, and so on? What I'm getting at here is that you must evaluate your own financial needs. How much income do you need to support yourself in the style to which you aspire or have become accustomed and how much (if at all) will your involvement in clay affect that income?

Your financial situation is directly related to your personal lifestyle, which in turn is related to your work, profession, and career. This is not a book about career counseling so you're not going to get a general lecture on the subject, only as it relates to your devotion to clay. A true professional devotion to crafts is difficult to explain to someone without direct experience. I believe that the best someone could do to understand the drive, interest, and commitment needed to pursue and be successful at an art or crafts career is to accept the fact that they don't understand.

To be successful and to feel rewarded, the desire to do clay and make craft objects must be an inseparable part of you. To a certain degree, you find yourself naturally eating, breathing, and sleeping craft and clay. This is not to say that you are always "talking shop" or that your interests are limited to craft and art related subjects, but the sensitivities and aesthetic awareness that makes the presence of art integral to your life is always at the forefront of your vision. You must want to do art more than anything and you must absolutely love the connection with, and pursuit of aesthetic principles and ideals. A drive to be connected to your craft must be ever present and if there is a stretch of time when you are separated from your craft, it should feel wrong, like there is something missing. An addiction to clay and craft might serve as an analogy.

How does this carry over to everyday life? In many ways. Consider the earlier discussion about the merits of using handmade objects over their machine made counterparts. An individual who believes making crafts objects is important would more than likely have a natural inclination to be a user of handmade objects. Contact with handcrafted objects on a regular basis would help to satisfy their craft "addiction." For me,

not only do I make an effort to use handmade objects as much as possible, but the drive that inclines me to do so carries over to a general sensitivity to the quality of objects, regardless of their handmade status. I might look at a piece of machinery and react to its design and packaging. I would choose to purchase an appliance that had a more satisfying aesthetic. I carefully examine all objects for flaws and defects not only in their manufacture, but in their design and appearance. Being sensitive and concerned about these issues might seem to be automatic, but many people don't pay the slightest bit of attention to the aesthetic merits of an object. This is clear by the amount of poorly designed objects that flood the marketplace. As a craftsperson, a *professional* craftsperson for whom good design is of paramount importance, these aesthetic concerns must be yours and must occupy a regular and unconscious part of your lifestyle. If they do not and a conscious effort must be expended to notice, choose, observe, and utilize good design over common generic objects, then you do not possess the kind of sensitivities required to excel and be rewarded by a craft career or deep involvement.

Clearly it is beyond the financial means of many of us to be able to surround ourselves completely with the highest quality objects, be they handmade or not, but it is well within the means of all of us to want to, to be aware of the differences, and to feel somewhat unsatisfied when we can't. Here is the essence of the issue and the point I am making. To be a successful artist or craftsperson, whether or not the goal is to market your work, requires a dedication to craft work as a whole. Pursuit of the making, using, viewing, and appreciating crafts, art, handmade objects and what they represent must fill a void in your life that cannot be filled by anything else. The crafted object is a part of you.

## Professional Needs and Goals

Have I made serious enough mention of the need to be mentally and emotionally devoted to your craft? To be dedicated and driven towards the pursuit of craft making and to have the attitude that your craft is integral to your life is of the utmost importance and cannot be stressed enough. However, as important as this state of mind is, it represents only half the effort needed to pursue clay work on a professional level. Sheer hard physical work is the other half. Working to master a craft, develop a personal style, produce objects, and even possibly market them requires an extraordinary amount of time and physical commitment. It requires undaunted perseverance in the face of discouragement and it requires a firm resolve that what you are engaged in is important and deserving of your attention.

In speaking with hundreds of craftspeople over the years, the overriding connection between the successful ones—those who consistently produce high quality, aesthetically sound work and love what they do—is their dedication to the integrity and honesty of their work. Apparently, there is a relationship between the ideals of integrity, honesty, and quality! Quality, as an idea and goal, should and must form the foundation to your making of ware. An understanding and fluency with the concepts of quality and aesthetics must also be learned and this is done through emulation, experience, and trial and error. Sound aesthetics can begin to materialize in isolation but cannot mature in that environment. Make no mistake, as much as quality is universally appealing and somewhat ubiquitous in recognizable traits, excellence is personal and the quest for excellence in your creative work needs to be an incessant goal that you relentlessly pursue. While there is a greater aesthetic that craft makers are bound to, right and wrong and good and bad are first measured in the parameters you establish for yourself. Only when your work meets your own rigorous standards should it be placed in the public eye for scrutiny and your response to public reaction will influence your next step. Don't become prey to inadvertently lowering your aesthetic standards in response to public mediocrity—the aesthetic standards of a particular population are not necessarily of the highest order. As important as it is, as much as you agree with its importance, and as true as you try to be to it, the highest quality and the most sound aesthetic ideals should always be ultimately unattainable. They are the perfect ideals we all strive for but can never reach. It is the effort to achieve these ideals and all of the education, information, experience, culture, wisdom, and enrichment gained along the way that must drive our creative energies and at the same time reward our efforts. This is why we make pots in the first place.

Situations and circumstances will present themselves almost as temptations to compromise the honesty and quality of your work. When I first began working in clay on my own, I faced the challenge of desperately wanting to develop a personal style, to work intently, slowly, and methodically. On the other hand, it seemed that making clay pots would be an easy way to make the extra money I needed to support my clay habit. Mugs, bowls, and flower pots could be churned out and sold at local craft fairs and to local shops. It worked. But soon after embarking on this entrepreneurial odyssey, the enjoyment factor grew less and less and I felt something I had never felt before. I didn't like making pots! After a little soul searching, I realized I had become a slave to the pots I was making. The artistic direction I had worked so hard to identify as a student became blurred and the overall quality of my work as well as my aesthetic spirit suffered a serious decline.

The anxiety and pressure to financially support my work in clay was real and I chose to use clay as the support mechanism. It was the wrong decision at the wrong time. Or maybe it was the right decision at the wrong time. Whatever it was, it didn't work the way I thought it would. I learned a valuable lesson: never compromise the integrity of your work for any reason. The real satisfaction in making craft objects comes only when you complete a high quality piece or from a body of work done to your own standards, at your own pace, to your own grand design. Never again did I compromise my aesthetics to please a client or close a sale and I have loved making pots ever since.

You may wonder how marketing your work fits into the professional potter scenario. It is an integral aspect of doing crafts on any serious level. For some, the sale is the emotional climax of the craft making process, while for others it is simply the final step in the creation of an object and offers no special satisfaction. And for others, the eventual sale of a piece is an absolute necessity and without it, the ultimate satisfaction in the creation of the object is not realized. Marketing your work, whether approached from a practical or personal point of view and regardless of how you view its importance to your craft making involvement, is a subject all to itself and will be discussed later on a grand scale.

Whether it is a short or long range business plan, the strategy for this afternoon's soccer match, or deciding to take an adult education course in French, setting goals is an important component of any type of planning. In deciding to focus more attention on pottery, some goal setting is appropriate. What is it that you want to achieve in the clay community? What accomplishments will you deem satisfactory for your efforts? What degree of involvement will satisfy your drive to work in clay? Realistic goals are fluid, they change with your degree of experience and the extent to which previous goals have been met. Set

your goals with this in mind and you will be less vulnerable to discouragement and disappointment. Set a series of short term goals that will require most of your creative energies and some long term goals that will coalesce as consecutive short term ones do. Examples of short term goals might be to find a local pottery shop, become a member, and begin to make pots. They might revolve around setting up your own workspace for the very first time. One goal might be to have an exhibit of your work for the very first time. Short term goals may be even more finite—to get that deep black glaze you've always lusted after or to throw a set of six identical tea bowls. Short term goals are the local stops for food, rest, and relief on your way to your long term destination. They are paramount to any kind of successful end. Only you can set your goals. Long term goals might seem to be more daring, challenging, and difficult to identify and formulate because they are likely to be two, five, or ten years down the road. You may think it impossible to predict what you'll be doing ten years from now and therein lies the fault. Setting goals is not playing soothsayer. You're not expected to predict the future, but rather to project the situation you think you'd like to find yourself in.

Getting back to the clay pit, set yourself a series of goals, for now and for the future. Ask yourself what you'd like to achieve in the clay community. For that matter, what is the clay community? It is your sphere of contact, the people who see your work and those who influence you. There are many closet craftspeople—folks who ply their craft in total or near total obscurity with great satisfaction. If this is you, then your clay community is you! If, on the other hand, your efforts reach out to a wider audience, then your clay community is as far as your reach. Perhaps regular exhibits of your work is a goal or perhaps a local exhibit once in a while would suffice. You may not be satisfied until your work is in The Freer Gallery. On the other hand, participating in a show of regional potters at the local arts center may make your year. Do you want to be influential, recognizable, and a regular contributor to a vibrant metropolitan clay scene or is being a quiet country potter with a loyal following more what you had in mind? Your vision of your connection with the clay community may be one of these or may be something totally different, but even the closet potter working in obscurity is not as invisible to a clay community as he may think.

Engaging in a craft involves much more than just working with materials to produce an object. At the very least, it also must include purchasing supplies, tools, and equipment, which requires talking to people and consulting magazines or books. While you're at it, you'll hear about other people's work and you'll talk about your own. Interaction with other members of the clay community is inevitable, so make the most of it. Involve yourself in a clay dialogue. Learn everything you can and offer some of your knowledge in return. One of the most rewarding aspects of being a craftsperson is interacting with other craft practitioners, sharing ideas, experiences, methods, and techniques. While your professional aspirations and desire for contact and recognition within the clay community may be grand, it may also be petite! At the very least, an interest in what's hap-

## Radios, Cows, and Clay Work

*Career changes are never easy. It takes vision and courage. Dan Taylor's road to clay has been unusual, to say the least, but it is one that we can all take some lessons from.*

My first career was in radio and TV and grew out of my interests as a high school student. I spent 15 years as a technician, announcer, and finally in broadcast management. When I was asked to transfer to a station in a large city and wasn't excited about the move, I realized that the only job I had ever had was in broadcasting and that it no longer held the interest and excitement for me that it once had. My options were to stagnate where I was or change careers. Not sure if I had any transferable skills, the only way to find out was to try. However, I had a family with five children, a home, and all the other trappings of a comfortable life. The thought of striking out into unknown territory was frightening, but the idea of being at the end of the line in a career that no longer appealed to me was even more dreadful. That was in 1969.

Never having milked a cow, I bought a dairy farm 600 miles away. Talk about naive! We survived farming for eight years, but more impor-tantly, I learned that I could survive as an individual. That lesson, as important as it was, cost me my marriage—a high price to pay. I left the farm for Medicine Hat where I taught carpentry (skills that I learned as a farmer), eventually starting a real estate company.

Branching out into insurance, I became an independent broker but again found myself in a career that lacked long term interest for me. I was 50, remarried, three teenagers at home, and had all the financial baggage that one accumulates by midlife, complicated by a second marriage. Having an artistic bent, I have been associated with the arts community throughout my life and had secretly wished that there was some way I could make my living as an artist. This, however, was rather pie-in-the-sky, particularly by this stage of my life, until I went to a pottery workshop. It was the first time I had ever watched anyone with any amount of speed and skill at the wheel. I sat there fascinated as the pile of pots being made grew in number as if by magic! My business background started the wheels spinning in my head as I began calculating how many pots it would take to make a living. I felt it was possible. My wife Joanne, who is also very artistic, had a potter's wheel downstairs gathering dust

pening around you and an effort towards building professional relationships will go a long way in securing your continued interest and excitement about clay and craft.

## Art and Craft Careers

Earlier I touched on some of the differences between traditional professions and those in the field of crafts. Basically, what it comes down to is that a craft career incorporates a lifestyle that revolves around your interest and dedication to craft. When an art or craft career is chosen, the decision more often grows out of an emotional connection and passion for the particular craft than through logically weighing the pros and cons of a certain profession. There are few other jobs that are as emotional and spiritual in their demands. Teaching, clergy, and community outreach professions come to mind. Other than that, it comes down to money. Most every craftsperson I know could be in another professional career making much more money than they do making pots, quilts, chairs, or wooden boxes and at the same time have professions that are much more socially successful. That is, jobs that are much more acceptable in the eyes of society.

Art and crafts are not professions and careers to pursue for monetary rewards. Yes, you can make a living as a craftsperson (and many make very fine livings), but the attraction to a craft or art career is a visceral one, not a tangible one. Call

*Figure 1-5. Dan Taylor in his studio, Taylor Clayworks, Medicine Hat, Alberta, Canada. (Photo courtesy of Dan Taylor)*

so I taught myself how to throw. I went to every workshop I could, bought many books on potting, and worked eight hours a day at learning, all the while keeping my insurance business going. It was two years until I felt I could produce enough sellable pots on an ongoing basis to approach some consignment stores.

I was now augmenting my insurance income with pottery sales. In 1989, four years after starting to make pots, I felt confident enough to sell my insurance business and dedicate all my time and energy to making pots. In 1991, our last major decision was to move the studio out of the basement and invest $30,000 in a new workshop where our garage used to be.

This career decision to be a potter has been one of the best I have made in my entire life and, in retrospect, I can understand why. I followed a lifelong interest, applied business basics in determining the economics of my decision, mapped out a plan for business and marketing success, and followed it, making adjustments along the way. I'll never look back.

it dedication or call it addiction. To some, it may come as a calling, to others it is simply in their blood. Whatever it is to you, the attraction to a craft career is different than that for most others.

Because of this indefinable desire, explaining why you want to be a potter or why it is so important for you to pursue a professional art education can be quite a daunting task. Some of you may be in situations that place you beyond having to explain your actions to anyone, and to you I say bravo! To the rest of you, I applaud and certainly encourage what you are about to embark on. So often in my role as a prep school teacher, I find myself going to bat for a student whose parents can't find any redeeming qualities or reasons for pursuing an art education or a potential art career. How can you justify a college education that doesn't prepare you for a specific job?

If supporting yourself through clay is something you want to pursue, then a little guidance in that direction is in order. The rest of this book will give you much of the nitty gritty you need in such areas as studio planning, marketing, production techniques, etc., but none of that will be of much use unless your efforts begin with setting goals, defining terms and conditions, and thinking long and hard about the kind of life you want to live.

Do you want to be a potter or do you want to have a career in clay? While this may sound like a matter of semantics, it is certainly not and differences do abound. In the context of earning a living, a potter is someone who does it by producing, marketing, and selling their wares. To me, having a career in clay means being involved in a variety of clay-related endeavors that contribute to your financial and emotional state.

Being a potter means becoming a manufacturer of objects. Your time is spent primarily designing and producing the wares you are going to market. As a full-time potter, most individuals find little time for other related activities that

might otherwise be fun, offer worthwhile distractions, or provide an opportunity to apply pottery knowledge to other areas. These other activities might include doing workshops and demonstrations, teaching part-time on a regular basis, writing, lecturing, etc.

Ralph and Sandy Terry are two full-time production potters who produce a line of wares including distinctive indoor and outdoor lighting that they market through designers, architects, and trade shows. While they have done workshops and demonstrations, and as much as they enjoy doing them, they find it very difficult to give up production or marketing time for teaching and interacting opportunities. They have made the decision to devote their professions to making and selling their clay work. Part of this decision comes from the fact that the ware they enjoy producing happens to be infinitely marketable. It can be reasonably priced, appeals to a wide range of aesthetic tastes, fits well in both commercial and residential environments, and the sales method is through a gallery or trade show. Ralph and Sandy, while they have certainly worked to design and direct their work to their market, have not drastically altered the kind of work they have always loved to do and they have not compromised the quality, integrity, or honesty of the objects they produce. The way they have assembled their professional lives satisfies and sustains their desire to be involved with clay and handmade objects. Sure there is sometimes a desire to do other clay things but there is no feeling of dissatisfaction or being unfulfilled. Being full-time production potters and spending their working hours making ware is what they want to do.

I, on the other hand, am not a production potter or even a full-time potter. My professional life is comprised of a combination of clay-related activities not focused on any one aspect of clay. I make pottery that I sell through galleries and exhibitions. I travel extensively presenting workshops and demonstrations. I teach part-time in a prep school and while I teach pottery and art history exclusively, I am also engaged in a variety of endeavors related to that teaching responsibility. For example, I am an academic advisor, I coach track, and I serve on several academic committees. I run my business, The Potters Shop and Potters School, which from an administrative point of view occupies much of my time. In my spare time (spare time?), I write books, articles, and reviews. The activities I am involved in fluctuate and are always in movement. At certain times, my pottery making occupies 90% of my time, usually when I am working towards an exhibition. At other times, running the studio takes almost all my time. Frustration over not being able to spend as much time with a particular project or responsibility is ever present but, for me, this negative is wholly outweighed by the positive aspects of the way I have assembled my professional life. Boredom is virtually nonexistent and I am always busy with something. The conversation and professional contacts cross over from one area to another as does inspiration, ideas, and motivation. If the phrase "jack of all trades, master of none" crosses your mind about now, it doesn't surprise me. However, there is a fine line between becoming adept and professional in several areas that funnel towards a common goal and spreading your interests so thin that you don't become properly trained or sufficiently experienced to do good work. Travel that line carefully lest it become your downfall.

Depending on your particular situation and the circumstances that bring you to this point, there may be no need to decide now what the extent of your clay involvement will be. If that's the case, relax and see what the clay spirits have in store for you!

# Carol Temkin:
# One Potter's Story

Becoming a potter was the furthest thing from my mind. Though I was an elementary education major in college, I had strong interests in art and took as many art history courses as my schedule would allow. However, except for one required course in art education, I did not take any studio art. My master's thesis was based on my belief that by focusing on and studying the art of a particular culture, children could develop an understanding of the society and people of that culture, and I developed a unit of study integrating art history into a social studies program.

When I took my first job in 1968 teaching sixth grade, I used my thesis ideas to teach the ancient history curriculum, but also found that a hands-on experience with pottery, a craft that was very important to the ancient Greeks and Egyptians, helped to make the culture come alive for the children. Admittedly, my clay skills were weak but I learned along with the kids.

As my personal interest in art and craft grew, I decided to test my own abilities by taking courses at a local adult education center. I took drawing and painting but was curious as to why the pottery classes were always filled. Finally, I got into one and from the first class, I was hooked! It was compelling! There was a special "click" with the clay.

Yearning for more challenge and opportunities, I found another community arts center, Project, in Cambridge, Massachusetts, that had more wheels and a much better facility. More importantly, I found inspiration in a teacher there, a self-taught potter named Norman. He threw beautiful functional forms and had a wonderful sense of glaze application and design. I had learned the basic hand building techniques before coming to Project but learned how to throw from Norman.

While taking Norman's class, my pottery skills grew but I also learned Norman's glaze techniques that continue to influence my work to this day. In addition, I worked as a studio assistant, learning how to mix glazes among other studio chores. I did all of this at night and on weekends while still working at my day job, teaching sixth grade.

Pregnant with my first child, I stopped teaching in 1973. I continued to work at Project and to take Norman's class, as I was determined to maintain my pottery work. After the birth of our second child in 1977, I was still working at the studio but was also teaching an after school pottery course at my son's elementary school. One day on the bulletin board of a local pottery supply I saw an ad for a pottery studio in Newton. The Potters Shop was not only more convenient to get to but it was much nicer and much better run than any of the other centers I had gone to. The only problem for me was that the shop opened late in the afternoon since Steve taught school during the day. We worked out a deal by which I would open the shop in the morning in exchange for use of the facilities during the day.

After some months, when Steve learned I was teaching a children's pottery class at my son's school, he asked if I would be interested in setting one up and teaching at the studio. Until this time, my interest in clay was personal and avocational. I had sold a few pots and I had taught the after school class, but these were somewhat low level activities. Setting up a children's program was a wonderful opportunity and it was at that moment that it occurred to me that I could have a career as a professional potter.

My own pottery work really blossomed as a result of my joining The Potters Shop. As my pottery training had been limited, there were many voids in my background. For example, I knew little glaze chemistry and had never stacked a kiln! The Potters Shop, and Steve in particular, have been a constant source of information and inspiration. Steve has always pointed me in new directions.

Both the quality and quantity of my pottery steadily improved over the years. I now dedicate my time and energy to throwing delicate, graceful, functional forms. I believe functional pottery combines a visual-aesthetic experience with a physical-sensual one.

I also learned some of the nuts and bolts of marketing my work. I went from selling my pottery at local holiday sales and on consignment, to wholesale marketing to galleries. I've been in many juried gallery, museum, and wholesale trade shows. I've also participated in juried crafts cooperatives. Marketing requires a continuous and endless effort.

As my role—first as a teacher and then as the director of The Potters School—expanded and at the same time my own pottery production increased, I had to learn more organizational skills. I planned a flow of work around kiln loads that also included time for me to attend to the responsibilities of the school and my family life. I hired an assistant to help me with my production, but because I have trouble, philosophically, with having someone else involved in making my own work, I do all the actual work in making the pots. My assistant stacks kilns, prepares pieces for glazing, wipes and touches up pieces after glazing, pugs clay, mixes glazes, keeps track of inventory, and packs for shipping. I do all the throwing, trimming, and glazing. Since I pride myself on well-crafted and refined pieces, I do not shortcut any production steps. This makes competing in the marketplace difficult in that my prices have to reflect that dedication to detail.

The time and money struggles are very difficult, and after all these years I feel I still do not have the best solutions. Keeping the production up and the hours under control is almost impossible. I often feel frustrated with my inability to keep some time open for experimentation and development of new work. However, in spite of any frustrations, I still love pottery and I will always find new challenges in the clay! I am struck by the way my career has evolved and how it became so central to my life. I am looking forward to continuing to make the porcelain pots I have worked so hard to design and create, to developing new pottery styles, to working in new areas, and to continue to reach out with our educational programs. In the end, no matter what difficulties I encounter, I never seem to lose the love I have for throwing, creating, and teaching pottery, and in fact, could not imagine a life without it!

*Figure 1-7. **Carol Temkin**. Dinnerware. Wheel-thrown porcelain, plate 12" D, electric fired. This set is also shown in the color section. (Photo by Warren Patterson)*

*Figure 1-6.* **Author.** *Covered Jar. 1979. Thrown and handbuilt, 12" H, raku fired. This piece is also shown in the color section. (Photo by author)*

*Figure 1-8. **Sandy and Ralph Terry**. Lighting Sconce. 1998. 17" x 10" x 5", hand-carved and press molded stoneware. (Photo courtesy of the artists)*

# Chapter 2

## The Transition to Professional

### Life After School

If you are a recent graduate of a university, college, or art school and are hoping that this book will give you some direction and guidance in the next phase of your craft careers, then this chapter's for you! If not, read on anyway so you can appreciate what someone might gain or lose from having had that kind of experience. A professional education in the arts and crafts will impart some real tangible benefits, though there can be some substantial negative baggage carried along with it.

Let's assume that the school you attended offered a quality program in the arts, one that included good facilities and abundant supplies. It provided the necessary academic resources to augment your studio work—library, museums or galleries—and was part of or even central to an active arts community. Most importantly, you were surrounded by experienced, dedicated, and craft-producing teachers. If your school sounds like that, then you most likely have a solid background in art, art history, artists, and the cultures that produced them. You have mastered many technical skills and your knowledge of materials, supplies, and use of tools is confident and solidly based. Intellectually, you are cognizant of the myriad of aesthetic, natural, and social forces that influence the creation of art and craft objects and you understand the role craft objects play in society. As a craftsperson, you actively seek out inspiration and input to make your objects relevant and meaningful. You want to be a potter when you grow up and, what do you know, you're grown up!

A professional art school education has the tendency to impart extreme confidence in a student's readiness to take the craft world by storm so my first bit of advice for you is to reach down into your artistic bag of tricks and pull out a hefty dose of humility. Confidence is good. Confidence in your ability is paramount to success. Confidence allows you to keep your eyes open and move ahead instead of getting bogged down in indecision. Overconfidence, though, can blind you to continued development and separate you from positive and necessary influences. Overconfidence can manifest itself in having an exaggerated sense of your experience, expertise, societal and professional impact, and importance. It can be a very destructive force in your growth as both a craftsperson and person. As a product of a professional art education myself, I have seen how this happens. When I speak to young craftspeople in workshops, social situations, or job interviews, I am prepared for their overconfidence yet the pervasive "know it all" attitude of many graduates never fails to irritate me. Certainly not all individuals come out of school like that and I am absolutely not suggesting that professional art schools intentionally try to communicate this attitude. What I am saying is that too often, a negative byproduct of a quality art education is this feeling of certitude and superiority. The art school graduate very often leaves school with the attitude that the years spent there were demanding and difficult and that they have "paid their dues." Nothing could be further from the truth. Your dues have yet to be paid!

In defense of the art school environment, the susceptibility to overconfidence is understandable and perhaps even impossible to avoid. Integral to a quality education in the arts is the development of self-confidence. Artists and craftspeople need to develop strong convictions about their goals and must be ready to tackle the obstacles (and there will be many) that will invariably get in their way. If the alternative to overconfidence is uncertainty, indecisiveness, or apprehension, then take the overconfidence and work to temper it after the fact!

An art school education certainly has its advantages, beginning with the resources mentioned earlier. There is probably no finer place to learn your craft. Facilities are certain to be at least adequate for the effective study and practice of pottery, metals, glass, etc. While space to work may not be generous in all situations, it too is usually adequate. Interaction with fellow students and visiting artists serves an important purpose, as does the stimulation of exhibits in the school galleries. Opportunities for unique study situations such as overseas travel and internships can be taken advantage of. Professional art school curriculums are generally physically as well as intellectually demanding, and the student is challenged to use all their creative energies in successfully completing their degree requirements.

I can go on and on extolling the many virtues of the art school institution and environment. My sentiments would be sincere and the list would be important. However, despite the great advantages and opportunities art school has to offer, there are often significant holes that remain after evaluating your experience there. I am not quibbling about details like not enough wheels in the throwing studio or kilns that are too small or in disrepair. I'm not even talking about deficiencies in the curriculum such as learning about building or finding a studio. I am talking about important skills and attitudes you need to carry on as a professional potter—skills you generally don't learn

in school but that you should, skills that are difficult to learn outside of school. Here is one of the great Catch-22s of craft education. Nobody teaches it to you, but you need to learn it!

I'm talking about how to establish yourself as an independent craftsperson and how (if this is a goal) to make a living at your craft. It is an issue that schools routinely neglect. I'll devote some significant space to this issue later, but it bears some mention now.

Before you get angry and decide not to send in that $500 donation to the alumni fund because your school failed you in a most important area, take stock of your educational experience and do a quick inventory of how you spent your time there and what you did learn. Schools have only a limited amount of time to teach you what they have determined to be essential to your education as a craftsperson. There is simply not enough time to teach you everything, so they've got to pick and choose.

If I were designing a craft school curriculum, I would devote the majority of the school's resources to teaching design and aesthetics, mastery of craft production skills, and technical knowledge of materials, equipment, tools, and safety practices. After all, do these not form the foundation of a knowledgeable craftsperson, competent and skilled in their discipline? To my view, absolutely basic to a profession is complete mastery of the skills necessary to carry out the responsibilities of that profession. This is not to say that education and growth in these areas stop when you leave school, quite the contrary, but there is a certain degree of technical and aesthetic competence that you must leave school with to be able to carry on. There is simply not enough time to teach everything and I am happy to report that most every art school I am familiar with shares my view in practice, and some even state it in print.

There are, of course, many aspects of being a professional craftsperson that aren't taught in school. In my mind, the most glaring omission is in the area of turning your craft-producing skill into a viable income-producing activity. I must remind you again that making a living at your craft does not necessarily make you a professional. And to be professional, you don't have to be engaged in your craft as an income-producing activity. But most craftspeople, at some point, are interested in earning some money at their craft.

Another potentially negative result of an art school or university art/craft education is a rather limited aesthetic experience and view. As an undergraduate building a foundation of skills, knowledge, and experiences, it is vital to maintain as broad a view of the variety of clay objects being produced as possible. This is important for several reasons. Most importantly, school is not the place or the time to arrive at a style or even a personal statement in your craft. It is not a time to decide that you are going to be a producer of utilitarian objects, that you are going to specialize in salt firing, that you are going to be the teapot maven, or that colossal ceramic fountains are going to put you in the *Guinness Book of Records!* School is not the place to eschew functional ware for the sake of sculpture or to extol the virtues and significance of high-fire reduction stoneware at the expense of low-fire earthenware. School is where you collect as much ammunition as you possibly can to enable you to spend the rest of your life working towards making important and significant creative statements! In short, school is what we all know it should be: preparation for our careers. It should promote an atmosphere that demands growth and should develop an attitude in its students that emphatically states that they must continue to seek education throughout their lives.

Unfortunately, school has become, in many situations, the "Establishment" of our career, the place where we lock into and onto styles, attitudes, philosophies, and biases. It is often a place where these are cast in stone, instead of a place where these are born, nurtured, and encouraged through continued development. One clear way this "fait du complit" is accomplished is through the emphasis and importance placed on the exhibition of student wares. An art school education usually culminates in a thesis, senior, or graduate exhibition where teachers and departments demand a body of work that makes a definitive statement of purpose, design, technical accomplishment, and style. This is the kind of exhibit that summarizes a period of time the student has presumably spent working towards a specific aesthetic and personal statement. Is that what a school should have their students working towards? Let me say again that absolutely not all schools are guilty of purveying this kind of message, but there are many that are.

Take a moment to review your own experience to see where you are in this melee. In my opinion, the school experience and environment should focus on and emphasize education through experimentation and fearlessness, resulting in an attitude of beginning and embarkation at graduation, not a message that the student has now developed their style and aesthetic sensibilities and the future is simply for the making of these wares.

My message here is that the school experience should, among other things, prepare you for growth, development, continuing expansion of your craft vocabulary and experience, as well as an always evolving style, statement, and emotional investment in the objects you produce. Having this kind of openness of mind is integral to maintaining an ever-present interest, love, and important personal involvement in the making of craft objects. Otherwise, making pots is going to get pretty boring pretty fast!

Having said all that, perhaps the greatest challenge facing you as a young graduate is finding a place to work at your craft. I say perhaps because when you are no longer part of a school environment, there are significant challenges to be met as well as voids to fill that don't make themselves clear right away. The most obvious problem for many at the outset is to find a workspace, furnishings, tools, and equipment. "What?" you say. "My studio with all the required accouterments, appurtenances, and equipage is not out there waiting for me? A reduction kiln with oxygen probe and computer equipped step up system is an unusual piece of equipment?" Welcome to the real world! To a certain degree, I'm being facetious. However, an additional disservice schools provide (for no extra charge) is often an over-dependence on equipment and technology— equipment, furnishings, and space that will be difficult or impossible to own or have access to after leaving school. Am I espousing primitive workspaces in schools? Of course not, for the opportunity to learn how to use the best tools, machinery, and technology is a great and invaluable experience and you should certainly weigh the quality of a school's facilities as a criteria for choosing one school over another. But if you are leaving school with the belief that a fully-equipped studio is the norm, then think again. Not only is that not the norm, but if you are destined to begin an independent career, you'd better decide what bare essentials are necessary for you to do your thing. If you are fortunate to have the opportunity to join an existing group studio (more on that later), the equipment available to you may be more copious. If you are independently wealthy, well, the sky's the limit and my words here may be falling on deaf ears.

Is all of this cause for depression? After all, you've lost your academic support system. No more spacious studio. Kick wheel instead of electric wheel. Small electric kiln instead of a reduction, gas-fired behemoth. Your unlimited supply of clay, fuel, and raw materials has been pulled out from under you. In some respects, the manner and style in which you face this present challenge will determine much about the success of your continued career as a potter. How frugal can you be? What essential pieces are necessary for you to make ware? In short, how resourceful can you be?

To be an artist, craftsman, or whatever you choose to call yourself, has as its central and consistently important core the ability to problem solve. As a potter, you may be willing and excited to face the aesthetic challenges, decisions, and crossroads that lie ahead. These certainly represent important examples of problem solving. But if you're not ready or able to apply problem solving skills to the current task, a successful and rewarding career or even a serious avocation in the crafts is unlikely. I suspect that if you've taken the initiative to purchase and read this book, the challenge, while formidable, is yours to meet!

## Taking the Next Step: You Can Be a Professional Too

Earlier I discussed the definitions and characteristics of being a professional. Perhaps at that time you plugged yourself in and you recognize where you are in this mystery. However, if recognizing yourself as a professional is still as far from reality as being a knight in King Arthur's Court, then relax and don't worry. I'll do my best to highlight your strong points and if I have to, talk you into thinking of yourself as a professional. Let's get one thing straight—you don't have to earn a living or any money at all from the practice of your craft to be considered a professional. So, just because you are not selling your work or even think you might be interested in selling your work, don't disqualify yourself from the professional ranks. Understand and accept that though you may not be in a marketing mood right now, at some point most everybody enters the selling zone! When the time is right for you, you'll enter it too.

During the preparation for this book, I solicited contributions from individuals in the form of stories, photos, and anecdotes to offer a variety of experiences on the subject of being a professional potter. I consider all the people I called on unquestionably professional, yet to many of them, the label professional was too high, too congratulatory, too flattering. Remarkably, in their eyes, I was the professional. I had to show them, and in some cases convince them that they too were professional. It's time for you to put yourself in the same category.

How you move from your present involvement in the craft to a professional one is a very personal journey. For some, it may be a long time-consuming effort with the ultimate goal to feel that you've finally earned the professional label. For others, it may be crossing an easily definable threshold—the sale of your first piece, making that first pot outside the school studio, or setting up your own workspace. Perhaps you've been able to do your pottery only on weekends and you feel it is now time to devote a more substantial amount of time to your craft. Or to go to the obvious extreme, perhaps you've decided that a career change is what you need and it's time to turn your pottery hobby into a "real" job. Whatever the move to becoming a professional involves for you, it will likely mean one or more of the following: a new studio situation or environment; becoming more knowledgeable about equipment selection and repair; locating local suppliers; photographing your wares; calling on galleries; and myriad other activities that you may not have any experience with.

Regardless of the scenarios that apply to you, there is one component that applies to us all—overcoming the fear about your ability to move on in this craft. Your fears may be concrete in nature, for instance, the doubts surrounding a career change. If a career change means giving up or substantially reducing an established income, then you are contemplating real risk taking. Or your fears may be more ephemeral and philosophical, having to do more with your technical knowledge, the quality of your work, or the likelihood of success in marketing your wares. No matter where your fears lie, they can be overcome, perhaps not in one fell swoop, but you can learn to deal with the challenges head on. Others have, I have, and so can you!

Uncertainty regarding your interest in working with clay is the first hurdle to jump. If you're not sure how much you enjoy working in the material, you must definitely put the next steps on hold. As I touched on earlier, love and devotion to the craft is essential to any kind of measurable success. Being uncertain at this point may sound a bit unlikely but there are many individuals doing clay who fear that if they spent more time at it, they would lose their interest, love, and devotion. Similarly, many are afraid that if working with clay becomes work, it will lose its luster, its appeal. Being a potter will be just like...well...work! These are real fears.

So let's start by exploring your uncertainty about your love of the craft. Ask yourself simple questions. How do you feel when using clay? Is it relaxing? Do you feel productive? Is what you're doing important to you? Does your involvement with the craft give you pleasure? Do you enjoy the clay community? Is it supportive of your efforts? How about your family? Are they supportive of your efforts?

Family can be a real thorny issue that warrants some mention here. The desire, need, and determination to do art and crafts is usually a deep-rooted one. It is a feeling that is often innate and basic to your individuality. In fact, most potters and students I encounter, especially in the workshops I do, are quick to admit and proud and anxious to share that doing pottery for them is an addiction. It is an indescribable love and something they cannot do without. Working with clay for them has become the single most enjoyable activity in their lives. My response is, of course, understanding, sympathy, and encouragement, along with a hope that they have not forsaken their other personal and family responsibilities in the name of mud! It is difficult, if not impossible, to understand these feelings if you don't share them. What this boils down to is the notion that unless someone is involved in the making of art and craft objects, they cannot feel the passion you feel. I have discovered that the best a friend or family member can do is understand that they don't understand while having the confidence that you know what you're doing, and that it's important and meaningful to you. There are no predetermined answers that qualify you to trash the uncertainty factor, but you begin to get the drift. All these queries can be boiled down to one question: "Are you enjoying this?" If you are, then it's time to shed your fears about enjoying the craft enough and move on.

Unquestionably, there are varying degrees of enjoyment. Call it conviction or dedication, if you will. Your likelihood of achieving success at different levels of involvement depends on the state of your passion, ardor, and zeal. Clearly, the more passionate you are, the less likely it is that you will be brought down by failures or discouraging experiences. Likewise, the more elemental you are in your love of the craft, the more likely you will be satisfied and rewarded by whatever successes you do experience. My love of pottery, pottery making, and all other clay-related activities that I am involved in is so basic to my existence that no matter what discouraging moments there are (and believe me, there have been and continue to be many), my dedication to clay is unwavering. One such experience has left me with an indelible mark.

Early in my career, the first year I made pots outside of school, I was working in a small group studio. I had been selling my wares to local gift and flower shops and was indeed enjoying what was, for me, great success. Through one of my accounts, I made a contact with a restaurant that needed 25 hanging planters to decorate their dining room. What a boon to my career! This was going to be the beginning of the big time. After some discussion of design, price, and delivery date, I set to work. Although I had plenty of experience making pots as well as selling them (so I thought), this was my first commission—pots to order. No need to worry, I loved this craft.

Leaving myself little time for re-do's (after all, what could go wrong?), I made the pots. Excellent! Little did I know that the making of the wares was to be the high point of the experience. As I contemplated loading the pots into the kiln for bisque firing, I was overcome with a totally crazy and irresponsible idea (although I didn't realize it was irresponsible at the time). I remembered some information on raw glazing and once-firing. Did I need to once-fire? No. Was this the time to experiment with new approaches to hanging planter making? No. Was I young and inexperienced? Yes. Did I think I knew it all? No, but I certainly thought that I knew how to do this. Was I a nut? Absolutely! I went about glazing the bone-dry pots. Can you imagine glazing bone-dry pots by dipping? And these were not tiny. I'm talking pots 6" to 8" in diameter and 8" to 10" tall. Miraculously, the pots survived the glazing process and I successfully loaded them in the kiln. As I began to unstack the kiln the next day, a small crowd (it was a small studio) gathered around. Not to see how the once-fired pots came out, for I hadn't told anyone about my new technique, but to give me their support and encouragement through my first commission. Try to imagine the ghastly expressions on the onlookers' faces when they saw defective pot after defective pot. A cracked rim here, an S crack there, a warped edge here, a huge area of crawled glaze there. Every single pot was defective to the point of being garbage! Perhaps if my friends weren't there to absorb some of the horror and I had to digest it all myself, I'd remember the incident as less comical. Although I was terribly disappointed and upset at the outcome of the firing, I didn't lose my love of the craft, not even for a minute. I immediately set about to re-do the pots, realizing that raw glazing and once-firing was either not the right technique for me or that I must have done something wrong. What I remember most about that experience were the comments from the other potters and how negative they were. Expressions like, "I would be devastated," "How can you ever make another pot again?" and, "I would be so disappointed I wouldn't know what to do next." The pots were truly a disaster, but the value of the experience was a revelation for me. I loved this craft and nothing was going to deter me from being a potter.

Take a moment to recall a personal disaster of your own or to realize for the first time that you've had one. Perhaps you've yet to experience your disaster. You will—it happens to us all.

I mentioned before that labeling an activity as work often signals its downfall as a fun thing to do. To begin with, for me and most other full-time potters, our clay involvement *is* work and that's exactly what is appealing about it. There is no potter I know who is not the envy of their friends. I've heard it so many times from so many people. They can't imagine what it's like being a potter, spending your working hours at something you love to do. And while, to be honest, I often get

bored responding, I never disparage the comments or minimize how strongly people feel about their observation of me. I am fortuitous in that not only do I love my work, but most of my friends—whose professions range from doctors to teachers, to scientists to laborers—enjoy their work as much as I do. Unfortunately, popular sentiment indicates that a large number of people don't like what they do and wish they could do something else. Further complicating matters is the fact that oftentimes they don't know what it is they would like to do. If you are contemplating a career change to pottery, within the sea of uncertainty and fear, at least revel in the satisfaction that you know what you want to do!

## My Beginnings as a Potter

Despite the fact that when I was born my mother said to my father, "Wouldn't it be nice if he grew up to be a sculptor?" having a career in art was far from certain and was, in fact, pretty far-fetched. My mother was a musician, having gone to Julliard School of Music, and she often spent time drawing as well. Her uncle, with whom I was very close, was a landscape painter who earned his living as a house painter. My great grandfather was a tailor who crafted fine clothing. As children, we were taken to museums, concerts, even Broadway shows. Our house was filled with art objects. My brothers and I took music lessons and were generally pretty well-rounded kids. Though art and craft was always a part of my life, to me it was a hobby, something to do to pass time and appease my parents but certainly not a serious endeavor. As a high school student, my interests were in sports. As my senior year began, while my friends hadn't even come up with their long list of college choices, I found myself applying early decision to a single, top-flight school to become a physical education teacher. As it was, having been a reasonably good student, combined with less than rigorous academic requirements, I found that I had enough credits to graduate from high school early. That sounded appealing until my parents pointed out that if I wasn't in school I would have to be somewhere. Since I feared that our respective concepts of "somewhere" were likely far apart, my only alternative was to stay in school and make the best of it by filling my day with the easiest courses available. What could be easier, I thought, than some art classes? Easy? Hardly. Little did I know that this was the start of something big.

For some reason, doing art as a high school senior wasn't the same as it had been for me as a child. Something about the activity, the material, or the other students around me now made a difference. It was clear that, for the first time, making art was necessary and I found that the art objects themselves spoke to me. Doing art was more than just fun, it had meaning and relevance. The major revelation turned out to be even more elemental and was made clear by my teacher. She showed me, not through words, but by how she lived and taught, that doing art or craft could not only be fun and have personal meaning, but it could be so important that someone could devote their life to it. She showed me that you could actually live a life where art was your central theme.

Needless to say, my life changed that year and although I arrived at college the following fall ready to join the jock ranks and take my place among the shorts, sports equipment, and goal posts, I was ready for, and knew inside, that it would take only the slightest push, the most minute inspiration, the easiest of influences to send me over the physical education edge rolling full steam to the art department. That push came in the form of my academic advisor. He was tall,

*Figure 2-1. Gallery and entrance to The Potters Shop and School, the author's studio and workplace, Needham, Mass. (Photo by Marna Kennedy)*

as fit as can be, crewcut and an attitude right out of boot camp. His t-shirt looked as if it was painted on. I was not as tall, sported shoulder length hair and a string of beads around my neck, and was just back from Woodstock. We were not of the same mold. As we worked on my schedule, filling it in with class after class of physiology, history of sport, and athletic skill courses, he announced that there was one schedule slot open and I could choose a course of my own liking. I responded with, "I'd like to take art history." He responded with an incredulous stare, a laugh, and remarked, "Are you kidding? I meant something like the Psychology of Coaching Baseball, or History of Athletics in America." I responded by getting up, thanking him for his time, leaving his office, and heading over to the art department. I was 17 years old and had just made what would end up being one of the most important decisions of my life. Thus began my career in art.

As a student, I took as many art courses as possible. Sculpture particularly interested me (kudos to my mother). As a degree requirement, each student had to take a course in crafts. Big of them! Not being attracted to any particular area, I chose pottery for no apparent reason. From the first moment I saw the material move, I fell in love with it. The teacher, John Jessiman, was a dynamic, charismatic individual who made the class fun. I couldn't get enough of it. After the first week of school, I decided I was going to be a potter. The decision was perhaps a bit premature (not to mention immature) but what the heck!

My undergraduate experience continued and I did major in ceramics, along with sculpture and art history. I had to petition the department almost every semester to allow me to take an overload of courses. I went on to graduate school at Rhode Island School of Design. The time I spent there completely reinforced any notion that I may have had to become a potter and to do whatever was necessary to support myself with and by my interest in art. My college and professional school experience was the same kind I spoke of earlier. Space, materials, teachers, equipment—I had it all. It was luscious and my education was privileged.

To many, my transition from school to profession and career appears to have been smooth and easy and in many ways it was. I attribute whatever degree of ease there was to a good education and family support, but most of all, to my own determination and self-confidence. Take stock of yourself and if you have to, pat yourself on the back and forge ahead. We all know that nothing is that easy and that's what this book is all about. But I did become a potter and this is how I did it. Indeed, in my mother's eyes, a potter is close enough!

## The Potters Shop and School

My studio and business, The Potters Shop and School, didn't just happen because I wanted it to. Nor did it happen according to an exact plan that I had formulated for myself. The establishment of my professional and business identity took a long time of evolution, growth, metamorphosis, luck, and of course, inevitable serendipity. Much of the story of how I developed my career and studio is discussed in the context of the various chapters in this book, but conceptually and chronologically it certainly bears a brief discussion here.

Upon graduation from college, my sights were set on being a studio potter, plying my wares, selling at craft fairs, shops, and galleries, and becoming famous. I thought I would also do some teaching to supplement my income from pottery sales. So what was stopping me? Attention. *Reality check.* I had no place to live, no workspace, no equipment, no supplies, no teaching job, no money, and no plan. Terrific, I had the world just where I wanted it. I needed a plan and it went something like the instructions for becoming a millionaire. You know—step one, go out and get a million dollars, step two, you're a millionaire. Here was my plan: decide where to live, get an apartment, get a studio, make pots, sell pots, get famous. It worked for me.

I don't advocate going about the establishment of your career using the same plan in the same way. The fact is that, after a fashion, that was indeed the plan I followed. No I'm not being facetious. With no business training or even a clue as to how to go about starting a career, that was the only plan I could come up with. To be honest, I wasn't totally in the dark. Rhode Island School of Design was a great place and even though there was no formal course or training in the business aspects of art and craft, I had been exposed, at least in informal and subliminal ways, to these vi-

tally important aspects of being an artist and somehow making a career of it. My plan, as you might suspect, did require the formulation of many mini steps and adjustments, as well as attending to a variety of details along the way. It worked in part because my circumstances, location, personality, and approach to problem solving worked with it. I learned along the way.

After spending the summer after graduation (1975) teaching at an art, music, and sports camp in Ontario, Canada, I moved in with a friend in Newton, Massachusetts, a suburb of Boston. I found work at a variety of short term jobs including waiting on tables, clerking at an art supply store, and crafting leather goods in an established shop, all the time looking for a place to make clay. Two big breaks came in the same week when I found a local clay studio with space to rent

*Figure 2-2. The main workspace in The Potters Shop and School is a combined classroom and open workshop for studio members. (Photo by Marna Kennedy)*

and a job at a local clay and pottery supply company. At last, a studio to work with clay and a job working with clay. This is it, I thought. So I'm not quite at the pinnacle of my career yet, but I am doing clay all of the time. After only a short time, it became apparent that this situation wasn't exactly what I had in mind. The clay company was a disorganized mess of a place and had little to do with pottery or pottery making. The atmosphere was less creative and artistically encouraging than an automobile dealership. The hours were long, clay mixing—which became my specialty—was dirty and arduous, and to add insult to injury, I barely got a discount on materials! I thought that being with people with a common interest in clay would be fun and supportive. On the contrary, the folks at this place were mostly nonpotters, blue collar laborers who simply worked there as a job, just as I had worked as a waiter or clerk. They took pride in their work as clay mixers, truck drivers, and the like, but couldn't care less about pottery or craft. Needless to say, I became so frustrated working at the clay company, even though I was around clay, it became more of a chore than working at some other meaningless job.

The clay studio was another story. Although it was small, dimly lit, and had only the barest of equipment, it became my sanctuary. Not having my own wheel or kiln or access to the owner's equipment forced me to do hand building just to stay in shape. It didn't matter. After some time, the owner allowed me to use her wheel after hours as well as pay her for the use of one of her kilns. I was now off and running. My job paid me just enough to support myself and pay the $25/month studio rent.

During this time, I began to make and market some wares on a very small level. But it was the contacts I was making that proved to be the real start to my career. Soon the owner of the studio announced that she was quitting clay, moving onto bigger and better things. She made me an offer to sublet the entire space along with all of her equipment, furnishings, tools, the entire ball of wax. Right place at the right time! It was an offer I couldn't refuse. Fortuitously, I had just quit the clay job and begun my career as a full-time substitute teacher. Though my teaching certification was in art, that was credential enough to be a general substitute teacher. I promised to teach any course, any grade, in any school, and that guaranteed me an assignment every day. The pay was meager, but better than I had been making and it was enough to afford the $250 or so that the entire studio was going to cost me per month. This is when my clay career really began.

The studio was in an old, dilapidated, second floor, two level apartment. The kitchen, which opened out to the roof of a commercial establishment below, served as the glaze and kiln room. There were two additional rooms on that first level which served as the clay workspace. Upstairs were three rooms I used as storage. After only a matter of weeks, I began to attract visitors and phone calls from people interested in taking classes, having their kids take classes, renting space, using the kilns, and even buying my pots! I then decided to open to the public. I advertised classes for kids and adults and thus began, in earnest, The Potters Shop and School. The year was 1977. So, 20-plus years, four locations, and thousands of students (and pots) later, The Potters Shop is going strong.

The Potters Shop and School has developed, grown, and matured into a multi-faceted business and facility. The entire operation includes a pottery school and open workspace for potters with a staff of 16. We have a large space, ten kilns, 18 wheels, and a variety of equipment. We have a gallery, sell supplies, and operate a mail order book/video/tool business. The Potters Shop and School houses my own workspace and has become a general resource for people working with clay. We've gone through many changes over the years, but the overall concept and idea have remained the same. The Potters Shop and School is my creative identity.

As I said before, the establishment of The Potters Shop and School came to pass because of many factors, not the least of which was luck. So how do you get luck? By working hard and making as much happen as you can. I had no blueprint to establish the kind of studio and business enterprise that I did, but I had the ability to evaluate opportunities and situations as they became apparent and to take advantage of them if they seemed to fit my "plan." Granted, it may be difficult (or impossible) to find an equipped studio and space for $250 a month, but in your own situation there too are opportunities to be had.

Formulating a realistic plan is important, but maintaining an open mind and being as flexible and experimental as possible is even more important. My plan, while thin in its content, was a plan nevertheless. I knew I wanted to be a potter, have a studio, and market my wares. And although teaching was a part of that plan, my idea did not include teaching in my studio or having the studio become a pottery facility. Successful plans are those that can be adapted to a changing focus. They can grow with new ideas and evolve over time. And while change, evolution, and adaptability are positive and necessary, don't confuse those characteristics with a lack of focus, intention, or professionalism. Likewise, don't confuse focus and intention with rigidity. Rigidity is confining and limits your vision. And let's be sure of one thing here, vision (and dedication) is what you need to maintain forward movement, progress, and ultimately success.

# Chapter 3

## Studio Concepts:
## Needs, Selection, Design, Construction

*The ideal studio is 40 by 120 feet of solar-paneled brick and clapboard, built atop a hot spring. It is set in a pristine wilderness two hours from every major art gallery in the country. To the north, a rich agricultural valley sweeps up into colorfully forested, snowcapped mountains. To the east, a fish-packed river flows between orchard banks. To the south, peaceful warm sands set off the crashing rhythms of the ocean. And to the west is a shimmering splendor of a night-flowering desert. The building includes a showroom, kitchen, den, and hot tub. There is an office, large shipping and storage areas, and a loading dock. Everywhere the air is filtered and temperature/moisture controlled. There is a central vacuum cleaner and a stereo system. And, let me not forget the wine cellar...*
*--Lili Krakowski from her article and handbook,* The $1200 Studio

### Types of Studios

The prospect of having your own studio space is certainly an exciting one. As a matter of fact, it may be the most exciting aspect of this entire professional potter thing. The thought of having your own place to work and the things that go along with it—the freedom to leave your works in progress out and unattended, privacy, and control of your workspace, etc.—can be so exciting that oftentimes inadequate thought goes into what must be considered when planning this space. Let's begin this process by defining certain kinds of studio situations to arrive at the type of workspace that would be suitable for you.

There are a variety of studio and workspaces used by potters and other craftspeople. Some are characterized by their size or style, organization or philosophy, or any number of other features. **Large group studios** are usually the most affordable and often the easiest to become part of. If you are new to pottery or just out of school and are looking for your first workspace, connecting with this type of studio situation probably makes the most sense. These kinds of spaces can be cooperatives, shared spaces, and studio spaces in schools and community art centers. If you live in

an urban or suburban area, chances are that this type of studio space exists near you.

Many cities and towns have established **community or neighborhood art centers** offering a schedule of classes in a variety of media, as well as a gallery, theater, auditorium, meeting space, etc. Sometimes, as part of the art offerings, an "open studio" may be available. Usually this is a block of time or certain hours during the week where, for a fee, individuals may use the space. This kind of opportunity can be a boon to those who are not interested or ready for a space of their own but would like to work when they want, independent from a class or teacher. While these facilities can be just what you need, oftentimes they are multi-use spaces that are ill-equipped and not well-maintained. The hours of availability may be limited, storage space may be tight, and with a variety of materials, tools, and individuals using the space, safe storage, particularly for works in progress, may be rare. However, if this is what is available to you right now, make the best of it, realizing that it may be your first step and is likely more than what many people have access to.

As you seek out bona fide clay studios, the most approachable and the least costly are those studios that offer some type of membership. These are existing enterprises that are self-contained, usually structured as either profit or non-profit corporations or schools. For a monthly, semester, or annual membership fee you are entitled to a variety of benefits. At The Potters Shop and School we offer different benefit packages depending on the level of membership. Resident potter members are entitled to 24-hour access to the facility, which includes a common workspace with ten wheels, slab roller, extruder, worktables, and hand tools. There is a glaze room, kiln room, outdoor raku facility, gallery space, and common library/lounge area. Members have their own storage areas for personal belongings and share common shelving for works in progress. A paid staff runs the shop and sees to all duties including studio maintenance, equipment repair, and cleaning. Membership fees cover all expenses for the use of the studio except firing and materials. One of the advantages of being part of this type of studio is that studio members have no shared chores, jobs, or studio responsibilities other than being good citizens, cleaning up after themselves, and treating the facilities with respect and care. Members have no financial responsibilities or headaches other than to pay their bills on time! Studios of this type are usually at least adequately equipped and maintained. The downside is that studios of this type solicit little, if any, input from their members with regard to the studio's operation, policies, and terms. Of course, there is always the influence of supply and demand and customer relations. Presumably, if the studio isn't meeting the needs of its members, those members will seek alternative spaces.

Perhaps you have been working in one of these kinds of large group studios as a member and feel that you are now ready to move to a smaller, more individual space, one where you can have a more personal connection and contribute more to the operation, atmosphere, and policies of the studio. Next on the scale of personal involvement is a cooperative type of arrangement. And while The Potters Shop and others like it appear to operate as a cooperative does, they are really very different. **Cooperatives** are usually a group of potters who, through a formal legal agreement, form a partnership of some kind to share space, equipment, and other resources under one business name. Oftentimes, each member of the coop will have their own private workspace. So as to not duplicate space usage, there are typically common, shared spaces in a coop such as glaze room, kiln room, raw materials storage, etc.

Depending on the extent of the business interests, which could include a gallery and classes in addition to the actual clay space, members of the coop divide the responsibilities of operating and maintaining the space on a daily, weekly, or monthly basis. There is usually a treasurer/bookkeeper to keep track of the group's finances. There might be a member in charge of inventory and ordering supplies and materials and a member who coordinates studio cleanup. One member might be particularly adept at technical chores and might be the studio technician.

A cooperative is defined more by how the space is shared than by its size or the activities that transpire in the space. A **group studio** can be similar to a coop but is usually defined by the singular goal of sharing the rent and maintenance costs of one large space in order to provide adequate workspace for a group of potters. There are usually less cooperative efforts involved in the operation of the space and more individual identity. Display space, glaze and kiln areas, materials storage, and other workspace features are often (but not always) left to each individual to incorporate into their own work areas. It may appear that this type of group studio arrangement, with its duplication of spaces, is a waste of space, but to some it offers advantages over a coop. These advantages lie mainly in the area of independence from others and the establishment of a more personal, individual identity to your workspace. That is not to say that being a part of a coop cannot be personal and individual, but by the very nature of it being a cooperative, you forfeit some of those individual characteristics.

**Small group studios** need not be much different than their larger counterparts as far as organization and concept are concerned. The primary difference is their size. I define a small group studio as having two to four members or participants. It is a small and much more intimate situation. The members usually are friends in tune with each other's needs, interests, work styles, and philosophies. Small group studios can be for-

*Figure 3-1. Mud Bug Pottery, John Jensen's studio is a converted garage with two open air, covered additions on the grounds of his home in Annapolis, Maryland. (Photo by John Jensen)*

*Figure 3-2. Interior of John Jensen's studio showing his throwing area. John originally set up his wheel to throw standing up in order to save space in the small shop, but this style quickly proved to be physically more comfortable and better for quickly being able to move around the studio. (Photo by John Jensen)*

mal cooperatives or just a few potters combining forces to be able to afford the expenses of a studio space.

For most craftspeople though, the ultimate goal is having your own **one-person studio/workshop**. Private, customized, individual—this is the life! The one-person studio is certainly the most common workspace among potters and for that matter, among artists of all kinds. Why? Well for one reason, most individuals who have created their own studios have done so in their homes or on their own property, be it in a garage, barn, or other outbuilding. Another reason is that most people who have assembled their own workspaces have, at least at first, done so on a very informal basis that required little in the way of planning, extensive building, or great expense. Bravo! However, a little planning can go a long way in making your space efficient, comfortable, and safe. And if you are doing clay work as an established business entity, your space and the planning that goes into it must be much more formal in physical as well as proper legal structure.

Almost everyone who contemplates any kind of dedicated clay workspace thinks in terms of a space of their own, and why not? You can be your own boss, set it up the way you want, change it on a whim or moment's notice, and not be concerned that another body might be occupying the space you need at that moment. There is nothing like your own space.

Before you get too enamored with the idea, though, realize that there are possible disadvantages to being in your own space. You will be alone and not part of an active, busy environment. For many, the lack of daily interaction with others proves to be extremely detrimental to the creative drive. For some, the isolation ultimately rings the death knell of craft involvement. There is much to be said for working in a space where there are other people, conversation being the least important attraction. Activity in and of itself, is an inspiration. Visual stimulation from objects around you and the absorption of ideas and tangible energy produced by the combination of individual identities and their wares can be an invaluable ingredient to your creative process. On the other hand, your work style may thrive in a quiet, self-contained space and you already may be part of a larger community of craftspeople outside your studio with whom you interact on a regular basis. Perhaps you belong to an association, guild, or cooperative gallery. Perhaps you live in an area that supports the presentation of guest artists. Whatever your creative and inspirational support system, consider it before you unwittingly remove yourself from it. Some members of The Potters Shop and School remain members although they have their own studio spaces elsewhere just to come in occasionally and work in an active environment where interaction with other potters can happen.

My references to, examples of, and apparent endorsement of the craft coop environment is not an attempt to discourage you from pursuing your own workspace. On the contrary, I still think an individual or small studio situation is the most ideal. Just consider as many of the ramifications as possible. In other words—plan ahead.

## Legal Considerations

Regardless of the type of studio—individual, group, or cooperative—any time there is more than one person involved, legal issues must not be overlooked. It is sad but true, but oftentimes a group of potter/friends will get together to rent a space and the only legal consideration they think of is the execution of the actual lease agreement, which details who is responsible for the rent, how much it is, when it is due, and whatever insurance is required by the landlord. Many times, this care-

# The Wesleyan Potters

If the idea and concept of establishing or belonging to a large potters' cooperative sounds intriguing, then a visit to The Wesleyan Potters Guild in Middletown, Connecticut, should be on your schedule. In the most important ways, it is typical of large craft coops. If a visit right now isn't possible, then the description here will have to suffice. However, you must visit a cooperative and experience the atmosphere for yourself at some point.

Founded in 1948 by some friends interested in learning how to make pottery, that group has evolved into a 100-member nonprofit craft coop. Though the vast majority (approximately 80) of those members are potters, the coop also provides space and programs in jewelry, basketry, and weaving crafts. It presently occupies a 9,000-square-foot building which includes a gallery/shop/office space, pottery studios and related spaces, weaving studio, and jewelry workspace.

*Figure 3-3. One of the studio areas of the Wesleyan Potters. In this space, members have their own equipment and workspaces. Adjacent to this space is the class area with its own wheels, tables, and shelves. (Photo by the author)*

The pottery facilities and equipment include separate class and member work areas, 15 wheels, open shared shelf space for work in progress, five electric kilns, a large commercial Alpine updraft kiln, a 90-cubic-foot car kiln, a soda kiln, two raku kilns, three test kilns, a slab roller, extruder, spray booth, pug mill, and a host of other pieces of equipment and tools.

The Wesleyan Potters is an incorporated non-profit institution and is operated and maintained by three categories of workers. A paid staff is comprised of a studio manager, assistant studio manager, office manager, gallery shop director, part-time assistant sales clerk, and two floor sweepers. The officers are elected from the membership and are a president, first vice president, second vice president, treasurer, and secretary. The membership comprises the remaining workers. Although there are highly qualified individuals as members, the teaching staff is intentionally not drawn from the membership, instead it is drawn from outside the coop. Since all members have a vote in the policies of the coop, the rationale is to eliminate conflict of interest issueardles that might arise when matters of teaching or classes are discussed and acted upon.

Over 1,000 adults and children take advantage of classes, workshops, and membership status on a yearly basis. A major happening at the guild is the annual winter sale representing the best work of the membership as well as some 250 outside craftspeople selected by jury or otherwise invited to participate. It has been held without fail since 1955 and is the major fundraising event of the year. For many, though, the great attraction to the guild is membership status. Membership slots are limited by the governing board and new members are accepted through an application process as slots open up. Each applicant must first have been a student at the guild for a minimum of two years, show a competent degree of skill in their chosen area of craft, and must be recommended by an instructor at the guild. Once accepted, a member is given a key and has unlimited access to the facility in exchange for a modest yearly fee (presently $250) and a commitment to serve on a specific committee and volunteer six hours of work per month to the guild. Committees cover the wide range of details and areas particular to the daily and long-term operation and viability of the guild and include publicity, glaze, gallery, space and design, buildings and grounds, education, hospitality, kilns, long-range planning, and many others.

Members have access to all the equipment in the studio and in addition may bring in their own wheels and set up their own small workspaces. Members also have private shelf space for the storage of personal tools, materials, and works in progress. As you would imagine, most of the members use the facility as their sole or primary studio space, though curiously, some also have other studios or workspaces at home where they produce most of their craft work. For them, membership in the guild offers other advantages. John Hampton the current president of the coop, has been a member since 1989. The attraction to the guild for him is the ever-present potential for interaction with others, exposure and access to the active schedule of visiting artists, good equipment, and up-to-date facilities.

Participation in the annual sale is also a major attraction. Diane Palmquist started making pots in 1972 while in high school and has been involved with the guild for the past 14 years (12 as a student and two as a member). She does all of her pottery making and glazing in her own studio and does her firing at the guild. She is a member of the coop for the camaraderie, interaction with other potters, social aspects, opportunity to sell in the gallery, and access to equipment that she wouldn't otherwise have at her disposal. "The Wesleyan Potters has been a great boost to my clay career. There should be more facilities like this for individuals to have access to," Diane believes.

lessness leads to, at best, misunderstandings, and at worst, dissolution of the friendship and bitter divorce!

And what about the one-person studio set up in the basement or garage? Are there legal considerations there as well? There are, as you might guess, many considerations that require legal attention. In my experience, these issues fall into two categories, contact with the public and the interpersonal relationships and connections between the members themselves.

Here's a typical scenario. A few friends or professional acquaintances think it would be a great idea to pool their resources of equipment, materials, contacts, and money in order to afford a large commercial space to share. Great idea! They talk about the concept, including design and layout, intended uses, hours of access, division of space, etc. Everyone speaks their mind, is heard and understood, and all agree to do it. A space is found and there is a frenzy of excitement. Now is the time to stop a potential runaway train and get off to a good start.

Craftspeople and artists have notorious reputations for being business retarded. This is partly because it's often true and partly because the side of the brain we tend to develop is, unfortunately, not the side of the brain with the highest capability and wherewithal when it comes to business and fiscal matters. Clearly, that has to be changed. If you suffer from business phobia syndrome and think that stuff is not for you, buckle down and get a grip on reality.

While I will discuss business and legal issues and considerations a bit later on, they bear mention now in general terms so you can begin to see their importance and relevance. Agreements are designed for the protection of the parties involved. Protection from outsiders as well as protection from one another. You can choose to treat that outlook as pessimistic, untrustworthy, self-

ish, or even distasteful. After all, who wants to have to be concerned about being taken advantage of, misunderstood, lied to, or worse? You are an honest, trusting person and are certainly not going to take advantage of anyone else. Who needs to be protected anyway? These agreements must be looked at as instruments that state clearly your intentions, expectations, responsibilities, and rights as much for your own understanding as for the understanding of others. By having it in writing, you are equally safeguarding yourself from miscommunication with others, and others from misrepresenting themselves and misinterpreting you.

Legal agreements are an absolute necessity and must never be overlooked. Some of the more obvious legal issues a group has to confront include lease and rental agreements, fire and theft insurance, and required liability insurance. Other equally important agreements to be arranged beforehand include the structure of the business being formed and what each member's responsibilities will be to that business entity. If money is being invested, each person's investment must be acknowledged with appropriate legality regarding repayment, interest, and other terms. If individually-owned equipment is being shared or contributed to this new business entity, what are the terms going to be? What happens if a member decides to withdraw from the coop? Do they lose their investment or initiation fee? Are they still responsible for their portion of the rent and maintenance until a new member is found?

The individual operating in their own space must be just as careful about tending to appropriate legal concerns as a group would be. Whether you realize it or not, even though your space is not shared, similar insurance and business issues apply and must not be overlooked. As you can see, the list of considerations is long. However, it is finite so don't get discouraged. More on legal issues later.

## Defining Your Needs

Now it's time to plug yourself into possible studio scenarios that may apply to you and see what feels good. I suggested earlier that first-time potters or those leaving the safety and security of a school environment would be wise to locate a group studio that offers membership. You may be beyond that now. Whether or not you are, you must identify and assess your work habits, personal style, and eccentricities. What? No eccentricities? Get out of town. We all have our own "mishigas" (Yiddish for craziness and idiosyncrasies) that have to be considered and if you can't begin this process with an honest evaluation of yourself, then I'm afraid the entire process is hopeless and doomed to fail! You are now about to step into the planning zone.

Most of you have done some amount of house painting, either inside or out. If you learned anything at all about house painting, either before, during, or after the experience, I hope it had to do with recognizing the importance of preparation. In painting, the finished job is the visible product and it is careful preparation that gets you there. Scraping, sanding, cleaning, priming, then and only then, painting. With careful preparation, the paint job is the easiest part of the process and is sure to last a long time. Planning for your studio situation can be compared to the importance of preparation in house painting. Don't neglect or shortchange the planning process.

Let's assume you are beyond plugging into an existing workspace and are contemplating one of your own design. Regardless of the type of space, planning for a workspace can be broken down into several areas, all of which need to be given equal and careful consideration. These areas include identifying the necessary spaces or work stations within, sharing the space, electrical, plumbing, ventilation, physical flow and how the spaces will be used, flooring, building materials, lighting, and a myriad of additional considerations.

The first question is who will use the space and what activities will go on there. Are you going to share the studio with a studio mate or is the studio yours exclusively? If the space is yours and yours alone, you have eliminated what may be the most difficult aspect of studio planning. That is, how to accommodate the needs of more than one person.

If you are embarking on the plans for a shared studio, the sharing must begin from the very start. All individuals involved must be involved equally in the planning and conceptual stages. Everyone must be confident that the space and its use is theirs equally.

If the studio you are contemplating will provide some degree of services for other potters such as firing facilities, gallery space, library, materials sales, etc., the way these services fit into the plan and the space must be considered and included. We're talking about a business plan as well as a floor plan that needs careful thought.

## Locating Space

How do you go about finding a space? With a lot of phone calling, newspaper reading, and legwork. End of advice. Period. Case closed. Okay, I'll give you more information than that, but be forewarned, it takes a heck of a lot of effort and oftentimes actually finding space is more work and ends up being even more rewarding than outfitting the space and moving in. Obviously, if the space you are going to be using is on your property, much of the following information will not apply, but it never hurts to be educated. Read on anyway.

Begin by setting some limitations. Of course, the broader your search and the less re-

# When You're Dealt Lemons, Make Lemonade

*Dick Lehman's studio and showroom is a beautifully assembled collection of spaces that flow in and out of each other with logic and harmony. But how he got there is a study of making the best of a potential disaster.*

I had long wished to someday have the opportunity and the means to build my own studio and assumed that if it happened it would be a decision made on my own. My studio was in an older building, my young business was becoming established, and I was comfortable. You can imagine my horror when I was notified by the county that the building was being taken by the provisions of eminent domain and I had 60 days to vacate. In shock, I actually considered folding my clay operation as the task of finding another space, moving, setting it up, getting re-established, disruption to my family, and all the costs involved seemed daunting. However, the building's owner (a furniture maker who also had his shop in the building) was encouraging and together we set about to find another building, determined to make this next situation even better. We looked at 13 potential sites and for each I drew up floor plans as a means of determining whether the space would work for us. Little did I realize that each drawing I did helped to form the basis for what was to be the plan for the eventual location.

In rather short time we found an 1890's brick, post, and beam constructed building. It was 60,000 square feet of open space and my mind went wild. This was it. I was now faced with some major life decisions. Taking up residence in this building would mean not only putting in the effort to move, set up, and re-establish my business including my customer base, but it meant securing a major business loan to finance the move, construction of the new space, and cover my living expenses until the pottery could support itself. It was very scary but my love of the craft and confidence in my abilities made my decision clear.

With a creative rental agreement with the building owner and a loan from a devoted and confident family member in hand, I set about designing my 3,500-square-foot portion of the building. I was keen on having a space that would give me ample production space along with necessary areas for office, shipping, packing, and photography, as well as generous showroom space to encourage retail sales, and have these spaces fully integrated. That is, to have privacy in the studio while giving the customer a feeling of welcome into the entire space. I achieved this by designing the space and my display cases allowing the customer's line of sight from almost anywhere in the showroom to travel directly into the studio space. Not only did this achieve my goal for the visitor, but it also allowed me and my three assistants to see customers as they entered the shop. (In the few areas that were out of sight, I discreetly installed rounded mirrors.) That first smile or nod from 35 feet away can mean the difference between a sale or not.

I was given an opportunity to design and envision an entire studio space as I eventually wanted to have it but realized that hastily made decisions could ruin my plan. What has emerged as the completed space is very much like the original vision but many details of the space and how it came to be ultimately designed and organized are the result of working in the developing space over a number of years. This strategy gave me the opportunity to fine tune many small decisions which in the end, have made the space far more usable and efficient than if I had made those decisions in the turmoil of those first few weeks following the forced move.

Looking back, it's hard for me to believe that I might have abandoned my dream to be a potter over a little thing like being thrown out of my building!

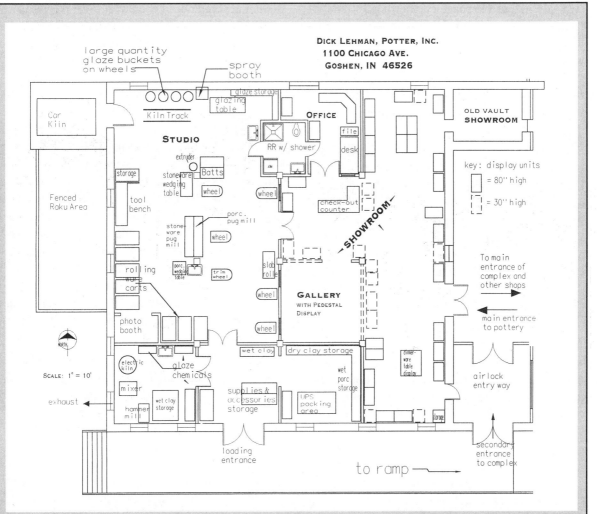

Figure 3-4. Floor plan of Dick Lehman's studio/showroom, Goshen, Ind. (Courtesy of Dick Lehman)

strictive your requirements, the better chance you have of finding something suitable. However, few people are in the position of having unlimited and unrestricted boundaries, so outlining these limitations will greatly facilitate the search. Are you planning to buy a building or rent a space? Most of you will be in a position to rent, though buying may be possible in areas where real estate values are not inflated. Smaller cities, towns, and hamlets can offer unbeatable deals on vacant or abandoned property and if these areas are appropriate for the type of operation you are planning, you should investigate availability.

Owning your own space is alluring and offers unparalleled security and the freedom to do whatever you like to the space (within legal limits, of course). Owning also means increased responsibility, expense, and headaches you might not want to take on. Circumstances that you took for granted as a tenant (leaky roofs, heating systems, storm damage, clogged plumbing) that were solved with a simple phone call to the landlord are now your burdens.

Renting is simpler in many ways and a lease with an expiration date allows the tenant to move to a better location if one is found. Of course, in a rental situation your development and use of the space is more closely regulated and if you do move, you must consider that the investment of materials and labor you made to improve the space may be lost and unrecoverable. And while that lease expiration date gives you the freedom to vacate, it also gives the landlord the freedom to raise the rent.

Larger cities and more populated areas may have artists' cooperatives or commercial condos that offer buyers affordable spaces for both working and living. One of the most well known developments in the Boston area is the Brickbottom Building in the neighboring city of Somerville. A group of artists and craftspeople looking for secure, affordable living and working space formed a corporation and began the search for a building. Guidelines were established for the kind of tenants who would occupy the space and the use of the space itself. A litany of regulations—from the design and construction of individual spaces, to the amount of equity each square foot would accrue, to the allowed resale prices of the apartment/studio—was put in place. Abandoned school buildings are popular subjects for purchase and renovation into artist's spaces and again, the Boston area is ripe with developments of that type.

Whether you are considering buying or renting, deciding the location is a sensible starting point and should be chosen with several criteria in mind. I find the most important of these criteria to be distance from home, type of neighborhood, and proximity to necessary services. By neighborhood I am referring more to zoning issues and any restrictions that might be placed on activities allowed than the beauty of the building or the desirability of its location. Don't overlook zoning laws when it comes to choosing a space. If you assume that because a space is commercial, it is suitable for your activity, you might very well assume incorrectly. Likewise, just because a space has been used similarly or even exactly in the way you intend to use it, it doesn't mean the space has been used legally and that you are entitled to continue its use in that way. I learned this well into my career, and when I did, it was the hard way. The following story illustrates all too well what can happen when you are a victim of ignorance and misguided trust.

Some years ago I was on a manhunt for a suitable space to relocate The Potters Shop. We had been renting a very comfortable space from a local college in their art building. We operated all our regular programs—classes, open studio space, services for potters, etc.—and in exchange for discounted rent and utilities, we also assumed the responsibility of being the school's ceramics program, offering three college level ceramics classes a week. After three years of what seemed to be a mutually beneficial arrangement for both the college and the shop, one day without any warning, I was told that the school's plans had changed and The Potters Shop was no longer a viable part of the program. Ooooooo, how I hate surprises. Our walking papers were served and my staff and I fanned out into the area in search of a space.

One of our resident potters came across what would eventually become our new home, an old mill building. It was in a convenient location (nice residential neighborhood), large enough, and apparently (according to preliminary information) affordable. It even had some interesting history (built as a corset factory over 100 years ago). I visited the building, assessed the space offered to me, and despite the desperation I was feeling in having to find a space before our present lease ran out, was able to maintain an objective view. The determination? It was too good to be true. It was large enough and I could divide it into areas for a glaze room, kiln room, main workspace, lounge, gallery, and my own studio. There was ample additional storage in the attic and a convenient area right outside to build a raku facility. It was a five minute drive from my house and my studio manager lived only two blocks away. It was a two minute walk to public transportation, easily accessible from major roads, and very close to the commercial services we use on a daily basis—bank, post office, hardware store, office supply, etc.

To keep things in perspective, though, it wasn't perfect. It was a second floor which meant hauling things like clay and materials up a long flight of stairs and it had wooden floors which, while quaint, are not ideal for a clay studio. It had a heating system that would be expensive to operate and presently had no water. Good thing, absolute perfection can be a bad omen! After successful negotiations with the building owner resulting in a comfortable rent, lease terms, satisfactory insurance, and attention to all the other necessary details, we moved in. Mind you, this was the fourth space the shop had occupied and by this time I had quite a bit of experience with leases, terms, rents, and other issues along those lines. Quite a bit perhaps, but as I would find out, there is always more to learn. The fun was about to begin.

Wanting to be good neighbors, we introduced ourselves to the community by delivering a letter to each house in a five block radius. The letter included a brief history of the shop, explaining that we were a group of potters and teachers who produced handmade craft objects and how we wanted to be a benefit to the neighborhood. It went on to say that we were quiet and would have little impact on the calm nature of the area. I ended with an invitation to come up for a visit and tour. Frankly, I anticipated at least a few inquiries or visits, if not out of interest in what we did, then at least out of curiosity. In hindsight, we did find it odd that no one took us up on our offer.

About three weeks later a letter arrived from the building inspector notifying me that necessary building and occupancy permits hadn't been procured and that The Potters Shop was in violation of town zoning laws and occupancy requirements. It went on to say that we would need to apply for a special permit from the zoning board in order to occupy the space. Thus began a chain of events that would take eight months and $25,000 to successfully resolve.

As it happened, we unwittingly put ourselves smack dab in the middle of a hornet's nest. This building, although absolutely commercial in nature, is in the middle of a residential neighborhood. Set back from the street to such a degree that we have to give visitors careful instructions so they don't pass by the driveway in search for us, it never occurred to me that any activity going on here, especially the quiet and benign existence of a clay shop, would bother or be a detriment to the area. I was wrong.

The hornet's nest turned out to be the residents living around the building. As we were to find out, they had been fighting the very existence of the building for years. After all, who wants to have the commercial tumult associated with business activities affect the peaceful, quiet enjoyment of their homes? To preserve their tranquillity, they challenged the legality of each

# School to Studio

Wendy Seller is an artist whose dream of a live-in studio came to life. She was one of a group of artists who, through passion, perseverance, resourcefulness, and courage, purchased a derelict school building and the surrounding three acres of land and turned it into 14 condos to live and work in. Once the initial purchase was made, it took about a year to complete general renovations to the building, including plumbing, electrical, heating, new floors, and interior walls. She moved into her space—half the former gym—with a completed bathroom, kitchen sink, and vision. That vision took six years, countless hours of work, and in other people's eyes, sacrifice beyond comprehension but for Wendy, the light at the end of the tunnel was forever in sight.

Always one to do things on her own and without a blueprint, Wendy planned the space as she went along, building, painting, and lugging materials while teaching and making art to support herself and her project. Building projects were undertaken and completed in stages as money became available. Lofts, stairs, cabinets, walls, windows, fixtures, furniture—all were designed and constructed by Wendy with help from an occasional paid assistant. Wendy attributes at least part of the success of the project to the fact that she didn't have the money to do it all at once. By doing it one step at a time, she was able to reflect on the completed portion and carefully integrate the next phase.

Wendy worked through injuries, family crises, financial crunches, and more. By the time she completed the final phase of construction, $31,000 had been added to the $78,000 she paid for her space. Was it worth it?

"I can't imagine a place I'd rather live," Wendy says. "This place was made for me."

*Figure 3-5. What was to become Wendy Seller's live-in studio, Newton, Mass. (Photo by Will Howcroft)*

*Figure 3-6. Partial view of Wendy Seller's finished studio condo. (Photo by Will Howcroft)*

new tenant's use of the space under the town's zoning laws, as these laws apply to areas of mixed use. The neighbors had been fairly successful over the years in getting the activity in the building reduced each time the use was about to change. To me, however, their arguments had some serious flaws. The building and its design as a commercial one predated all the homes in the area. As a matter of fact, the homes and the neighborhood had sprung up in response to the build-

ing. People who worked in the building built their homes there so they would be close to their work. Clearly, the folks who lived there now were no longer associated with the building. They did, however, buy homes next door knowing full well what was going on there. In addition, I thought, surely our use of the building would be considered less intrusive than other types of interests that were presently there. After all, we had no large trucks coming on a daily basis. Our activity was quiet, no loud machinery. Our daily retail activity was minimal and didn't generate high levels of walk-in customers causing traffic to clog up the street. Our parking requirements were more than adequately met, thereby eliminating the need for on-street parking. The final convincing factor was that we were serving the neighborhood and town by offering a cultural resource to children and adults that did not currently exist in this town. Who could deny the children of the area the opportunity to learn pottery and broaden their craft and art experiences?

Back to the letter. It sounded ominous. I called the building inspector, who was actually quite pleasant. We talked and he invited me in to discuss how we might proceed. At the same time, I thought it prudent to consult an attorney and was put in touch with an individual from town who had, at one time, served on the zoning board. What a connection, I thought! We met informally as a favor to a mutual friend. He gave me some advice and minimized the seriousness of the situation. We would have to make a formal application to the zoning board and present it at a public hearing.

"Routine stuff, happens all the time, no problem," he said.

"Are you sure? The letter sounds pretty serious. A special permit, zoning board, building inspector. Do we have a problem here?" I asked.

"All they want you to do is go through the process and get the required permit to satisfy the zoning requirement. There's never been a pottery studio in that space before and since it is a new use for the space, a special permit is needed."

"How should I prepare for the hearing? What do I have to bring? What do I have to be prepared to talk about?"

"Just tell the board what you do and how you will use the space. Tell them about the classes you teach and how this will be a great boon to the children of the neighborhood. Tell them about your history of success and the popularity of the operation. No one ever comes to these hearings. It'll be a piece of cake," he assured me.

I filed the appropriate application with town hall and was informed of the hearing date. Well, it was no piece of cake. The room in town hall was packed. People I had never seen before were mulling around and when I walked in, head after head turned and I could hear whispers. The members of the zoning board began by announcing that The Potters Shop was here to support its application for a special permit to occupy the building at 31 Thorpe Rd. I was asked to make a statement and did so, addressing the issues that my friendly (but absent) attorney advised me to address. After my statement, which I thought was well stated, to the point, and convincing, the board simply asked, "How does your application address the requirements of the zoning law?" Boy, was I on the wrong track. I had no answer. I hadn't studied the zoning law. I had no idea what they were talking about. It was the most uncomfortable situation I had ever been in. The neighbors were well versed in zoning law and even better prepared in their presentation. They were poised to squash me and my merry band of potters like ants. In the four weeks between the day we moved in and the hearing before the zoning board, they had gathered statements from neighbors (themselves) attesting to the fact that we were loud and a nuisance. Photos were presented showing delivery trucks coming into the neighborhood at ungodly hours. They had lists of "dangerous and polluting materials" we were spurting into the environment. They even had statements from our previous landlord about how irresponsible we were fiscally! It made no difference that the trucks delivering goods were not ours or delivering to us. It didn't seem to matter that the list of materials had nothing to do with anything we used. We hadn't even begun to operate out of the new space yet. And while "fiscal irresponsibility" couldn't be further from the truth, I was not prepared to respond to this or any of the allegations except to say that they weren't true. I felt like a business baron who, through some shady or undesirable deal, had become the target of hate and disdain. What I had thought I was prepared for turned into a personal and business fiasco. It didn't take long to figure out what was going on here and where the neighbors were coming from.

Since it was clear that we hadn't been in the neighborhood long enough for anyone to get to know us and that the allegations made against us were totally fabricated, the opposition must have had some underlying motive. Either they were being discriminatory on some arbitrary basis or they just didn't want that building occupied. I dismissed the discrimination theory out of disbelief. As far as the occupancy of the building, I couldn't think of any other operation that would be as quiet and unobtrusive as we would be. If our use of the space wasn't being supported, then whose would be? As it turned out, there was (unknown to us) a well-established feud between the building owner and the neighbors that, in its most simple terms, came down to the fact that the neighbors (in the formal term, "abutters") didn't want the building occupied at all! They contended that the building was in a residential neighborhood and should be used for residential purposes or torn down. No matter that the building predated all the houses that surround it. No matter that the homes were built in response to the jobs provided by the business in the building. No matter what the history, they wanted it to go away.

The hearing was continued to another date and even rescheduled for a larger space. I never make the same mistake twice. I hired an attorney whose specialty was town, land use, and occupancy law and we went to work.

It soon became clear that the zoning board as well as the building inspector were in sympathy with the neighbors. Hearing after hearing we would be faced with allegations and questions that we would seem to respond to adequately and positively, only to be met with more allegations and questions. Despite the Perry Mason-like expertise of my attorney, we were outgunned. No matter how we responded, whether it was with expert testimony, citing past cases of state zoning rulings, or what-have-you, the zoning board continued to acquiesce to the loud-mouthed neighbors who had their ear. It was a nightmare that I wouldn't wish on anybody.

So how did we prevail? By identifying the few substantive issues that directly related to our situation and limiting our arguments to those issues, and realizing that the neighbors would continue their vigilant opposition to us without regard to good conscience or to their own rational behavior. In our case, the substantive issues related to building size verses open space and the type of business (profit-making corporation, school, nonprofit, etc.) that was occupying the space. After three or four more hearings and through a chain of ironic events and actions on our part, the zoning board determined that our proposed use of the space was in compliance with the laws that governed the use of that space and that the ratio of open space to building space conformed to the required percentage. We finally received our occupancy permits.

There were compromises we had to make, but none that adversely affected the way we would operate the studio and certainly nothing that compromised my integrity or honesty. Financially, it was a disaster. Not only did the legal fees amount to a small fortune, but while the hearings were going on we couldn't operate on the weekends or at night, essentially closing down our school and access to the studio for studio members. That lost income would never be recovered.

What lessons can be learned from this experience? There are a few to be sure. Ask questions. It never occurred to me to ask about whether a pottery studio would be allowed to operate in this building. Why would it? It was never an issue before. It's an issue now. In this case, the building owner should have informed me about the history of the building and its occupants, but the fact is, he was as surprised at the turn of events as I was and had made no disingenuous effort to conceal information from me.

Get reliable professional help when you find yourself on unfamiliar ground. Consulting an experienced attorney from the beginning would likely have gotten me off to a better start. Know when to cut your losses and go back to the drawing board. During the initial stages of the proceedings, the objections raised against us appeared logical, seemed minor, and we anticipated being able to provide easy answers and explanations. Issues like noise, traffic, parking, and the like were concerns that deserved acceptable responses. But an answer on our part led to a question on theirs and this escalated into an uncontrollable frenzy of allegations that would make any reasonable person's ten-best list. In our case, we did discuss giving up the fight but several factors kept us going. Most importantly, and what had gotten us into this whole mess in the first place, was that the quality of the space and its appropriateness to our use was outstanding. But what had given us a false sense of confidence was that, in our eye, this frenzy of accusations made against us, along with the apparent shaky foundation of the allegations, appeared so ludicrous as to be humorous. It was obvious to us from the start that it was likely that our use of the space would be found legal and this entire proceeding would

be short and sweet. It wasn't, and I'll never be as overconfident as that again!

There is also the personal aspect of a confrontation like this. I would be less than truthful if I didn't admit that there was a certain amount of pride at stake here as well. I had endured serious attacks on my social and business integrity and honesty that I felt couldn't go unanswered. In hindsight, I was able to more clearly see what my attorney and friends had recognized early on—this was a strategy on the part of the neighbors and it was very effective. While I felt compelled to retaliate with equally personal attacks, better judgment reigned.

So, the usual conclusions. We shouldn't have had to go through this, it shouldn't have cost us so much in time, money, and emotion, we shouldn't have been so unprepared, we shouldn't have been so naive. It happened to us but it shouldn't have to happen to you!

## Studio Design

Before the actual studio design process can begin, consider the old question, "What came first, the chicken or the egg?" Do you have a space to work with or do you have to find a space? The design phase hinges on the actual space you have at your disposal but until that space is identified or you determine that you will find a space to conform to your design, you can't proceed. Of course, I'm primarily talking about mental activity here because for this activity to be successful at all, you have to maintain a considerable degree of flexibility in your plans and expectations. Before you begin looking for this elusive space, you should have already spent time assessing its intended use.

While I am not talking about a full fledged studio design yet, you should have some ideas regarding basic requirements to find one that will be suitable. The more space considerations you can apply to your search, the easier and more comfortable it will be to ultimately design, customize, fine tune, and furnish the space. For instance, how much total space do you need or want? Must you be on a ground floor? If not, is an elevator necessary? Do you need your own bathroom or is a shared common lavatory on the same floor acceptable? What are the characteristics of the space's natural light? Is the ceiling height a consideration? How much work and expense are you willing to do to customize the space? Identifying some of these basic requirements and features of your future space will greatly simplify the next step in your quest for your own studio.

Once you have tackled the daunting task of acquiring a space, the first consideration in designing or planning the workspace is to assess the space itself. This step is essentially a continuation of your earlier efforts to identify a suitable space. Most studios and work places are in an existing space, so you probably won't be able to design from scratch, which means there are certain limitations at the outset. If the space is in your home or on your own property, these limitations may be more flexible and you may be able to work around them more easily than if the space is in a commercial, industrial, or retail location. Nevertheless, there are always going to be limitations in what you can do to and with a particular space.

If you can build a space from the ground up, there is a significant difference in the design process that you can and should take advantage of. You have the ability to design the space from the inside-out rather than from the outside-in. What does this mean for you? It means you are not under the constraints of a wall two feet from where you would really like it to be. It means the overhead door area that makes sense for storing clay and materials can be where you want it to be. It means you can design your studio using the experience you've gleaned from working in studio spaces and you don't have to be anxious because you're not an architect. Think about it. When you work in a space, you are always moving around, continuing to move until a wall, door, window, or some other obstruction gets in your way. How many times have you wished a wall were a foot further back or the door was at the opposite end of the wall? The opportunity to design a space from the inside-out can free you in wonderful ways.

In assessing an existing space, a number of important factors must be taken into consideration. Begin with its shape and configuration. Note the existing divisions of the space and whether these areas are adequate as they exist. If not, are they removable or alterable? Note the materials used in the construction of the space and how the materials already in place may affect what you can do. For example, if the walls and floors are wood, it's easy to add walls, but if the existing walls and floors are concrete or cement block, construction methods are going to be a bit more technical and may require more outside help. Note the location of doors and windows and how these features may or may not fit into how you envision the space working. Windows can function not only as passive cooling in the summer, but as part of an active ventilation system for your kilns or spray booth. It's always easier and less costly to use existing features than to build them from scratch.

A major, and I mean *major,* consideration in any workspace is water. Be very careful to assess where the present water supply is, whether it's adequate, and what's involved in moving it, if necessary. You might assume that just because there's a water supply, you are halfway to getting it exactly the way you want it. Not necessarily. What matters most when it comes to water is where it presently is and where you ultimately want it to be, not whether there's water in the space. Don't be discouraged if the water supply and drainage system isn't already in your space, it may be just on the other side of a wall. On the other hand, it may be physically in your space but at the opposite end of where you want it to be. Note whether the water supply is hot and cold or just cold. If it's just a cold supply, you are going to be responsible for installing a water heater. The major consideration in installing a water heater is the choice of gas or electric and installing it properly to safeguard against the inevitable leaking tank. If you are on the ground floor, leakage may not be as critical as if you are on a higher floor where a leaking water heater can cause serious damage below. Plumbing can be a very costly proposition and in some cases, it may not be possible to bring the water where you want it. Time to redesign.

Electricity is another major factor in assessing the viability of a space. Examine the existing electrical service. What is the voltage and total amperage available? This question can be easily answered by looking at the service panel and reading the numbers, however, understanding and assessing the voltage and amperage of an electrical service can be much less obvious and may require an electrician. Where are the outlets, wall switches, and overhead lighting fixtures located? Keep in mind that you will have to augment the existing electrical service if you plan to install kilns or other specialized types of equipment such as a compressor, fans, etc. Augmenting the electrical service means bringing more power and service to the space and may mean bringing more power to the building. Where does the power enter the building? Where is the main electrical distribution panel for the building and what is involved in installing lines from that panel to your space? If you are renting, is each unit's electricity independent? That is, does each of the rented units have its own electric meter and service panel?

You can see that there are many things to consider in deciding whether a particular space may be suitable for your intended use. Don't take this step of assessing the space and its characteristics for granted. At best, outfitting the space will be more costly than you anticipated and at worst, the space you end up with may be unsuitable.

Once you have determined that the space is perfect for a pot shop, you're ready to begin the actual design phase and before you know it, you'll be potting away happily ever after. However, few raw spaces are perfect, and you'll have to make some sacrifices or compromises to make the space work. Design is as much about altering and changing the space as it is about altering and changing your work style and preconceptions about your workspace. Again, unless you are starting from scratch and building a new space from the bottom-up, there will be some compromises to be made. Not to worry. You can make it work!

## Making the Space Your Own

You're ready to design the actual interior. Whether you are building from scratch or retrofitting an existing space, the next phase—design and planning—is very similar. Here is where you plan your work areas, predict traffic patterns, place equipment, tables, shelves, lighting, and try to figure out every detail down to the placement of the telephone! This is the fun part.

Where do you start? Everyone reading this with the intention of designing a studio will have already had some experience working in one. You can't do this otherwise. Spending some time either in a pottery classroom, group studio, community center, or some other clay workspace is an absolute prerequisite for designing and planning one of your own. Having worked in a studio gives you a wealth of knowledge about studio design you may not even know you have.

The phase of design and planning is very similar whether you are building and designing from the ground up or within an existing space. But as I mentioned earlier, there are some significant advantages if you are designing from the inside-out. Keep in mind that you should begin your design in the center of your studio (where you'll spend the most time). This will most likely be your production area. For convenience and the sensible relationship between your various work areas, all other spaces should radiate (to a degree) from this central area as much as possible. Design the studio so there is the least amount of walking from one end of the studio to the other.

A good place to start your design is to do a couple of mental exercises to recall your own work habits. Begin by writing down the features of the workspaces or studios you have worked in. The more detail the better. Categorize the work areas, starting with those you found yourself in most often. Depending on the kind of studio you worked in, there may have been a main work area, glaze/materials room, kiln area, storage space, office, etc. Within these spaces, there were probably subdivisions. For instance, the main work area may have had potters wheels against one wall with a hand building area opposite. Were the potters wheels facing the interior of the space or were they turned to face the wall? Perhaps there was an area with a slab roller and extruder. Maybe there was a large worktable or two smaller ones. Where did you wedge or prepare clay? Was the wedging surface plaster, wood, laminate, or concrete, and was it covered with canvas or left bare? Was the clay stored out in the open or in a separate area? Was the clay kept in boxes and plastic bags or was it in a container on wheels? What kind of seating was there in the studio? Stools or chairs? Metal or wood? Did they have backs to sit back against? Keep going, keep thinking. What other features do you recall? Do this with every area of the studio.

**Glaze area.** Observe the work surfaces. Countertops or tables? Can you walk around them or are they accessible only from one side? How are raw materials and prepared glazes and slips stored and what type of containers are they in? Are they stacked for storage? Where and how are glaze room tools (brushes, scales, spatulas, screens, cups, bins, basins, buckets, etc.) stored? Is there a water source in the glaze room or do you have to use the sink from another area of the studio?

**Kiln area.** Is it a separate room? Observe ventilation, storage of kiln furniture, cones, and other kiln and firing supplies, electrical connections, and the amount of space left to maneuver between the kilns.

**Storage area.** Is there a separate storage area and if so, what's stored in it? How large is it? Is it situated logically in the studio? Is it equipped with shelves, bins, or other storage devices?

**Office area.** Don't overlook the need for a clean space for you to store business records and to carry on the everyday chores of business management. Desk space and space for your business machines (calculator, phone, answering machine, fax machine, computer, copier, etc.), file cabinets, and a storage cabinet for paper and other business items are essential.

**Display area.** If you plan on a display area, observe others you have seen, even if your display area is to be informal and noncommercial. Perhaps you simply want a place to store your finished work. This might as well be an outward display area so visitors can see your work. Who knows, you might sell something. It can be a closet or room or a corner of the studio. Whatever it is, keep it neat and clean. Will it be pots on shelves or pedestals? Commercial shelving or more elegant gallery-style shelves?

**Lounge/kitchen area.** Are you planning an area for rest and relaxation where you can sit

*Figure 3-7. Glaze room at The Potters Shop. (Photo by Marna Kennedy)*

*Figure 3-8. Partial view of the kiln room at The Potters Shop. Note the wall fan for exit ventilation, kiln shelf rack, and shelving units. (Photo by Marna Kennedy)*

down with your lunch and a good book or video? Don't overlook the comfort of a couch in front of a TV and VCR, with a refrigerator nearby. An area like this is a good place to keep your library and magazine collection as well as an appropriate place to sit down with a client or customer for a chat.

**Other areas.** Studios and workspaces you've been in may have had other specialty areas. Recall them and observe how they were used and whether they would be appropriate for the space you are designing.

Now that you have thoroughly dismantled every studio space you've ever set foot in, it's time to get more detailed about your own studio requirements and work habits. With the information you now have in hand about other studios, along with your own experience as a potter in those spaces, you can plug your own requirements in and come up with your ideal work environment.

With a rough sketch of the space, begin to draw out the placement of your areas and furnishings. Use graph paper and scale cutouts of the wheel, tables, counters, kilns, and other equipment. This technique and process will give you a good sense of how the space will work and how you will fit into the space. It's much easier and faster to move a paper cutout of your kiln and wheel on a paper floor plan than to move the real things around the studio! As you do this, keep in mind that there are two main factors you will use to determine the design of your studio: how the furnishings fit into the space, and how you plan to function with and around these items.

Your work habits and working style are details you now need to analyze and assess. Where should the glaze area be in relation to your clay working space? Where should the kilns be located in relation to the glaze area? How will clay and materials be delivered and stored and should that

**Work Flow**
  * Receiving area/clay and materials delivery
  * Storage for clay and materials
  * Clay preparation area
  * Production space
  * Trimming and finishing area
  * Storage of work in progress
  * Bisque firing
  * Unloading and storage of bisque ware
  * Glazing
  * Glaze firing
  * Unloading and display/storage of finished ware
  * Packing/shipping area

be near your wheel area? All these considerations have to do with your movement in the studio and making your studio as efficient as possible. I refer to this aspect of studio design working routine as work flow. That is, how your production and use of the space moves from one area to the next. A work flow list can help in organizing your thoughts.

Obviously, this list doesn't include all the possible and necessary areas of your studio. It really only considers the actual workspaces. Other areas I have mentioned are just as important and need to be sensibly incorporated into your design.

Figure 3-12 shows the rough floor plan of Bonnie Hellman's studio. Though this plan is for a studio built from the ground up, the approach to the planning and drawing is universal. The components, including doors, are drawn to scale, aiding in the comprehension of how the space will function. Notable features of this particular design include a radiant heat system in a cement

*Figure 3-9. The nerve center at The Potters Shop. (Photo by Bethany Versoy)*

*Figure 3-10. The Potters Shop library and lounge area. Books, magazines, and video tapes are conveniently accessible for all members of the studio in an area away from the muck of the workplace. (Photo by Bethany Versoy)*

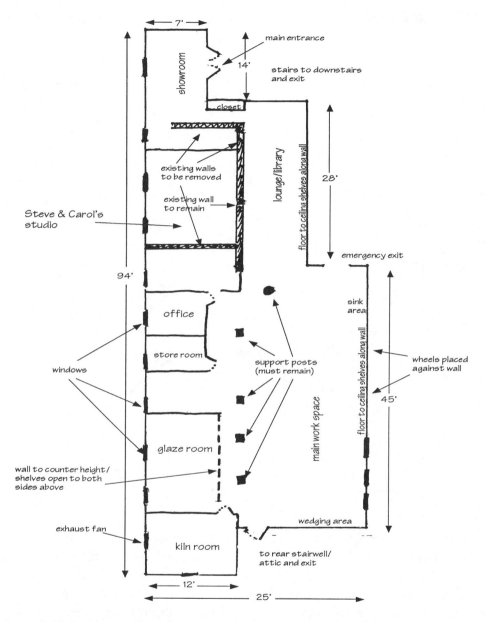

7'

showroom

main entrance

stairs to downstairs
and exit

14'

closet

existing walls
to be removed

existing wall
to remain

lounge/library

Steve & Carol's
studio

floor to ceiling shelves along wall

28'

94'

emergency exit

office

sink
area

store room

support posts
(must remain)

wheels placed
against wall

floor to ceiling shelves along wall

windows

main work space

45'

glaze room

wall to counter height/
shelves open to both
sides above

exhaust fan

kiln room

wedging area

to rear stairwell/
attic and exit

12'

25'

*Figure 3-11. Preliminary floor plan drawing for The Potters Shop, 1989. The entire space was
open except for the existing walls as indicated. After doing this initial plan, a detailed drawing
was done on graph paper with cutouts of equipment and furnishings to help validate the sensible uses of the spaces. (Drawing by the author)*

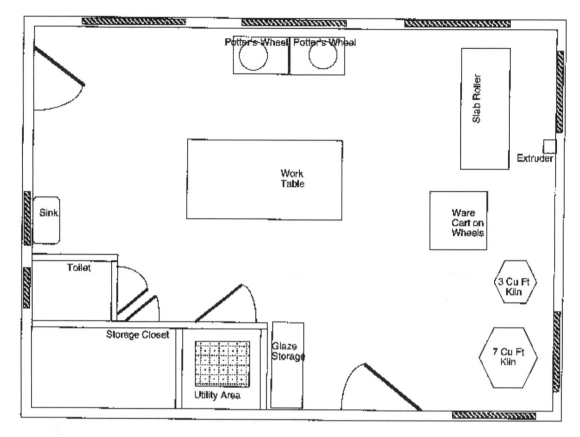

*Figure 3-12. Floor plan of Bonnie Hellman's studio designed by Bonnie and Jeremy Hellman. Additional features include electrical outlets in the ceiling for added convenience and the kiln venting directly to the outside with individual venting systems. Not indicated are shelves which will be on all the walls between the windows. (Courtesy of Bonnie Hellman)*

floor that comes up one foot high around the perimeter with floor drains so the floor can be easily hosed down for cleaning.

Efficiency in floor plan is important and becomes much more so when you have a tight space to begin with. If you have the luxury of an abundance of space to work with, you can afford to apply a little less scrutiny to this area of studio design, but even the grandest studios are much more functional and comfortable to work in when the floor plans reflect the style, work habits, and personality of the inhabitants. You say you have a garage you are turning into your clay heaven and all of this planning seems overkill? No way. With careful planning and the layout of your equipment and work surfaces according to this plan, even the smallest and simplest of spaces can be made into enviable studios.

*Figure 3-13. The author's studio at The Potters Shop. (Photo by the author)*

It's very likely that your space will be small and not able to accommodate separate clay working, glazing, storage, and kiln areas. Yours will have to be the one-room schoolhouse studio. That's fine. With careful planning, you can roll out your glazes, store your clay and materials, and have your kiln ventilated to the outside, and function comfortably all within four walls. Careful studio design and vigilance in neatness and keeping things orderly will insure your success!

## Construction of Your Space

While anyone is capable of designing and planning the space, not everyone is capable of undertaking the actual construction. Many reasons may prevent you from taking hammer and saw in hand and pounding away. You may not be interested, you may be physically unable, you may have terrible construction skills, or you may simply be too intimidated by the whole ordeal. I'm not going to talk you into taking this on, but I will say that simple framing and construction techniques are within the capabilities of most of us and if you want to give it a try, you certainly can. Building partitions, tables, counters, hanging doors, laying a floor, or installing a light are simple enough for the most inexperienced to learn if you have the interest and desire. On the other hand, installing the electrical service for your kiln, plumbing, pouring a concrete foundation, or any number of more complex processes necessary for the completion of your space may not be within the realm of your ability and it's important to recognize that early in the construction phase. Certainly there are pros and cons to contracting out the construction of your studio. The pros are easy—professional construction workers will apply their expertise to your project and you can usually assume it will be done well. The cons are that it will cost you more and the work schedule may not be as fast as you like. Let's take this aspect of studio construction slowly and logically.

With your space and plan in hand, take a look at the amount and complexity of the needed alterations. Break these down into projects you think you can do or learn to do, and those you feel are out of your league. No machismo here! With each studio space that I moved into, I was able to take on more of the construction work myself from the experience I had gained previously. In the space I presently occupy, my staff and I constructed all the interior partitions and installed much of the electrical wiring for the usual outlets, lights, and wall switches. We built the counters in the glaze room, wedging tables, work tables, and all the shelving. Of course, we did all the painting as well. The major projects we didn't undertake were the plumbing and electrical service for the kilns.

Since almost all studio construction projects require building walls and partitions, start with that. Before you do, though, before you pick up a nail, hammer, screwdriver, or screw, check into the world of construction permits and building inspectors. Warning: it may not be a pretty sight!

## Construction Permits/Building Inspectors

Inevitably there will come a time when you must deal with the local building or fire inspector. This will usually be in the context of either building or remodeling a structure for use as a studio or installing or building a kiln. Let's focus on the former first, since I deal with issues pertaining to kilns later.

Sometimes, depending on the town or city, even the simple act of moving into and occupying a space may require formal approval and an occupancy permit signifying that the space is suitable for your intended use. But whether you are simply moving into an existing space, doing minor remodeling, or a major renovation, contact with the building department is necessary to secure the necessary permits and schedule the subsequent inspections. The complexity of the structure or degree to which you plan to alter the existing space is not the issue when it comes to whether or not some kind of permit is needed. Any work you plan to do to a space will most likely require a permit and inspection upon completion. For many, this step in the studio process is a difficult one that generates an unhealthy amount of anxiety. Before I attempt to quell your fears, you should understand the purpose of it all.

I'm sure some of you have had experiences with building inspectors and have already formed attitudes about them. I hope that at least some of the experiences were positive. However, regardless of what you think of building inspectors and what you believe their motives may be, building permits and the subsequent inspection of the work in progress and the finished job are in place for the safety of those who will ultimately use the space. Although the process, including the hoops you sometimes have to jump through, may be time consuming, frustrating, and often appear ludicrous, the permit and building process is an absolute necessity. If you are doing your own construction, you benefit twice from the process, both as a construction worker and as the ultimate user of the space. Requirements concerning construction codes, regulations, materials, and other considerations vary from town to town, but you can be sure they exist and that your town or city, not the state or federal government, issues and is responsible for the regulations.

Generally, the process begins when you present your plan to the inspector. Depending on the requirements of the town, the plan can be as informal as a sketch or even a walk-through where you point out the changes you are planning, or it may need to be a professionally prepared blueprint indicating every minute detail of the work to be done. Whatever the requirements are, that's what you have to do! There is no way around it and if you try to circumvent the process, it will undoubtedly catch up with you at some unfortunate point. Realize, too, that not knowing you had to get a permit is never going to be an acceptable response to the zoning board or planning department. I have heard of situations where a building inspector, upon being made aware of changes to a space, inspected the space and ordered the work taken down and rebuilt so it could be inspected during construction. There was even a case in the town where my studio is located where the entire top floor of a new building had to be removed to comply with zoning codes. Don't you hate having to do the same thing twice?

Certain towns have regulations covering what kind of work an unlicensed individual can do. For example, they might dictate that electrical or plumbing work of a certain complexity can only be done by a licensed electrician or plumber. If you are planning to do some or all the building yourself, this is an area that merits some investigation. In addition, there are often requirements that specify the kind of materials allowed and disallowed. In the town where my studio is located, plastic plumbing components are adequate and allowed in residential installations but only copper and iron are allowed in commercial buildings. There may be regulations regarding the use of metal verses wood studs in wall construction or other restrictions placed on the use of certain materials. The bottom line regarding building permits is to check with the local building inspector before you begin any work on a space. In the long run, you'll be glad you did.

Now you know the reasons for contacting the building department and securing the necessary permits. Should you bother getting a permit to divide a room in half? Do you need to go through all this red tape to install new lights or a larger window? How about getting a permit to install a larger sink or clay trap? The choice is still yours, but I'd say better safe than sorry.

## Simple Framing and Construction Techniques

Since you are now getting into building things, the first order of business should be to assemble a collection of tools. These tools will serve you not only through any studio construction projects you are planning now, but through everyday repair, building, and maintenance. Speaking from experience, I advise you to buy the highest quality tools you can afford. They will pay for themselves in the long run, not only in the quality of the work you will be able to perform, but in their reliability, ease of use, and longevity. Many manufacturers and retailers of quality tools such as Husky, Craftsman, and others offer lifetime warranties that guarantees that they will replace a tool at no cost if it should break or fail in some way.

Other tools to add to your collection as you need them include open-end wrenches, socket wrenches, chisels, files, and clamps. The list above should get you off to a good start. In addition to the tools, you'll need screws, nails, bolts, washers, and a whole mess of additional pieces of fastening hardware. Buy these items as you need them for projects, buying more than you need to stock your supply.

# From Basement to Sanctuary

*Rick Malmgren is a successful potter with very uncertain and modest beginnings. He is dedicated to his craft and serious about what he makes and has forged a career out of an enduring commitment to aesthetics and lifestyle.*

In 1975 I got started working in a basement apartment. It was one big room with only a shelf unit separating my bed, bathroom, and small kitchen from the potting area. I was living and working in the same room. I had an 18" electric kiln and I stored my work on metal shelving from a hardware store. Clay came to me in boxes, commercially prepared from Westwood Clays. It was kind of crazy for a Maryland potter to be using California prepared clay, but it was the best available and I found it easy to throw in a time when I was just learning how to handle clay.

I bisqued and glazed my work in the apartment and then drove it a mile up and down some of the steepest hills in Maryland to my parents' house where I had a gas kiln that I fired to cone 10 reduction. I usually lost several pieces on the journey or at least had to retouch the glaze while loading pieces into the kiln. Little margarine cups came in handy for holding repair glazes for each trip. Those 8 a.m. to 11 p.m. firing days were long, but they also came to be my rest-and-reading days. While my body would take a break, my mind would engage itself in books about clay. In retrospect, I see that those hours away from the studio were very important to my growth. When the firings were finished, I would pack everything up carefully and carry it home to be sorted out and shipped off. It was a surprisingly productive year.

After that first year, I knew I wanted to be a potter and that I should set up my own kiln and a more proper studio. I was also teaching in a ceramics program in Columbia, Maryland, and the hour-long commute from Annapolis to Columbia was beginning to wear on me. One day I saw an ad for a house with a full basement, stable, outbuildings, garage, and shed. It was a great "starter home," convenient and affordable, though tiny. It also backed up to woods and had over an acre of land separating it from the houses around it. One of my concerns in buying the home was whether I could legally set up a studio on the property. The county does provide for home occupation, but potters are never mentioned in its rules and regulations. The closest category I could find was "custom woodworking." I wrote to the head of the zoning department for clarification and received a letter back that I interpreted as approval. Now over 20 years later, I have had no problems with zoning and don't expect to, but it is always a gray area. Feelings about zoning seem to change as the community changes, and the county is responsive to community pressure. My wife and I wonder whether we are just one step away from a complaint or argument with a neighbor that might cause us great grief and expense.

The cinder block building where I work was unheated when I moved in, so I hired two carpenters to put in sliding glass doors, install a propane furnace, and enclose a tin frame lean-to that was next to the garage. They were fast and it was cheap. The workspace is 22 by 22 feet with half devoted to firing, storing bisque work, finished work, my clay mixer, and glaze materials. All my clay work takes place in the other half.

I make the space work by being organized.

*Figure 3-14. Rick Malmgren's studio, a converted garage in Severn, Maryland. Behind and out of view is a separate small building housing his downdraft gas fired kiln. (Photo courtesy of Rick Malmgren)*

Sometimes it feels like working or living on a boat. Like most potters, I work in cycles, spending my days throwing, trimming, decorating, and glazing. For several years, the cycles were fairly long—three weeks throwing, a week glazing and decorating, and a week or two to fire everything. In more recent years, I have switched to a weekly cycle, throwing and trimming for three or four days, and firing at the end of the week. My body responds well to the more frequent activity shift.

We no longer live in that tiny starter home. We've since moved to a 650-acre wildlife sanctuary where my wife works and we are the caretakers. Though it's a 45-minute drive from the studio, I love it and I make the best of the ride by making notes to myself and pondering the day's work schedule.

One thing that repeatedly strikes me is how few young or new potters there are. I see lots of people from my generation who are interested in pottery as a lucrative hobby when they retire, and a few of the traditional college-age students who are drawn to pottery as a hobby. Almost no one in my experience is doing what so many of us did 20 years ago, striking off to make it in clay.

*Figure 3-15. Interior of a portion of Rick Malmgren's studio. (Photo courtesy of Rick Malmgren)*

As I said earlier, most every studio construction project involves the building of walls or partitions. Walls are simple to build and the construction techniques involved can be used to build tables, counters, shelving systems, and other features of your studio. There are essentially two components to a wall: the framework and the wall covering. Lumber used to build walls is commonly 2" by 3", 2" by 4", or 2" by 6" dimensional lumber with 2" by 4" the most common. Boards 2" by 3" are usually reserved for partitions

in closets or other tight spaces or for other uses. Studs 2" by 6" are usually used for outside walls where the additional thickness allows for more insulation. Studs are generally available in 8, 10, 12, 14, 16, 18, and 20 foot lengths.

One of the first things to learn about lumber is that the labeled measurement of the board is not the actual measurement. Dimensional lumber and boards are known by their nominal size. Thus a 2" by 4" is not 2" thick by 4" wide. It is actually 1-1/2" by 3-1/2". The original 2" by 4" measurement comes from the lumber before it is milled down and then shrinks to precise construction standard sizes. Common pine boards that you might use for shelving are labeled in the same fashion. A 1" by 12" pine board actually measures 3/4" by 11-1/2". Plywood, on the other hand, which you might use for a tabletop, countertops, shelves, or wall covering, is sold by its exact measurement. It is very important to realize this when planning a project.

To build a nonstructural, nonloadbearing wall or partition, assemble the wall on the floor and raise it into position when completed. Make the

framework with 2" by 4" studs. A simple wall consists of the sole plate, vertical studs, and top plate. Studs are generally placed 16" on center, though you may place the studs 24" on center. More studs make a stronger wall, better for heavy shelving loads or to hang an extruder from. Why 16" or 24" on center and not some other measurement? Wall covering goods such as sheet rock, paneling, or plywood are manufactured in 4 by 8 foot sheets and the relationship between these measurements allows for accurate fastening to the stud wall. It also gives you a sense of where the

*Figure 3-16. A typical wall of 2" x 4" stud construction—this one with plywood sheathing on the exterior. Note the electrical box installation. (Photo by the author)*

## Tools to have on hand:

Carpenter's claw hammer with
   12-16 oz. head
Screwdriver set including slotted
   and Phillips head in various sizes
Carpenter's awl
Slip joint pliers
Channel lock pliers
Needle nose pliers
Lineman pliers
8" vice grip pliers
Adjustable open end wrenches,
   6", 8", 12" long
Allen end wrenches, set of
   metric and SAE sizes
Crosscut saw
Hacksaw
25-foot tape measure
36" metal straight edge
24" carpenter's steel square
24" level
Bench vice
2 sawhorses
3/8" electric corded drill
7-1/4" circular saw

studs are after they're covered, so you can find them to hang shelves or other objects.

The first step is to measure the width (or length) of the wall. Then cut the top and sole plates to size. Next measure and mark on the top and sole plates for either 16" or 24" on-center studs. Measure and cut the studs to height. Position the studs on your marks and nail in place with 16-penny, 3" nails. Raise the wall, level it, and nail it into place.

There you have it—your first wall! Not so fast, not so easy. There are plenty of considerations I haven't raised yet. Building the wall itself is easy but getting the measurements correct and being able to actually raise the wall and fasten it in place could be difficult. First think about the height of the wall. If you are building a floor-to-ceiling wall, you have to consider the ceiling height and build a wall on the floor to that height. As you raise it into place you realize that because of the thickness of the wall, it is just a little too tall to clear the ceiling height and be raised into place. Ooops! The solution is to build the wall 1-1/2" shorter than the ceiling height. Cut a second sole plate and nail it in position on the floor. Raise your wall, lift it onto the sole plate, and snug the wall into position. Your wall must be securely fastened to the floor, ceiling, and adjoining walls, to existing studs, floor joists, or ceiling rafters.

Other specialized features of wall construction are corners where walls come together, fitting walls around existing objects, floors that may not be level, door openings, and other components.

I also haven't discussed the wall sheathing or covering. The purpose the wall surface will serve will help you decide what kind of covering to apply. The most common wall covering is sheet rock, also known as drywall. This has a core of gypsum covered on both sides with paper. The panels are normally sold in 4 by 8 foot sheets though 10, 12, or even 16 foot lengths can be or-dered. Standard thicknesses are 3/8", 1/2", and 5/8" with 1/2" being the most common. Sheet rock cuts easily with a matt knife and is designed to have its seams taped, puttied, and sanded to perfection before painting. Applying wall board tape, putty, and sanding, is a thankless, filthy, dusty, and utterly disgusting job that should be avoided at all costs if possible. However, if your goal is to have a beautifully smooth wall surface, then sheet rock is the way to go. Though the process is time consuming and tiresome, a quality finished wall surface is within the ability of most everyone who has the patience to see it through. Other acceptable wall coverings include commercially available paneling and plywood of various grades and wood types.

While the actual construction of walls and partitions is relatively easy, much more preparation and education is necessary before you can confidently work on these projects in all situations. Because more homeowners want to do it themselves, there has been a proliferation of quality step-by-step instruction manuals and books on all phases of construction including basic carpentry, home repairs, and maintenance. You'll find some of the best listed in the bibliography. I have a collection of these books myself and they have come in handy many times over. I urge you to have a few of them in your own library. Also, home centers such as Home Depot and others offer free weekend workshops on a variety of home construction projects including wall construction, laying floors, painting, and other building projects that are really quite good! They even offer workshops on the use and care of tools and choosing fasteners for the right applications. Take advantage of what these places have to offer. In addition to formal workshops, local lumberyards may be happy to offer you some help and advice in planning and building your project. Don't be afraid to ask!

# Electrical Needs

In addition to building simple walls and partitions, the next most likely area of construction you might be tempted to try is simple electrical wiring. Do-it-yourself wiring for outlets, switches, and lights is relatively easy if you have some basic electrical knowledge. Experience and familiarity with volts, amperage, watts, ohms, electrical grounding, circuits, and wire gauge are essential. So is understanding the various components of electrical circuits and connections such as single pole and three-way switches, metal and plastic wall boxes, fuses and circuit breakers, romex and bx cable, and other segments of electrical systems. If you have some experience, then by all means go ahead and do your thing, but I won't give instructions on wiring here. Even the easiest aspects of wiring can be complex, dangerous, and require the utmost attention to safety. Again, the home maintenance books mentioned above offer very complete and detailed instructions for do-it-yourself wiring and electrical maintenance. What I will offer is some basic electrical knowledge, advice on planning for your electrical needs and the placing of your outlets, switches, and other components.

Begin by thinking of your studio's electrical needs in two parts. First are your regular electrical demands such as outlets for your wheels, office machines, power tools, grinding wheel, air compressor, lights, general heating and ventilation, kitchen appliances, TV, and radio. Second are the special demands of kilns and kiln components such as power burners (if you use them with a gas kiln), fans, kiln room ventilation, electric kiln ventilation systems and computerized controls, and any other items specific to the kiln room and firing.

I have always found it practical and helpful to maintain separate electrical service in this way for a few reasons. In any studio larger than a one-person shop where you have several wheels, a few different workspaces, and other equipment as well as two or three electric kilns and ventilation, your electrical demands will be high, electrical service boxes can be complicated, and your own understanding of the system can be limited. Having separate service simplifies things and allows you to organize your understanding of electrical needs a bit better. Knowing that the circuit breakers for your kilns and related equipment are in electrical box "A" and the circuit breakers for ev-

*Figure 3-17. Circuit breaker box where electricity is distributed to the outlets, lights, and appliances. The small box to the left is an automatic timer for outside lights. (Photo by Bethany Versoy)*

erything else are in electrical box "B" makes it easy to locate a tripped breaker. If you need work done on your kiln, you won't have to shut down the rest of the studio while the work is being done. Taking this one step further, you can sometimes have these separate systems drawn from separate transformers in your town's electrical grid so that if there's a power outage, brownout (where voltage is temporarily reduced by a small percentage), or other electrical system failure, your entire studio is not affected. In my studio, there are two separate services of 200 amps each, just as I have described.

Let's talk a little about electric supply and your needs. Electric service is discussed in terms of volts and amps and is supplied the same way. Typically, 240 volts of electricity come into your home or studio where they are divided at the circuit panel into 110-120 volt circuits. This means you have 110-120 volts available at any outlet to power what you plug in there. In addition, you have the full 240 volts available to operate higher voltage appliances like electric ranges, clothes dryers, and kilns. You do have items that don't require 110 volts to operate and would fail dangerously if they were subjected to that much voltage—desktop calculators, telephone answering machines, cordless phones, battery chargers, and other like appliances that plug into 110-120 volt receptacles but do so via small mysterious black boxes called AC adapters. These adapters are small transformers that greatly reduce the voltage from your outlet to an amount that is usable for the object it powers. In fact, many electrical devices and appliances actually operate on less than the full voltage coming into it and have some sort of internal voltage regulator that adjusts the voltage for that device.

To form a practical understanding of your electrical system, you need to be familiar with volts, amps, wire gauge, circuit, and circuit breakers.

Anything electrical needs a certain amount of voltage and draws a certain number of amps as it operates. The term volt is analogous to pressure. Think of water pressure and you'll get the idea. The higher the pressure, the more force there is pushing the water through your pipes. The higher the voltage, the more pressure is behind the current. Amperage refers to the amount or quantity of current flowing to or being used by an appliance. It gets this voltage and draws the amps through the electrical wiring of a certain gauge that runs through your house or studio. The gauge is indicative of the amount of electricity a wire can supply, which in our water analogy is similar to the diameter of your hose or water pipe. The larger the pipe diameter, the more water can flow. In electrical terms, the heavier the wire gauge, the more electrical current can be delivered.

Total electrical consumption is measured by the combination of volts and amps, or watts. Watts are computed by multiplying voltage by the amps being used. A kiln that draws 60 amps at 240 volts is said to draw 14,400 watts or 14.4 kilowatts (Kw). Look at the specifications of your electric kiln and note the wattage for yourself. This will come in handy later when I discuss how to assess your kiln's operating costs.

A home or studio electrical system is divided into several circuits, with each one able to handle a certain demand. As the amperage demand on your circuit increases (the more appliances you operate at once), the wiring heats up. This temperature increase is of no concern unless it reaches a point beyond the safe limits of the wiring and of the circuit as a whole. If this happens, a circuit breaker automatically shuts the system down by sensing too much amperage being drawn through the wiring, thus preventing a potential fire hazard. It is also useful to understand that as an additional safeguard, a circuit is designed to handle only 80% to 90% of its rated load. This means that if you have a kiln that indicates a draw of 40 amps, it will have to be on a circuit with a 50 amp circuit breaker. I have often come across situations where a 50 amp kiln is connected to a 50 amp circuit, resulting in a tripped breaker. The combination of the electrical appliances you want to operate and the voltage and amperage these appliances require and draw dictates the wire gauge, number of separate electrical circuits, circuit breaker size, and ultimately the design of your electrical system.

So what good is all this mumbo jumbo if you're not going to do the electrical work yourself? Aside from the satisfaction that you have knowing just what it is that makes those fancy little electrons ramble through your walls and into your kilns and lights, how about the ability to discuss electricity with your electrical contractor when you talk about the system for your studio? How about knowing a little something about electricity when the repairman comes to fix your lights or to install your new kiln? Or better yet, how about not having to scratch your head when the circuit breaker trips during a firing and shuts off your new kiln? (A good illustration of how a little knowledge can be useful and can make your workplace safer.) It is true that sometimes a breaker will trip for no apparent reason, and after you reset the switch, all is well. But more often, a tripped circuit breaker is an indication that something has gone awry. Using the kiln as an example, the cause of the tripped breaker might be a short circuit where a hot wire has come in contact with the metal case. This can happen if a wire attached to one of the switches corrodes or otherwise separates from the switch. The resulting contact causes electrical current to flow to the ground, which trips the circuit breaker. This happens at the speed of light and is a built-in safety feature of all modern electrical devices and circuits. If there was no safety mechanism, coming

in contact with that electrified kiln shell could prove seriously shocking. Anytime a circuit breaker trips, you should examine the appliance and/or the circuit itself.

Another common but often overlooked cause for a circuit breaker trip is an overheated circuit breaker. Through age and use, the electrical draw through a breaker can eventually cause it to fail. A contributing factor can be if your service panel is located in your kiln room where both the air in the room and the panel itself can reach unusually high temperatures. The kiln room in The Potters Shop can get as hot as 120 degrees and we have experienced premature failure of circuit breakers. My advice? Locate your kiln room's service panel just outside the room, not in it! I wish someone had told me that ten years ago!

While the actual installation of your electrical system may be best left up to a professional, you should at least be involved in planning the system and the placement of outlets, switches, lights, and other features. You, after all, will be the one to live with it after it is completed. Although changes can be made to fine tune the system (and expect there to be some), there is nothing better than doing it right the first time.

To plan the system and layout of outlets and wall switches, you must have already laid out your tentative floor plan, denoting workspaces and the placement of your equipment. With this done, you can easily "walk through the plan" and "see" where things need to be plugged in. Once that bit of design is finished, you must decide on the number and placement of outlets. Next will be the placement of equipment that will need to be installed such as fans, spray booth, and similar appliances. At this point, you can more intelligently design your lighting to provide maximum visibility and comfort, based on the tasks you will be performing in the different areas of the studio.

While lighting may seem like a simple concept, there are reasons why some people make their living as lighting designers and consultants. Lighting design is a complicated craft and if you have the opportunity to design a lighting system from scratch, you should absolutely get some professional help and advice. The obvious factor to consider is the placement of your lights, but there are others that may not be as obvious. Even the placement of lights requires some thought because the difference between placing an overhead fixture 6" to 12" in either direction can make the difference between distracting shadows falling on your work surface or having a clear view. Some other factors to consider include the size and wattage of lights and the type of lighting source. We can all recognize the difference between incandescent and fluorescent lights but within these two categories exist quite a few variations of light quality, appearance, and physical comfort. Generally speaking, you want a combination of incandescent and fluorescent lighting, but fluorescent lights have come a long way in recent years and the quality of some is comparable to that of incandescent lights. Don't overlook the importance of the placement of wall switches to operate your lights. The convenience of being able to turn on a light from a handy spot in the studio can be immeasurable. Remember that you are not limited to one switch in one location for your lights. They can be put on three- or four-way switches, giving you the flexibility to switch them on or off from multiple locations.

Another lighting consideration should be an emergency lighting system. These are lights that will automatically come on in the event of a power outage. Emergency lights are battery powered and wired into an electrical circuit. This circuit essentially powers a switching mechanism in the emergency light that, when turned off due to a power outage, engages the battery power in the light. The purpose of emergency lights is not so much for you to be able to continue to work during an outage, but to help you find your way around in the dark. I have found emergency lights to be very useful and valuable. While there is no need to make this aspect of studio and electrical system design any more complicated than it needs to be, a visit with a lighting expert should be on your schedule.

After outlet, appliance, and lighting placement are determined, take a look at the number of circuits that will be needed to power all the equipment that will operate at the same time.

*Figure 3-18. A typical emergency lighting system. (Photo by Bethany Versoy)*

Remember the discussion on electrical circuits and load. Just because you have an abundance of outlets doesn't mean you can have an infinite number of appliances operating at the same time. When I set up my first studio, the electrical system was so outdated that I couldn't have two electric wheels plugged in next to each other because the circuit couldn't handle the load!

Planning your electrical system may seem like a daunting task but with a little electrical knowledge, proper preparation, and perhaps consultation with experts, this phase of studio design need not be difficult. Spend the necessary time to do it right the first time. A properly designed system will function quietly and imperceptibly in the background while you take the whole thing for granted!

## Contractors and Tradesmen

All this advice to consult experts and professionals for studio construction and electrical work may raise the question of how to find reputable and competent contractors. It's a simple procedure, but one that can take some time and it's not easy. The next chapter deals with this subject in detail, but let me say a few words about it now in the context of electricians and builders.

Calling in the services of an electrician, plumber, or builder should never be thought of as a one-time event. You will undeniably need these services time and time again throughout your career and throughout the life of your studio. With this in mind, you might as well go through the task of properly and responsibly identifying quality tradesmen so you can rely on them for your future needs as well as your immediate one. Once you have found a good plumber, electrician, or any personal service provider, guard them like jewels or babysitters (if you have preschool age children, you know what I mean!).

You can begin the search in any number of ways, including cold-calling from the Yellow Pages, but don't ever let anyone put a wrench to your pipes without some sort of a personal recommendation. I have never hired an electrician, plumber, contractor, painter, or any tradesman without the recommendation of a friend, professional colleague, or some other acquaintance. If you are new to a location and have no friends to ask, even the recommendation from a neighbor or other business owner is better than nothing. You will be confident that at least someone has had a successful experience with this particular person. Mind you, this is far from foolproof. Just because Sam the Electrical Man did some good work in a timely fashion for the guy down the street doesn't necessarily mean that this is his usual style. But a recommendation is a good start and an essential one at that.

After you have a potential individual or company identified, a bit of an interview is necessary to make sure you are comfortable with their personal characteristics, business style, fees, prices, and terms. You have to be able to communicate your needs to them and know that they can fulfill those needs. If this seems like too much to get into with someone who is simply going to fix your sink or install a new electrical circuit, think again. Don't make a costly mistake by making an uninformed and careless choice. There is much more to consider on this topic and we'll cover it in the next chapter.

## Furnishing and Outfitting Your Space

By now, you undoubtedly realize that there is much more to setting up a studio/workspace than having a wheel, kiln, and some tools. Even the selection of those items—ones you have had some experience with—will require careful research and planning. But your studio has other furnishings and components that you may not have thought of or have taken for granted. Items like flooring, walls, ceilings, sinks, and lights are essential to a comfortable workspace. Work tables, shelves, and counters are personal items that should be designed or at least modified to suit your own tastes. Some of these furnishings are best purchased ready-made while others are best left for your own design and construction. Of course, anything I suggest you build can be done by another person under your employ.

**Walls** are most likely going to be a wall board material as I discussed earlier. Wall board or sheet rock is strong, smooth, and easy to paint and repair. You can hang things like pictures, posters, shelves, and other hardware for installing and hanging additional objects that will inevitably adorn your studio. Avoid wood surfaces like paneling because they are more difficult to construct with and certainly to repair. Besides, they generally don't look that good. Homosote is a wonderful wall board material that is soft yet sturdy, easy to cut and shape, and great for soundproofing and hanging objects from. If you don't recognize the name, picture the usual backing material for cork surfaced bulletin boards.

**Ceilings** are best left plain and white to aid in light dispersion and visibility. Avoid getting fancy with exposed beams and the like, as they simply serve as additional surfaces to collect dust. Wherever possible, avoid any exposed pipes, conduit, etc. for the same reason. Getting up there to clean those surfaces (and you will have to) is a real pain.

**Flooring** surfaces can vary tremendously. In my opinion, too much concern is placed on flooring. Flooring should be simple. The most important characteristics are durability, smoothness (without being slippery), and washability. The floor must be durable enough to stand up to the movement and weight of rolling carts and wag-

ons, dragging of equipment, pressure of wheels and casters found on ware carts, dollies, clay barrels, and many other heavy objects in the studio. A smooth floor makes moving these items easier and makes cleanup more efficient. You must have a floor that will withstand constant wetness from clay, slop, and spilled water, and one that allows for safe and hygienic cleanup. Since everyone knows that sweeping a clay studio is a major no-no, a floor that can be mopped and wet vacuumed is a must.

Many different materials can conform to these requirements, with the most popular and common being concrete, wood, vinyl, or tile. Concrete is wonderful—it's waterproof, durable, and can be polished to a very smooth and quite lovely surface when it is being poured. A concrete floor is a wonderful surface to roll wheeled objects on and you can drag things to your heart's content without wearing the floor down. Contrary to popular belief, a concrete floor doesn't need to be sealed in any way to insure its durability but if you like, it can be painted for aesthetic reasons.

Laura Chandler of Laura Chandler Decorative Painting in Kensington, Maryland, is a painter with more years of experience than she cares to admit, doing custom murals and other onsite work. She has painted over cement floors for a couple of clients and here's how she does it.

1) Etch the floor with muriatic acid, followed by many washes. (Laura hired people to do this.)

2) Base coat and decorate with an all-acrylic commercial (not artist's) product. Two companies (among others), Bruning and Fuller-O'Brien, make such products called Versa-Flex and Silathane, respectively.

3) Seal and top coat with a product from Bona-Kemi called Pacific-Strong. The top coat here is in two parts (you add a catalyst,

which they sell). It is water-based so your colors stay bright and accurate, quick drying, and tough as nails (it's used for gym floors). Laura has used this on bar tops and even on Formica, which was primed with a stinky but effective product called XIM. She's had no problems from anyone so far, and some of these jobs were a while ago.

While wood flooring would not be my choice, if your studio presently has wood floors there is no need to cover or remove them, as wood is a perfectly acceptable surface. Indeed, the previous studio space as well as the one I occupy now both have wood floors. A hardwood floor is durable and will withstand the rigors of washing. One advantage of wood floors is that they are easy to build into and otherwise attach things like shelving units, cabinets, walls and dividers, and other furnishings to. If you are concerned about keeping the floor in better than mediocre condition, wood does require some serious maintenance and this can be inconvenient. Keep in mind that even with the highest degree of maintenance, a wood floor in a studio space will take a lot of work to restore it to a condition suitable for a home.

Vinyl as sheet goods or tile can make for acceptable floors but you must be careful not to go for the cheap stuff that is so common. If purchased in a high quality grade, vinyl possesses all the necessary characteristics for a suitable flooring surface. Inexpensive material is thin, soft, and will wear down and tear through in a very short time.

Avoid carpeted surfaces at all cost. Even in office or gallery spaces (unless they are well isolated from the rest of the studio), carpet and rugs will attract and hold clay dust. Not only is cleaning difficult, but every time you walk on the soft surface of a carpet, the trapped clay dust will be made airborne, contributing to an unhealthy studio environment.

**Doors and windows** should be well considered if you are able to specify or change them. Doors are built for either interior or exterior use, usually of steel or wood, and constructed in hollow or solid core varieties. Hollow core doors are built for interior use, are lightweight, transmit sound, and are not very energy efficient. Solid core doors are for both interior and exterior applications, are strong and sturdy, more soundproof, and are energy efficient. Solid core doors are also more expensive and, for this reason, I suggest you use them where you want the durability. Ware carts, kiln shelves, and other objects can easily put a hole in a hollow core door. Another feature to contemplate is the width of the door opening. Think about what will have to go through the opening and be sure the opening is wide enough. Think also about the swing of the door (left or right) and whether it would be more convenient for the door to swing in or out of a particular space. Perhaps it would be convenient if a particular door had a window in it so you could see through it. The door to your office may fit the bill. Also, is the door going to be an unsecured passageway or is a lock necessary?

Windows need to be chosen mostly for size, aesthetic style, and energy efficiency, though within those considerations, function is an important component. Will they be double hung windows where the two sashes slide up and down like the windows in a home, or would casement windows that crank open be better? Think about the purpose the windows will serve and you will be better able to make intelligent decisions about them. Are they for light? For ventilation? For the view? For access to the outside? Make a list.

**Lighting** has already been discussed in the previous section but don't forget the aesthetic aspects of the lighting fixture that you choose. Remember that you will be looking at these lights as well as being illuminated by them.

**Sinks and faucets** offer many options and you will have to take a good look at what you will be doing at the sink to make a wise choice here. Your sink must be large enough, durable, and made of a material that will be kind to the objects that come in contact with it. For instance, if you do raku and will be using the sink to wash your wares after firing, a sink made of a softer material will not as likely cause a chip or crack in your ware if you inadvertently bang your pot against it. Size refers to not only the obvious width and length, but also to depth. Sinks can be single or double bowls or you can have two or more sinks installed side-by-side. The faucet must be tall enough to allow you to get objects such as pails and buckets under it and it must be far enough away from the back of the sink to accommodate those same large objects. Don't skimp on the faucet. A high quality faucet will pay for itself in a very short time. A low quality inexpensive unit will not stand up to the daily rigors and abuse of use. Having a separate connection for a hose at the sink is a very convenient feature as well. A hose is much more useful to the potter than the spray attachments common to most household applications. A hose can be extended to other areas of the studio, is useful for glaze mixing and washing larger objects, and is generally handy to have.

While I'm on the subject of sinks, a discussion of clay, plaster, and sediment traps fits in well. Your studio must be equipped with some sort of clay reclamation system that not only allows you to reclaim as much slip and slop as possible for

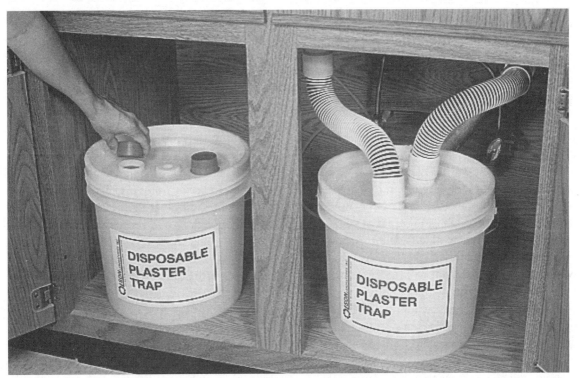

*Figure 3-19. Disposable plaster or sediment trap. One of the flexible hoses leads from the sink, the other to the drain. The container is see-through and is disconnected from the hoses and replaced when full. (Courtesy of Olson Labs, Port Washington, Wis.)*

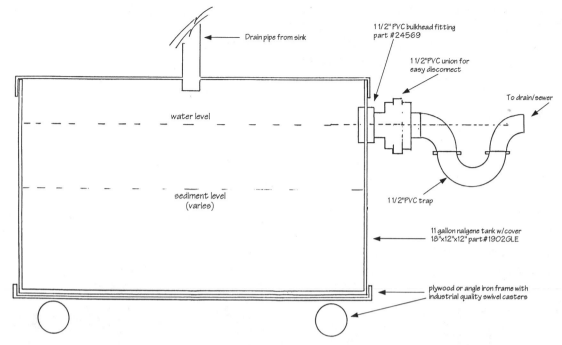

*Figure 3-20. Plaster trap designed by Jonathan Kaplan. Use a hole saw or sabre saw to drill the tank and lid for the pipe fittings. PVC fittings should be schedule 40 rated. For the specific parts indicated by number, see Consolidated Plastics in the Addendum of suppliers. (Courtesy of Jonathan Kaplan, Ceramic Design Group, Steamboat Springs, Colo.)*

recycling, but also serves to keep clay out of the drainage system. It is not so much that clay or the materials that you wash down the sink are harmful to the environment as much as it is a problem of clogging. Continued washing of clay down the drain will clog the drains and be a real pain in the neck. A plaster trap is a self-contained unit designed to allow materials that are heavier than water to sink to the bottom of a large basin or tank. The incoming and outgoing pipes are situated on the sides toward the top of the basin and only when the water level is at or above the outgoing pipe does the water drain. Presumably, when the water reaches this height, it is free of much of the clay and other sediment you want to keep out of the drain. As a rule, commercial traps have a removable screened insert that helps a bit

in cleaning the trap, but don't be fooled. It is a dirty mess with or without it!

An innovative idea is the disposable trap made by Olson Labs shown in Fig. 3-20. The entire trap is disposable, eliminating the cleanup, and is reasonably priced. I've never seen this trap in use but it appears to be worth a look. Plaster traps can be homemade and are often more practical for the potter because commercial traps tend to be small and very expensive.

A plan for a simple trap as designed by Jonathan Kaplan is illustrated in Fig. 3-20. Outstanding features of this design are that the tank is on wheels and the quick release feature of the drain pipe makes it easy to disconnect the trap from the system and wheel it away from the sink for more convenient cleaning. Be sure you don't

*Figure 3-21. Close-up showing construction features of one of the glaze counters at The Potters Shop. (Photo by Bethany Versoy)*

inadvertently turn on the water while the trap is out of position! I hate when that happens.

**Work surfaces** such as tables and counters need to thought out carefully. Some areas of the studio will be more aptly furnished with tables of different sizes, while others are better served by permanently installed counters. At The Potters Shop we have a few tables in the general workspace but permanent counters in the glaze room and wedging area. Counters are more stable and are obviously suitable where you don't need to alter the space for different activities.

The work surface itself is also an area of contention. Our glazing counters are Formica (melamine or any other similar commercial surface) for durability and ease of cleaning. Our general workshop tables are plywood because wood is a softer, more earthy material that is more comfortable to work on. I simply like working on a wood surface better than on a synthetic one. Wood surfaces are also kinder to clay and allow the clay to be rolled and slammed onto it with minimal sticking. For water protection and durability, seal the wood with polyurethane. A good coating should last about five years, at which time you can recoat the wood.

Fig. 3-21 shows the construction of the counters at my shop. Note the use of 2" by 4" studs and 3/4" plywood for shelves. The entire unit is fastened to the wall for stability. You can certainly alter the design to accommodate your own needs. For instance, the shelves are fixed, but yours can be adjustable. The countertops are preformed and available at any home center in a variety of precut lengths and colors. Some centers will miter the ends, making installation a bit easier, but using a circular saw is not that difficult to do if you choose to take on the task yourself.

The worktable shown is constructed from 2" by 4" stock with an old solid core door as the foundation of the top. The door is covered with

*Figure 3-22. A worktable showing the typical construction method. (Photo by Bethany Versoy)*

*Figure 3-23. A wedging table with a plaster surface. The table is built of 2" x 4" boards and is bolted to the wall for stability. (Photo by Bethany Versoy)*

to these dimensions, but I wouldn't recommend straying too far because most stools and chairs fit nicely with these heights. Wedging tables are another matter altogether and this is where a custom height is necessary. Wedging is a very physical activity that is hard on the arms, neck, and back. It's amazing to me how many wedging tables are at standard table or even counter height, making the act of wedging a battle beyond reason. An optimum height for a wedging surface is personal but is going to be about the height of your thigh, midway between your knee and waist. At this height, you can lean over your clay and comfortably get your body weight behind the wedging process. If you are building a wedging table for general studio use, make it about 28" high (to the top of the surface) and provide a flat, stable, step stool for those who may find the surface a bit high.

Wedging surfaces can vary but they should be durable and absorbent. Plaster is the most commonly used material but I've seen stone slabs, concrete, wood, and other materials used as well. Many potters will pour a plaster surface and cover it in canvas for protection. I prefer a plaster surface unadorned or covered. It is true that an exposed plaster surface is susceptible to scratching, gouging, scraping, and other abuses and if yours is for general studio/class use, you might want to consider some other surface or a protective cover such as canvas. If you treat it well, though, plaster will last a long time and will do the things for your clay that you want it to. I find that canvas has a tendency to rip and clay dries on it, allowing your soft clay to pick up unwanted dry bits. Make your wedging surface larger than you think it should be. The extra surface areas will come in handy for laying out slip for recycling, setting out clay slabs for drying, and for usual wedging and clay preparation. A surface 24" deep is not too

3/4" plywood and the table is edged in 1" by 4" #2 pine stock. Solid core doors are great for tables and the only reason this one is covered with plywood is that it is a raised panel door, not flat and suitable as a table. You can get inexpensive solid core doors for tabletops at home centers that specialize in seconds, manufacturer's overruns, and other discontinued items.

Pay attention to the height of your tables and counters as you design and build them. Standard table height is about 30" and standard counter height is about 36". Of course, you are not bound

*Figure 3-24. A typical shelving unit. This one is built of #2 pine with 48" wide shelves. Note the details of construction as referred to in the text. (Photo by Bethany Versoy)*

large if you have the space. The wedging table needs to be the most sturdy and stable table in the studio. Build it either next to a wall so you can lean the table against it or better yet, attach it to the wall for maximum steadiness. A rickety, rocking wedging table is uncomfortable and frustrating to use.

**Shelving** is an absolute must. Intelligently designed and appropriately installed shelving will not only allow you to organize and store your pots, materials, and supplies off the floor and in accessible places, but will free your workspace of clutter and mess that is both dangerous and distracting. The first rule of thumb is that you can never have too much (or enough, for that matter) shelving.

All shelves should be adjustable and individual shelves should be easily removable. Each shelf must be strong enough to hold your materials. Shelves must be deep enough. The entire shelving unit must be solidly built and installed.

There are many different types and styles of shelving units both commercially available and homemade, but when it comes to conforming to

the standards set above, the choices become fewer. Avoid inexpensive metal shelving units sold under the category of "heavy-duty utility shelving" at hardware stores and home centers. These units are generally lightweight, narrow, and unstable. The shelves are not conveniently adjustable and although shelving of this style (with some reinforcement or modification) can be useful in the studio for raw materials storage and the like, they are totally unsuitable for the everyday storage of ware. In addition to the inconvenience of not being adjustable, metal shelves will eventually rust and corrode. Some of these units are heavy-duty and will take very heavy loads but again, because of their nonadjustable shelves and metal construction, they are not suitable for the everyday storage of wares in progress. Many other types of commercial shelving units are available and have some application in pottery studios. These include plastic units, also labeled "utility shelving," and shelving units sold at office supply stores such as Office Max, Office Depot, and Staples. Be careful when evaluating the potential uses of these products. They are probably unsuitable for the storage of work in progress due to their instability and inappropriate construction materials.

In designing your own shelving for the studio, focus on simplicity of construction and a standardization of dimensions. I have seen many different shelving designs, all with their own particular attractions, but the simplest and most functional system I have come across is shown in Fig. 3-24. It is designed around a system of 1" by 2" cleats spaced 6" apart. Shelves cut from either 3/4" plywood or #2 common pine easily slide in and out. The uprights are cut from either plywood (1/2" or 3/4"), particle board, or #2 pine. The cleats are glued and screwed into place. The uprights are fastened to the wall and floor. All shelves are removable and the units are quite stable and sturdy since each one butts up to the next, adding to the overall strength of the system. Shelves should not be longer than four feet or they're likely to sag. Never use particle board as shelves! Particle board is extremely dense, heavy, and solid but it has very little rigidity. It is also inexpensive and that is why its application is useful as the upright component.

Design your units to fit a limited variety of shelf sizes, for instance two, three, and four foot lengths. This will allow you to interchange shelves all around the shop. Standard 12" deep uprights can accommodate shelves up to 18" deep, even though the shelf will protrude beyond the front edge of the upright. To design and install your shelves follow these steps and refer to the details of construction in Fig. 3-24:

1) Limit yourself to two, three, and four foot shelf lengths regardless of what your installation space measures.

2) Decide on the shelf length or combination of lengths and the number of units that a particular space will accommodate, figuring in the 3/4" width of the uprights.

3) Measure and mark the placement of the shelf cleats and cut all the cleats you will need.

4) Cut to size at least three shelves per unit.

5) Working from one end of the wall, install the first upright. While a helper holds the second upright in its approximate location, place three shelves in the unit towards the top, middle, and bottom.

6) Secure the second upright in place.

7) Repeat along the length of the wall until all the units are in place.

Building your shelving units this way will accurately place the uprights the correct width apart, maintaining this standard throughout your studio. I use 1-1/2" to 2" "L" brackets and screws to secure the uprights to the floor and the wall. If your floor is concrete, don't bother. The units will be sturdy enough without the floor attachment. While most of the weight of the units and the ware is vertical, some weight will be pulling the units from the wall so when screwing the units to the wall be sure to screw into a wall stud or use a molly or butterfly bolt.

As far as the shelving material is concerned, most of the shelves in my shop are #2 common pine. If you want to be as economical as possible, cutting your own shelves from 3/4" plywood is usually less expensive. Plywood comes in a variety of grades with some finished on one side, oth-

*Figure 3-25. John Baymore's throwing area. The shelves are supported by 1" dowels inserted into a pair of 2" x 4" uprights secured to the floor and ceiling. (Photo by John Baymore)*

*Figure 3-26. A common standard and bracket shelving systems. (Photo by Bethany Versoy)*

brackets (Fig. 3-26) can be used in display, office, and library areas but are unsuitable for the storage of works in progress. Another very functional commercial system consists of upright standards with small "L" shaped shelf supports that clip into slots in the standards. I have found this system to be especially useful where extreme strength is important, occasional adjustability is necessary, and you want the units to be at least somewhat nice to look at. Fig. 3-27 shows this system in place. The standards can be recessed so they are flush with the surface of the wood or they can be installed on the surface. The recessed technique is more desirable for both appearance and a neat fit between the wooden uprights.

ers on two sides. Choose the type of plywood to use when you visit the lumberyard when the viability of the different grades will become apparent. The wood should be sealed with a polyurethane for protection against moisture, warping, etc. However, often in my haste to get more shelves into place, I have skipped the finishing step and have found little problems using unfinished shelves. Sure, an occasional shelf will bend and warp but surprisingly not very often!

As discussed above, other types of shelving systems are suitable in other locations and applications in the studio. Common wall standards and

*Figure 3-27. Recessed standards with clip-in shelf supports. (Photo by Bethany Versoy)*

Shelving can also take the form of movable units such as commercial ware carts. You can build your own ware cart, or for that matter, you can build entire shelving units that move on casters. You will need to assess the relative value of an entire shelving unit on wheels (I can't see its practical application in most pottery studios). Ware carts are of immense value and can add significantly to the storage capabilities of any studio, regardless of size. Ware carts are available from a variety of manufacturers in many different configurations and sizes. Some come with precut shelves, others allow you to cut your own. Commercial ware carts are generally built from metal angle stock, are extremely solid and rigid, and have large heavy-duty casters for wheels. Fig. 3-28 shows common commercial cart. Fig. 3-29 shows a cart built from scratch, using 2" by 2" pine stock, outside edge pine molding as the shelf supports, 3/4" plywood shelving, and casters. This cart is used for porcelain and is covered with a polyethylene cover attached with Velcro to keep dust off the ware.

Carts can be built from readily available metal or aluminum stock as well. The advantages of a homemade cart are the lower cost and the ability

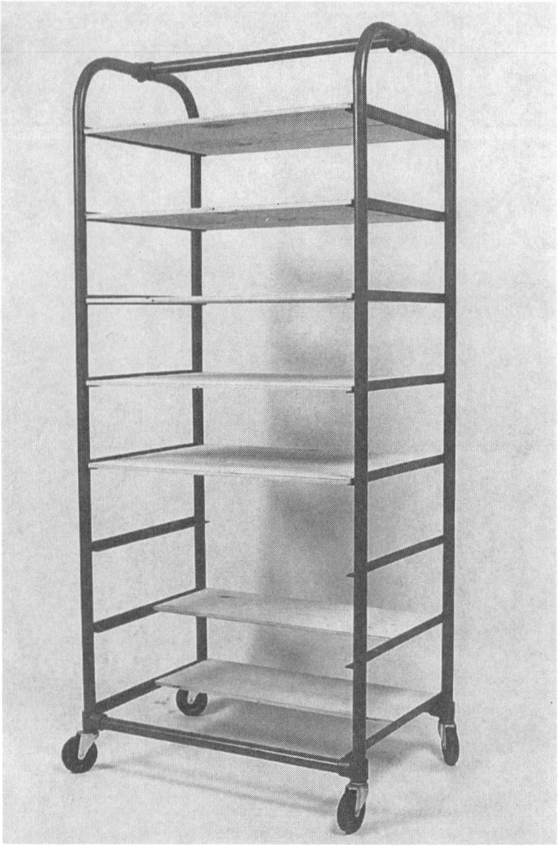

Figure 3-28. Brent® ware cart. (Courtesy of American Art Clay Co.)

*Figure 3-29. Ware cart built by the author. The cart is covered with plastic and secured with Velcro, keeping dust off bisque and glazed ware. (Photo by Bethany Versoy)*

*Figure 3-30. A commercial baker's cart as a ware cart. (Photo by Bethany Versoy)*

to build one to conform to a custom size. Although I built the cart in Fig. 3-29 and have built others, I recommend purchasing a commercial cart for the convenience and quality of construction. You can absolutely save money on a cart built from scratch but once you compare the actual outlay of materials and time, you can often do better by buying one.

An alternative to carts built for potters and sold through pottery supply companies are the many types of similar carts manufactured for the food industry. Carts for bakers, supermarkets, restaurants, and other establishments are usually perfectly suitable for potters' applications and are

often less expensive. Be careful when evaluating one of these products. They are often not as heavy or sturdy as a potter's ware cart, but they are usually heavy enough. If you can find a commercial restaurant or food service supply, you may be able to purchase used equipment at real bargain prices (not only carts, but all sorts of other items).

You will also need to store kiln furniture so it is safely out of the way and yet convenient to access. The same cleated shelving units described above are suitable for kiln posts, stilts, cones, etc. Kiln shelves present their own storage peculiarities though. Kiln shelves are heavy, somewhat awkward, and are handled at various times during their use. They are placed in the kiln when stacking for firing, removed after firing, handled again for scraping and kiln washing, set aside to dry after washing, then stored. Each time the shelves are handled, they need to be put back somewhere! Heavy-duty stationary racks are useful, as are carts that wheel the shelves to different places. Kiln shelves should be stored low to the ground and in racks that allow for their easy removal and replacement. Refer back to Fig. 3-8 and note the kiln shelf rack as well as the shelves holding kiln furniture and supplies. This rack is designed to hold full round 18" and half round 18" to 28" diameter shelves, and could easily be converted to a cart with the addition of heavy-duty industrial casters. Of course, you can alter the dimensions to suit the size shelves you are using. Fig. 3-31 shows a commercial kiln shelf cart constructed of iron pipe and pipe fittings.

In addition to shelves and carts, you also need to think about storing clay and other materials. I've already mentioned using commercial metal shelving to store raw materials and a system like that can be very useful. Depending on the variety of materials and the quantities you have on hand, storage systems will vary. Containers and buckets are usually the preferred method (see Fig. 3-7). Keeping materials in their original bags can be a viable method in some applications but not when you must access the contents of the bags on a regular basis. Opening and closing paper bags is messy and creates an abundance of dust. The bags are not easily closed and contamination is possible. An accidental spill of water can also ruin the contents of a bag. I use original bags to store materials only in the overstock area, which is separate from the rest of the studio. Be sure to label all materials, including those in original bags, with clear descriptive tags. While the covers of containers can be labeled, the bucket or container itself must have a label on it. It's too easy to misplace a container lid and be left with a bucket filled with a mystery material.

Resolving the issues of shelving and storing ware, materials, and all the other items you presently have and will collect, as well as building or purchasing functional work surfaces, carts, and other furnishings is an ongoing challenge. As your work habits, style, and space evolves and expands, so will your needs. Flexibility and a degree of standardization in design will enable you to grow and refine your studio systems with the least disruption and most continued improvement pos-

*Figure 3-31. Brent kiln shelf cart. (Courtesy of American Art Clay Co.)*

sible. Remember that nothing need be permanent and everything can be altered to suit your changing needs.

**Bacia Edelman**. Lichen-Glaze Teapot. 1995. Hand-built, 10-3/4" H, stoneware. (Photo by the artist)

**Warren MacKenzie**. Teapot. 1997. 8" H with handle, wheel-thrown, faceted surface, reduction fired. (Photo by Peter Lee)

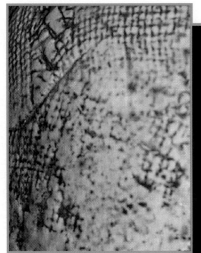

**Author**.
Covered Jar. 1979.
Thrown and handbuilt,
12" H, raku fired.
(Photo by author)

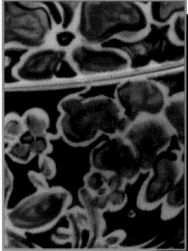

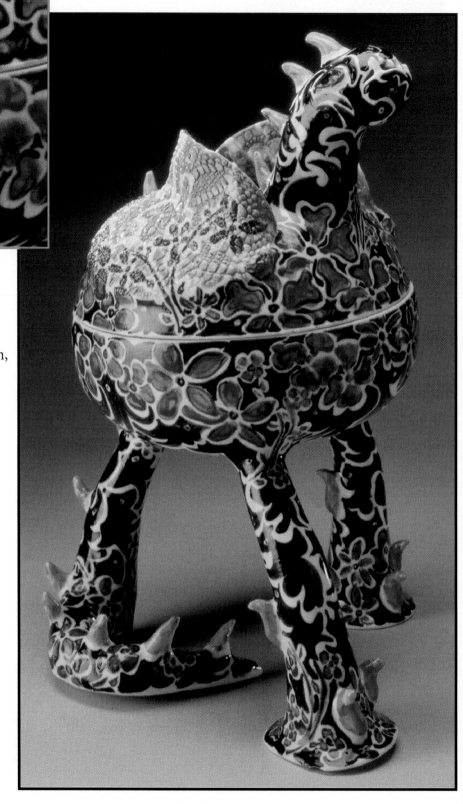

**Jill Gross**.
Beastcake. 1997.
Wheel-thrown and
handbuilt porcelain
covered vessel, 18" H,
underglaze decoration,
electric fired. (Photo
by Bob Arruda)

**Bryan McGrath**. Bowl. 1998. Wheel-thrown
porcelain, 3" H x 7" D, wood fired, shino glaze.
(Photo by the artist)

**Author**.
Vase. 1997.
Wheel-thrown textured
and altered surface. 22"
H, raku fired. (Photo by
the author)

**Bill Capshaw**. Meshak. 1995. 19-1/2" H, wheel-thrown with wheel-thrown additions, raku fired. (Photo courtesy of the artist)

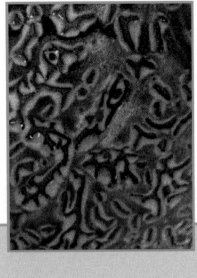

**John Baymore.** Side Handled Teapot (Kyusu). 1997. 6" H, wheel-thrown with carved pattern, shino glaze. (Photo courtesy of the artist)

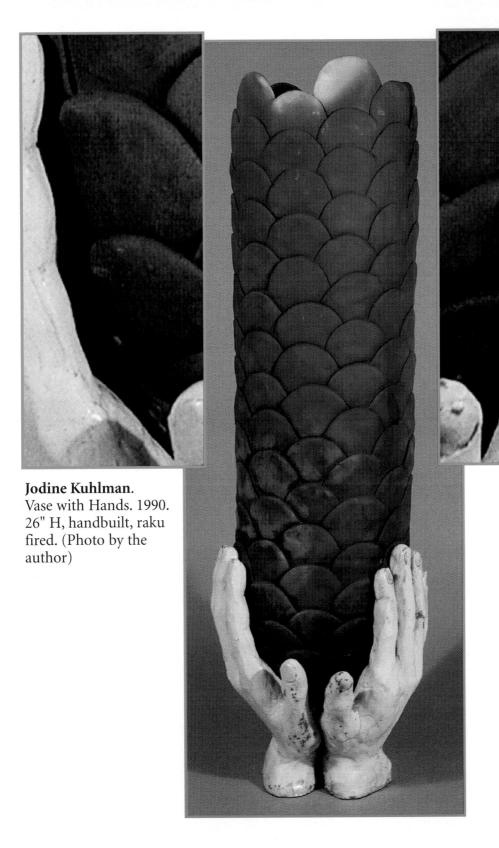

**Jodine Kuhlman**.
Vase with Hands. 1990.
26" H, handbuilt, raku
fired. (Photo by the
author)

**Bob Kinzie.**
Double Walled Vessel.
1998. 35" H, thrown
and handbuilt with
extruded sections,
carved surface.
(Photo by the artist)

**Author**. Vase. 1998. 15" H, wheel-thrown with inlaid colored glass, raku fired. (Photo by the author)

**Jack Troy.**
Pitcher. 1998.
14" H, wheel-thrown,
natural ash glaze,
anagama fired, cone
10. (Photo by Hubert
Gentry)

**Author**.
Vase. 1998.
16" H, wheel-
thrown, textured
and altered
surface, raku
fired. (Photo by
the author)

**Carol Temkin**. Dinnerware. Wheel-thrown porcelain, plate 12" D, electric fired. (Photo by Warren Patterson)

**Dan Finch**.
Barn Pot. 1998.
13" H, wheel-thrown
and handbuilt, cone 10
reduction fired. This is
one of Dan's sought
after signature pots in
his production line.
(Photo by Spectrum
Multi Media)

**Carol Temkin**. Teapot. 1997. Wheel-thrown porcelain, 11" H, electric fired. (Photo by Warren Patterson)

**John Jensen**. Toad House. 1998. 5" H, stoneware. Attached is his descriptive card which serves as a sales and marketing tool. (Photo by the artist)

# Chapter 4

## Suppliers, Vendors, Tradesmen, and Contractors

Despite even the highest level of self-sufficiency, you will always have to rely on others for a significant part of your dealings. This dependence spans the gaumt from minor purchases to contracting out the design and installation of a major system such as plumbing or electrical. Most of your dealings with others will fall somewhere in between. Purchases of raw materials, tools, studio furnishings, paper goods, equipment, and a myriad of additional items will occur on an everyday basis. Too often, not enough thought and planning is spent determining where to best make these purchases. You can save time and money and have the added benefit of better product if you apply some careful yet simple strategies to dealing with suppliers, vendors, and contractors.

A useful practice, and one that will forever pay dividends, is to learn and establish a way to identify reputable vendors and contractors. Try to strike a comfortable and advantageous balance between quality, honesty, value, and reliability when identifying sources. My experience has taught me that in order of importance these features are honesty, quality, reliability, and price. Making life more complicated is the fact that as a consumer, you literally have the world at your fingertips. Not only do you have the ability and responsibility to choose wisely among local shops, stores, warehouses, and other local vendors, but the vast resources of phone and mail order (and now the Internet) is at your disposal. Choice is a wonderful thing, but it can sure make life complicated!

Certainly there are categories of purchases that are more critical and require more care when choosing a vendor, but looking for those qualities mentioned earlier should remain steadfast. To aim an appropriate amount of effort in the right direction and put the whole activity into perspective, categorize your purchases as minor or major. Minor purchases are everyday items easily obtainable and, for all practical purposes, available only from local sources. Some examples are common hardware items (screws, nuts, staples, nails, fasteners, adhesives), cleaning supplies, paper and office supplies, general hand tools, shelving materials, and a variety of other expendable supplies. This is not to say that these can't be purchased from a catalog, often at a price that beats the local competition, but to take advantage of mail order sources you must be confident and comfortable in your ability to evaluate, specify, and select the objects you need without seeing or handling them. This may not be as easy as it seems. You can solve that problem by inspecting items locally, then ordering them by mail. Whether that strategy is practical depends on the item in question and whether there is a local source so you can examine it.

There are other questions to ponder regarding the advisability of mail order purchasing. Clearly, if the item may require servicing or technical support of some complicated fashion, it's wise to consider a local source. However, even those fears can be put to rest if you feel confident and comfortable with the company you are doing business with.

So, enough about nails and masking tape. How about clay, kilns, wheels, potter's tools, and all the other real stuff you need? Enough people are either without a local pottery supply company or are unhappy with the one they have to make this a point worth discussing. If that's your situation, you are by circumstance forced to peruse catalogs and buy over the phone. Look through ceramics magazines, make some phone calls, and get your hands on as many catalogs as possible. Here's a word about catalogs, though. Catalogs cost a company money to produce, sometimes big money. If you think producing and mailing a catalog is simply part of the cost of doing business, you are right...partially. From the company's point of view, their catalog is meant to help you purchase supplies from them, not to serve as a reference book. It irks companies to think they are sending you a catalog so you can use it to shop around and end up spending your money with someone else. I say all this to prepare you for the company that charges for their catalog. This practice, while not common, shouldn't cause you to think ill about a particular company. Indeed, it's common practice to deduct the cost of the catalog from your first order. So there! You get your money back and the company gets at least a little of your business. It all works out.

When it comes to making a purchase, how do you choose one company over the other? Not by price alone I hope! The answer is plain and simple: reputation, word of mouth, and personal recommendations. I don't care how big they are or how many inches their ad takes up in *Ceramics Monthly* or *Clay Times*. It doesn't matter how large their catalog is, whether it's in color or black and white, or how many square feet their showroom is. Ask around and get advice from folks who have dealt with the company in question. Often the best test of a company's true character is how they deal with a problem: a defective item, an unwanted item, a misrepresented item. Find someone who has had a piece of equipment repaired or replaced. Are they still doing business with the company? Have you ever needed any-thing yesterday? How does the company handle emergency requests or deliveries needed by a certain date or only on a certain day of the week? How about the clay supplier who you've asked to let you know the planned delivery date so you can gather extra hands to unload the truck, only to discover the driver ringing your doorbell unannounced with only you and a buttered bagel in the studio to greet him? These are the true tests of a company's intestinal fortitude. Do not, under any circumstances, do business with a place without a personal recommendation. And furthermore, don't base your buying decision on price. Reliable, honest, and informed service costs money and you usually get what you pay for. Pay a little more if those qualities mean something to you.

Who can you ask and how can you get recommendations? Making contact with other professionals who have some experience is not all that difficult. It's likely that there are some potters in your area. If not, there are probably some schools with teachers in them. If not, there is someone you know who knows someone. And there's the Internet, magazine resources, and other ways to get information. Be creative and resourceful. After all, I suspect that reading this book isn't your first brush with clay or pottery.

When evaluating a potential supplier, vendor, or contractor, be sensitive and aware of the following:

1) How pleasant do they sound on the phone?
2) Are they generally helpful?
3) Are they generous with their time and patient in answering questions and offering assistance and information?
4) Are they knowledgeable about their products, availability, and delivery time?

Use your intuition when talking on the phone or in person. Read the body language. Do they really know what they are talking about? If they don't know the answer to a question, do they willingly go to someone else to get help? Do you get the feeling that they want your business and value you as a customer? If you don't get a good feeling, go somewhere else.

Curiously (and quite frustrating), many professional pottery suppliers simply don't know all that much about the equipment and materials they sell. I have experienced this time and again and it never fails to amaze me, not only because someone is purporting to represent a piece of equipment and is not equipped to do so, but because some suppliers, through their ignorance, disburse serious misinformation that can come only from a lack of concern or interest in the correct information! In the end, this attitude is bad for us all. Just for fun and as an experiment while writing this book, I called ten suppliers chosen randomly from the pages of a well known ceramics magazine. I asked a series of questions about a specific potter's wheel, making it clear that while I had used electric wheels before, this would be the first time I was going to be buying one of my own. In other words, I put myself at their mercy. I chose a wheel rather than another piece of equipment like a kiln, slab roller, or pug mill because wheels are relatively simple, the specifications are easy to compare and are subject to practically no subjective analysis. I asked about the size of the motor and wheel head. I asked what direction the wheel spins and how much is weighs. And just to give them a hard time and throw what might be considered a question requiring a subjective answer, I asked if I would be able to center 50 pounds of clay with their wheel.

Well, you can guess where I'm going with this. I got a variety of answers ranging from dancing around the question to blatantly incorrect information. Some of the more captivating and creative answers were that the motor size is 5000 RPMs and 14" long, the wheel head is "regular" size, the size of a dinner plate, and that the wheel spins the "normal" direction. As far as the 50 pounds of clay question, answers ranged from no, yes, maybe, to why would you want to throw that much clay?

The lesson to be learned from this exercise is to do your own research and try not to have to rely on the knowledge or experience of the supplier. Again, ask friends, teachers, and other potters and get product information from the manufacturers. Remember that a pottery supply doesn't have to carry everything to be a valuable resource. The trick is to know exactly what their limitations are and operate within those limitations. Locally, there's a clay supply company that I recommend because I know they generally have a good stock of clay, raw materials, and equipment. I also tell people that the staff there doesn't have even the most basic knowledge of raw materials, clay processes, or the use of the equipment that they sell. Worse yet is the fact that if you ask a question, they won't say they don't know because they *think* they do! If they have what you need at a price you're willing to pay, make the purchase. The folks are nice and they'll load your vehicle and say "good day."

Whether you are in the process of establishing your own studio for the first time or have been in a workspace for some time, there are at least two tradesmen you will have to hire—a plumber and electrician. Let's face it, most of us don't have the knowledge to do our own plumbing or electrical work. If you are lucky enough to have experience in either of these critical areas, your life has been or will be made easier, but even if you are reasonably competent, there will likely come a project that is too advanced for you. Despite the reverence I have for the Yellow Pages, never, under any circumstances, call a plumber or electrician cold from that book of yellow. Ask around before you need one and always get a personal recommendation. Look for someone who is not only licensed and insured, but is neat, careful in their surroundings, and a good craftsman. Clean-looking installations and an interest in providing the best solution to a particular problem or project are important and, for me, absolutely critical in evaluating an individual. The person who is interested in putting a little more effort and thought into a job to accommodate your specialized needs and aesthetic concerns is worth the extra money. Emergency service is something, that at one time or another, you will need. It is very satisfying and reassuring to be able to call a familiar electrician and hear that they will be right over. That kind of attention is as much a result of the way you treat those that work for you as it is the way that particular individual runs their business. Cultivate, develop, and maintain positive professional relationships and they will pay valuable dividends.

If you find yourself in a situation where you must choose between two or three bids to do a large job, like the installation of an entire new electrical service, the impulse to choose by price will be hard to resist. As difficult as it may be, don't fall prey to the low bid. To begin with, be unquestionably certain that you have presented the scope, specifications, and expectations of the project in the identical fashion to each of the bidders. Be sure to ask if they use their own employees or if they contract out some or all of the work. Once you have chosen the individual to do the work, assemble a contract specifying the work to be done and the way payment is to be made. Do not make the last payment until you have inspected the job and determined that it is complete to your satisfaction. It's very difficult to get an electrician or plumber to return to the job site to finish up small details once final payment has been made. Forget about it!

There are, of course, other services and supplies you will require as your business grows and your needs expand. One I have depended on from the first day I hung out a potter's shingle is a printing and graphic design service. It may seem unusual for me to devote a section to a service that is so readily available in all areas. Local printers, copy shops, office supply stores that do printing, and the like have proliferated to the point of being as common as convenience stores and gas stations. Not only are they all over the place, but it seems like each one, regardless of size or name recognition, is a full-service company offering everything from two-cent black and white copies to four color printing, binding, design, typesetting and layout, self inking stamps, and wedding invitations! It's exactly these characteristics that make the printer a good example of other services and supplies.

Keep in mind that there are really only three avenues for you to get your message out to the public: your work itself, your personality and in-person delivery, and the printed word or image. Choose a printer carefully. Sure, you can go anywhere to get copies made, but it won't take long for your printing needs to go beyond the scope of copies and into some serious advertising and promotional material. It is true that the day of the truly full-service graphics and printing supplier is here, but you do have to choose carefully and wisely. Understand that full-service doesn't necessarily mean that your local printer actually performs all of their advertised services themselves in their facility. In fact, much work is often done by other specialized companies, with your local printer acting as the conduit for customers. There is nothing wrong with that as long as you get quality and control in the job and the responsibility for the work is assumed by your print shop. I have been using the same local printer (who is a national chain franchise) for over 20 years. During this time, we have built a relationship of trust and reliance that has become extremely valuable to both of us as business owners. Valuable to me (in addition to those traits important in any vendor mentioned earlier) is the quality, speed, reliability, and pricing that I receive. Valuable to my printer is my repeat and reliable business and the new business that I refer to him. To know that he is able to complete a printing job for me within the two days that I need it allows me to concentrate on other things and sleep a whole lot better. Having the services of a vendor who knows their business and who you can trust to know their business well is important and allows you to use their services with confidence. While I have learned a lot about printing over the years, I don't know it all, nor do I care to. But I do want to know that the person I trust with my printing knows it all and will look out for my best interests.

Despite how comfortable you become with a vendor, you still need to be cognizant of your own needs and how well your local supplier can service those needs. If you have a trusted and confident relationship with a vendor, you can often rely on their judgment and recommendations. However, never take yourself out of the equation completely. For instance, one area of printing that few local shops can compete with is color cards, invitations, and promotional material. Nationally advertised companies such as Modern Postcard are the kings and queens of this kind of work, not only in terms of pricing but in speed and delivery time. By now, I'm sure you have a handle on my attitude regarding comparison by price alone—don't do it. In the case of color printing, costs can vary significantly. When you factor in the price with the experience and specialization these companies offer, the decision to use one becomes clear and shouldn't affect your relationship with your local supplier. I bring all my printing needs to my local company. Every job I need done, from a few copies to my major catalog needs, I offer to him first and it is only the most unusual or spe-

cialized jobs he can't do for me with his usual quick, reliable style and competitive pricing. He appreciates this approach, recognizes his own limitations, and refers me to other sources when he can't fill my needs. Do I always get the absolute lowest price for my printing? Probably not, but that's not the most important thing, for the immediate advantage and satisfaction of low prices work themselves out in the long run. How? In extra copies, personal service, assuming responsibility for a questionable error, and so many other intangible ways.

## Nontraditional Sources for Supplies and Materials

As you might expect, almost every item you can imagine is available through a catalog. The value of catalogs lies not only in the buying power they put in your hands, but in the valuable information you get from them—information on available equipment, ideas for shelving and studio furnishings, systems for storing small items, etc. My collection of catalogs is vast and if you are asking yourself what could possibly be in that collection, you are probably thinking of the usual kinds of catalogs—clay companies, computer supplies and equipment, and maybe even office and packaging supplies. But there are companies and catalogs out there you haven't begun to consider or imagine. Within each catalog, there is merchandise you didn't even know you needed. In the back of this book is a listing of catalogs to call or write for, but once you get on a single mailing list, the rest is history. Catalogs will come fairly consistently and in no time, you will be faced with the problem of how to store and file these valuable resources for quick and easy reference. Don't remove yourself from these mailing lists. Regardless of how many useless and frivolous catalogs you get, the inconvenience of examining one that you will toss in the trash is worth the gem that is on its way to you. Besides, don't be so quick to play Frisbee with a catalog that looks like it might be a waste of time. Okay, so you're not a library, but in that library supply catalog are unique office supplies, video cases, magazine holders and filing systems, tape, glue, step stools, and more. In that industrial building supply catalog are heavy-duty shelving systems, organizing bins, hand trucks, commercial quality storage containers, rubberized flooring, and more. Get the idea?

The single most comprehensive catalog of everything you need, will need, think you may need, or don't even know that you need is from the WR Grainger Co. This is a virtual encyclopedia of everything from electrical and plumbing supplies to ventilation systems, adhesives, raw materials, and motors. You can find screws, bolts, expanded metal, plastic and metal containers, and organizing bins. There is shop furniture, tools, paint spraying equipment, rubber matting, and much, much more. No craftsperson should be without it. Period. You can request a copy and they will be happy to send it to you as long as you can show that you are a business. Professional looking letterhead will usually suffice. In addition to the catalog, they have warehouse locations nationwide. A similar institution is McMaster-Carr Inc. Both are listed in the back of this book.

While on the subject of catalogs, there is one catalog you probably have in your home or studio right now. It's large and you get a free updated issue every year whether you want it or not. It's such a common piece of print media that you not only take it for granted, you probably don't use it enough or know how to use it. Maybe you guessed it: the Yellow Pages! I admit I may have exaggerated a bit about its infrequent use, but it is far more useful than to simply find the location and phone number of a sporting goods or computer store. The Yellow Pages are a great resource to help you link a particular object to a retail source. Larger cities like New York, Boston, or San Francisco have Yellow Pages to die for. They are complete with indexes that cross reference subject titles and are virtual encyclopedias. But even perusing a small version in a small city can be an eye-opening experience. I needed some metal barrels in unusual sizes for post firing raku reduction. The local hardware store couldn't really help me so where did I turn? The Yellow Pages. Under barrels was a selection of manufacturers and suppliers of everything from high tech stainless steel for clean rooms and hospitals to used metal containers of all sizes and shapes. I've been a believer in the Yellow Pages from that day on. Call the phone company and, for a charge, you can get any city's Yellow Pages delivered to your door. Better yet, call a friend in that city and have them get one free!

Catalogs, as I have been referring to them, have been limited to print media. Just a few short years ago that would have been it. Finished. End of information on catalogs. But now we have the Internet and it seems that almost every company with a print catalog also has a web site and an online listing of its products. Poke around and see what you can find.

Greatly overlooked outlets for necessary items exist all around us. When you think shelves, for instance, you probably think of a home center or lumberyard and if you live some distance from a major shopping area, your sources are going to be limited to the usual and customary. In this case, think catalog and mail order. But if you live in or near a large city, opportunities abound. Used office and industrial furniture warehouses can supply you with great deals on furniture of all kinds, carts, storage systems, and more. Commercial food, restaurant, and bakery supply outlets are exciting caches of a variety of things like heavy-duty spatulas for mixing glaze, buckets, brushes (designed for the food service industry but great for slips and glaze), steel bowls that make great molds, and a zillion other things. Wooden scrapers and sticks made for bakers make terrific and unique ribs, scratching, drawing, and trimming tools, while oversized spoons and other utensils make outstanding throwing sticks and paddles. Are you on the lookout for a mega rolling pin? Forget the clay company, head to the nearest commercial bakery or kitchen supply. Scales and containers? You'll find those as well. In the previous chapter I suggested baker's carts as substitutes for potter's ware carts.

Certainly home centers can be treasure troves, but they are totally inferior when it comes to metal cans and containers for raku, tubs for mixing glazes or recycling clay, large plastic containers for storing clay and raw materials, wire fencing, straw, and a myriad of other things. For these and additional industrial strength supplies, head to the local feed, farm, or agricultural supplier. This is where our country friends have the advantage. If you've never been to a rural farm supply, prepare yourself for a great experience. I relish hardware-type stores and no matter where I am or what I'm doing, if I see one that looks out of the ordinary, I go in. I must admit that I do get a variety of incredulous stares and reactions when, in response to the question, "Can I help you?" I answer, "No, just looking." Go and have some fun.

Another category of purchases often overlooked is that of studio maintenance and the repair and upkeep of equipment and studio systems. When you need replacement firebrick for a kiln, your immediate thoughts turn to a pottery supply company. When an electrical connector, plug, receptacle, or wire in your kiln fizzes out, where do you turn? Where else but a pottery supply company. If you are more resourceful, you might go directly to the kiln manufacturer. When you need a new triple beam balance or a scale of a different

standard, who is going to have it? The pottery supply. You're beginning to see the pattern. It's time to broaden your spectrum and branch out. Commercial firebrick and furnace companies deal with exactly what you need, often at a lower price and might even have a stock of used brick on hand at tremendous savings. A commercial electrical supply company that caters to the trade will likely have just what you need, not only at a lower price than your usual source, but they will often have an industrial quality component that will last longer and give better service.

There is a caveat, though, to being able to take advantage of these commercial or trade oriented supply outlets. You need to know the language. The parts counter of a large commercial electrical supply company can be an intimidating and even disgusting place. Men in work clothes, smoking cigarettes, using foul language, and often with little patience for questions from "homeowners." A local supply house I frequent has a sign prominently displayed indicating when the homeowner hours are and that licensed electricians and contractors will be serviced first at all times. Now isn't that friendly and helpful sounding? Never mind, you're not there to make friends and have brunch. To be fair, these places do not have our education as their mission. They are there to supply knowledgeable professionals with the supplies and information they need to carry on in their trade.

If you want to take advantage of the quality components and reasonable prices that are out there, you have a responsibility to do your homework. Have some idea of what you're looking for, what it does, and what it's called. Bring in the part you are replacing and take responsibility for the purchase, whether it turns out to be correct or the wrong item altogether. Learn the language of the trade and I don't mean fake it or you'll be looked at with utter disdain and all you'll be shown is the door! Refreshingly, you might come across an individual who is genuinely intrigued by what you do, who you are, and that you are looking for an expert to help solve a problem. In fact, taking an approach of expert in your field yet ignorant in theirs is one that sometimes turns out to be fruitful. I've developed some satisfying professional relationships with counter folks who love to help solve a problem or find a suitable replacement part. Indeed, you may pique someone's interest and curiosity with the unusual nature of your craft and its associated equipment and paraphernalia. You do need to be cautious when purchasing an item recommended by one of these experts, particularly when you bring in a part hoping to replace it with an exact duplicate. I have no doubt that their intentions are good and that they are offering you the part they believe is the same or better, but here is where intimate knowledge of the equipment and its specifications are necessary. If you're not certain and completely confident that you are getting the correct information, you are usually better off leaving well enough alone and returning to the manufacturer. I once replaced a motor in a wheel with what was purported to be an exact equivalent. It turned out that the motor was the same in voltage, wattage, power, size, and other important characteristics but it was not the same in smoothness, quietness, and vibration. Every time I turned on the wheel I felt like I was throwing on a barreling freight train. On the other hand, I have greatly upgraded the electrical components of my kilns by going to a commercial electrical supply and getting industrial outlets, wire, receptacles, connectors, and more. Proceed, but proceed with an educated approach!

Be creative and ingenious in your search for supplies and resources to help you find items you need now and will need in the future. Think with an unconventional mind and you'll have the advantage. Apply the example of the printer to your quest for any supplier, vendor, tradesman, or contractor. It may take a bit longer to find someone you feel comfortable with, but it will be worth the extra effort.

# Chapter 5

# Equipment Selection, Repair, and Studio Maintenance

Evaluating and choosing equipment and learning how to keep it running are essential skills for the craftsperson. Manufacturers abound, each touting the absolute superiority of their equipment from both a performance point of view and a durability and longevity perspective. How do you choose? What do you do when a tool needs repair and the Yellow Pages (Potters Equipment—Repair) yields a shortage of choices? How about a leaky faucet, flickering light, or no dial tone? Who do you call? Not Ghostbusters, that's for sure.

## Building Your Own Equipment

This is going to be a short section. Not because I don't approve of building your own wheel or slab roller or don't think it can be done, but rather because in recent years, the practicality of building your own equipment has been reduced. As pottery making in schools and by individuals has become more widespread, the market for these products has grown, forcing competition between manufacturers, resulting in higher quality equipment, more choices, and reasonable prices. One indication of this is the decreasing the number of articles and books written on building your own equipment, to the point now where there is only an occasional piece about building equipment.

With the exception of building your own fuel-fired kiln, another reason for my lack of enthusiasm for building your own extruder or clay mixer is the issue of how you can most efficiently spend your time, energy, and resources. I believe they

are best spent in setting up your studio, establishing yourself in the field, making pots, and learning how to maintain and repair equipment.

If you are headstrong about building your own equipment, you'll find the most information on building electric kilns, kick and electric wheels, slab rollers, extruders, and clay mixers, with an occasional ball mill or pug mill thrown in for good measure. *Ceramics Monthly* magazine has been the most fertile source of information, along with a few articles in *The Studio Potter* and a few books on the subject (see the following books in the Bibliography: *Building Pottery Equipment*, *Getting Into Pots*, *The Potter's Alternative*, *Pioneer Pottery*, *The Self Reliant Potter*, as well as the yearly indexes of *Ceramics Monthly*).

I'll not give any instruction here but I will give some advice for the adventuresome. There is nothing more frustrating than trying to work on a piece of inferior equipment, and a poorly functioning wheel should not be standing between your present skills and abilities and your ultimate accomplishments. The highest quality materials and construction techniques produce the highest quality products. If there is a choice between wooden framework and steel when building a wheel, go for the steel. If that means having someone weld it for you because you don't have the equipment or ability, then go for it. The choice to build your own might be about trying to save money or designing something to suit your own particular needs, but it should never be about speed or cutting corners. My bottom line? Do your research and spend the money on commercially available equipment. They'll be plenty of headaches that come about over other aspects of pottery making that are unavoidable. This is one headache you can sidestep!

## Choosing Equipment

Unfortunately, the local availability of potter's equipment is generally weak. Even if you are lucky enough to be within a reasonable drive of a potter's supply, few have a wide variety of equipment on display for you to examine or try. The reasons for this are easy to understand. Equipment is expensive, sales may not be brisk, and it is a financial risk to have too much money tied up in inventory. However, understanding the reasons doesn't make it any easier to make informed decisions about equipment purchases without being able to see the equipment. Without this ability, you are relegated to making choices based on what you may have experience with, reputation, word of mouth, and recommendations. Of these avenues, the one you'll trust the most is your own experience with equipment that you've used in school or group studio situations. And although this is not a bad or inferior way to make choices when it comes to purchasing, it does limit you by not giving you the widest range of choices. You must be as resourceful as possible in gathering pertinent information about equipment and go beyond your immediate experience.

### Wheels

Using the potter's wheel as an example, what's wrong with simply buying the wheel that you used as a student or are now using as a studio member? Nothing at all if you are completely happy, but there are some limitations to this practice. First, just because you are satisfied with what you've been using doesn't preclude the possibility that you would be happier with a different brand or model. Second, the wheel you have been using may no longer be available. And third, you may have experience with more than one wheel and be in a quandary about which one to get. Assuming there is no pottery supplier with a selection of equipment in your area, you can visit local potters, schools, and studios to see the equipment they have. Ask questions about the operation, maintenance, and repair records of the equipment that interests you. Ask to try the wheel and be sure to bring your own clay. Why? It is both courteous to the studio and sensible to test the wheel under as close to realistic conditions as possible. The choice of clay goes a long way to simulate real conditions. Once you have narrowed down the choice, rather than asking the supplier additional questions, consult the manufacturer for accurate answers to any technical questions you may have.

**Power:** A wheel's power in practical terms is a function of horsepower and torque. What you really want to know is whether you can apply the necessary force to the largest amount of clay you will work with and not have the pug mill slow down or stop.

**Speed:** Speed is related to power but is really a different performance issue. Your style of working will dictate the speed or RPMs of the wheel head you require.

**Control Sensitivity:** Your sensitivity to extremely slow speeds and the degree of gradual increase as you apply it will dictate any concerns you have in this area.

**Smoothness and Vibration:** Again, personal style and expectations will make this more or less of an issue.

**Weight:** If you use 30 or more pounds of clay, the weight and stability of the wheel could be an issue. You don't want the wheel crawling along the floor as you pressure the clay!

**Wheel Head Diameter:** Although you can use bats of almost any size, the diameter of the wheel head may be a concern. The smallest head is 12", with heads going as large as 16" or larger.

**Misc Features:** Splash pan, integrated seat, attached work table, height adjustability, and choice of wheel head rotation are examples of additional features you should be aware of.

After your research, call around and make your choice of supplier based on the considerations discussed in length in the previous chapter. Remember—do not make your choice on the basis of price alone!

Here are some questions to consider when choosing other popular potter's equipment. This isn't the complete litany of questions but should get you off to a good start and get your mind thinking along an appropriately inquisitive direction.

## Slab Roller

1) Is it manual or electric? If electric, what's the motor size, switching mechanism, etc.?

*Figure 5-2. Brent SR-36 slab roller. (Courtesy of American Art Clay Co.)*

*Figure 5-1. Slab roller manufactured by North Star Equipment Co. (Photo by Bethany Versoy)*

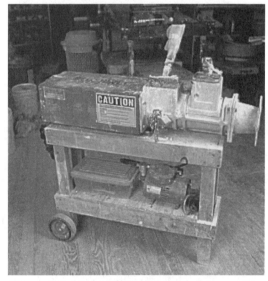

*Figure 5-3. Model #400 pug mill manufactured by Bluebird Manufacturing Co. set on a rolling stand constructed by the author. (Photo by Bethany Versoy)*

2) What is the maximum size slab that can be rolled out?

3) Is it a tabletop model or does it come with an integral table? If it does, is the table suitable as a general work surface as well?

4) What size are the rollers?

5) What is the mechanism for adjusting the thickness of the slab? How accurate and sensitive is that adjustment?

6) What is the machine and its various components (gears, rollers, knobs, tabletop, etc.) made of? Plastic, steel, aluminum, stainless steel?

## Pug Mill

1) What is the size of the motor?

2) What components are steel, stainless steel, other materials?

3) What is the maximum production by weight per hour?

4) What is the size of the hopper?

5) Is the drive mechanism direct, chain, shaft, or by other means?

6) Is there a de-airing feature and if so, can you bypass it?

7) Are there different size nozzles and can you attach dies to covert the machine into a power extruder?

8) How convenient is it to dismantle the machine for cleaning?

## Extruder

1) What is it made of?

2) Does it mount on a table or wall and is all the mounting hardware included?

3) How large is the barrel? Are different barrel sizes available and interchangeable?

4) How do the dies attach? What dies are available and is a die set included?

5) What is the plunging mechanism?

*Figure 5-4. An extruder manufactured by Bailey Pottery Equipment Corp. (Photo by Bethany Versoy)*

6) What is the longest extrusion the machine is capable of?

## Kilns

Shopping for a kiln can be more complicated because the choices are wide ranging. Not only are there gas and electric kilns, but it seems there are so many kiln manufacturers as to make gathering information complicated and confusing. Obviously, the first decision is between gas and electric firing. This will be dictated by your experience, the proposed location of your kiln, local fire and building codes, and your immediate and long term pottery production plans. One of the primary factors that may affect your choice of a gas or electric kiln is whether you can provide an adequate shelter for the gas kiln. Electric kilns can be placed in almost any location, from a garage or other outbuilding to a room in your house. Common sense and manufacturer recommendations regarding proximity to combustible materials and surfaces will dictate exactly what areas of your house or studio are appropriate. Electric kilns are self-contained, require no chimney, and although a ventilation system is an absolute necessity, it need not be particularly complicated. Fuel burning kilns, on the other hand, are not as easily located. They are usually placed outdoors in areas sheltered by an open shed or other roof supporting structure, although indoor locations are not uncommon as long as there's adequate ventilation and isolation from combustibles.

Once you have decided gas or electric, it's time to organize your thoughts regarding the requirements you have in a kiln. Although the options for brand, size, style, and other features seems confusing, your ultimate choice of a kiln need not be any more difficult than choosing a wheel.

**Gas Kilns:** Gas kilns offer the choice of home built models and commercially available ones. The choice between building a kiln of your own and purchasing a commercial kiln can be cut and dried for some and rather exasperating for others. Building a kiln of your own involves designing, purchasing materials, preparing the site, and doing the actual construction. This is more than many people are willing to do. The advantages of a home built kiln are personal, but may reflect a specific need that is not addressed in a commercial model—a need to be more self-sufficient, the desire to save significant money by building a kiln of your own, or the intellectual curiosity and desire to be more familiar with kiln construction. Any advantages you might think exist in the actu-al operation or construction of home built kilns are mostly outdated and erroneous. Manufacturers have incorporated up-to-date technology in the design and construction of kilns to include efficient combustion systems, convenient door mechanisms, well insulated construction, and ease of firing control.

If building a kiln is your choice and you have limited or no experience, some serious study is in your immediate future. You may want to consult or hire someone who specializes in the design and construction of fuel-fired kilns. For a fee, they will act as both the architect and contractor, with you supplying the labor. As in the design phase of any project, the kiln designer will ask you about details such as chamber size, type of firing you plan to do, frequency of firing, type of fuel available, and other questions aimed at arriving at the kiln that will meet your needs. Many kilns have been built in kiln building workshops where a host organizes a weekend presentation by the kiln guru. The participants build the kiln with the host and the fee charged pays for the materials and design work. A good deal for both the host and the participants!

Some features to compare in commercial gas kilns are:

1) **Design**. Consider the shape—flat top or arch design, stacking space, door mechanism.

2) **Package**. Welded steel frame or some other method of support?

3) **Construction Materials**. Are insulating bricks or refractory fiber the primary or sole insulating material?

4) **Combustion System**. Updraft, downdraft, or crossdraft design? Power, venturi, or atmospheric burners? What kind of chimney and flue control is there?

As you assemble literature on the various designs from different manufacturers, you will make note of other variations and considerations. Compare them all and ask questions before making your choice.

**Electric Kilns:** The technology that has been applied to electric kilns over the past 20 years has been refreshing, especially in the areas of insulation, ventilation of components, and general durability—all features that have plagued electric kilns in the past. Efficiency has been upgraded, sizes have been increased, and the longevity of elements and other electrical components has been lengthened. When shopping for an electric kiln or any kiln for that matter, first get a handle on the size kiln you need. Compare the amount of your production with the frequency you like to have loads fired. You may produce truckloads of work over the course of a month but your style of working may demand that you fire small loads on a frequent basis rather than huge loads every few weeks. Firing temperature is a consideration. It used to be that kilns were built in either low-fire or high-fire configurations. This is no longer the case and if you do come across a manufacturer who offers low- and high-fire variations, select the high-fire model for durability, longevity, and versatility in your firing options.

After size, compare the following:

1) **Controls.** Look at the number of switches and note whether they offer infinite heat control or low/medium/high settings only. Is there a built-in timer or kiln sitter? Is there an option for computer control?

2) **Power Requirements**. Be sure you are capable of supplying adequate electrical power for your kiln.

3) **Insulating Material and Construction**. Compare the thickness of the brick used in the walls, floor, and top, and whether there is additional insulation in the form of refractory fiber. Is the floor reversible for longevity? Is the top a one-piece cast form or is it

constructed of brick? Is the kiln sectional or one-piece? If it is sectional, can it be fired with a section removed?

4) **Elements**. How many are there and how are they arranged? Is there an element in the floor or top and is this an important feature?

5) **Hardware**. Examine the hardware used in the general construction, hinges, handles, electrical boxes and their attachment. Do the electrical boxes offer adequate isolation and ventilation from the heat of the kiln? If the lid is particularly heavy, is there a counter balance system?

Just as in comparing gas kilns or other pieces of equipment, as you learn more and ask more questions, you will become aware of additional considerations.

### Other Equipment

There is a variety of other equipment you will outfit your studio with at some time, and I have already mentioned a lot of it in the context of studio design. Items like fans, scales, banding wheels, spraying equipment, compressors, and other pieces of equipment of varying magnitude need to be examined, evaluated, and chosen according to your specific needs and requirements. Use the same criteria with the same probing mindset you used in choosing the items discussed above.

## Repairing and Maintaining Equipment

Though my philosophy about self-sufficiency must be clear to you by now, here's a little reminder—the degree to which you rely on your own knowledge and personal resources must be within a realm of practicality. There is only so much time in the day to divide between the activities you have to tend to, like making pots, ordering supplies, and running your operation, and indeed there is a level of reasonable knowledge and skill that a person can be expected to master in their lifetime. Of course, there are vastly differing degrees of self-sufficiency and I know potters who seem to be able to do it all, from welding a ware cart to changing the bearings in their pug mill to clearing the back 40 in the seat of an eight-speed tractor. When emergencies or predicaments arise that are out of the ordinary, you'll have to decide whether they require your attention or whether your time would be better spent having someone else tend to them.

Achieving a minimal degree of general handyman ability is a necessity if you are going to operate a studio. Enough minor repair work will need to be done to make it impractical and very expensive to call a repairman every time something goes awry. The wherewithal to properly maintain your equipment and systems is also a necessity because timely maintenance will reduce the frequency of needed repairs. I have already discussed some of the issues relating to being able to "do it yourself" in the section on studio design and construction. Simple electrical and plumbing troubleshooting and repair is well within the reach of most people and you should make an effort to become familiar with them. That leaky faucet might only need tightening or a new washer or gasket. If you do it, it will probably cost less than $10 (depending on the need for parts) and take less than half an hour of your time, with immediate satisfaction and no downtime waiting for the plumber. Bring in a plumber and the cost climbs. Call and arrange for him to come over and you are told that tomorrow afternoon is the earliest appointment. Minimum charge is $50 plus parts.

Learn how to do it yourself. With the variety of systems and equipment you have in the shop, the same or similar scenarios will be played out many, many times over the course of a year. Take the time to learn something about your equipment and you'll not only save yourself money but will be more in tune with how your equipment operates, being able to fine tune and prevent costly repairs or replacement down the road. Learning just how to do this is a matter of being resourceful, self-confident, and sensible.

When it comes to general studio maintenance such as plumbing, electrical, telephone, and tending to other systems and components, home repair do-it-yourself books are wonderfully helpful manuals that guide you through the processes with step-by-step instructions, leaving almost no stone unturned. Equip yourself with two or three of these and you'll be in good shape. However, regardless of the comprehensive and thorough nature of these guides, you ultimately have to use your good sense in deciding just what repairs you feel comfortable tackling. I advocate a bold approach, but within reason. Don't hurt yourself!

When it comes to repair and maintenance of your equipment—wheel, kiln, mixers, power tools, fans, carts—a degree of self-sufficiency is even more useful and powerful. These items are subject to heavy use and will absolutely require care, repair, and maintenance. It is really a necessity for you to learn at least the basics of how these machines work and feel confident in performing regular maintenance and minor repair. It is totally impractical to hire someone to tend to these items on a regular basis.

Maintenance, general troubleshooting, and repair usually fall under two main areas—mechanical and electrical. Mechanical workings are the nuts and bolts, how things are held together, the way components mesh, and basically how they work. Dealing with the mechanical components of an item is usually within the reach of most people and if you can't actually fix the problem, you can almost always diagnose and understand what the problem is. Electrical issues can be problematic because they can be difficult to locate and diagnose and many electrical systems and

*Figure 5-5. Brent E-J motorized kick wheel. (Courtesy of American Art Clay Co.)*

components are designed to be replaced rather than repaired. Sometimes repairing is impractical and not worth the effort or cost. Before you attempt a repair, become familiar with the technical specifications of the equipment and the manufacturer's suggested maintenance schedule and procedures.

A very common maintenance measure is lubrication. Any piece of equipment that has even a single moving part will require lubrication. Not all oils are the same and different components require different types of oils for their maintenance. Consult the manuals that came with your tools. If there is no recommendation made, call the manufacturer before choosing an oil on your own. Not only is the type of oil important, but the area or spot of lubrication can be critical. Lubricating something doesn't mean an indiscriminate drenching of the apparent squeaky part. Lubricant placed on the wrong component can, in the case of motors and other electrical parts, mean doom and gloom. One method to reduce the amount and frequency of lubrication necessary is the advent and widespread use of sealed bearings. These are rotating collars that are lubricated at the factory

and are often designed as a no maintenance component. That is, when they begin to squeak, squeal, and make horrible grinding noises, they are ready to be replaced. Depending on the bearing and the way it's installed, removing and replacing may require special tools called bearing pullers and pressers. Again, a consultation with the manufacturer is in order before you destroy anything! If a bearing on a machine does need to be replaced, be resourceful in finding someone capable of doing the work. Logical places to look are auto repair shops, machine shops, and, believe it or not, bearing suppliers. A look in the Yellow Pages will yield results.

## Wheels

Potter's wheels fall into two broad categories—kick wheels and electric wheels. Of course, nothing is ever that simple and in this case there are also kick wheels powered by motors and a style of kick wheel called a treadle wheel. A treadle wheel is powered by a pumping action similar to an old style sewing machine.

A kick wheel, whether constructed around a sturdy metal frame or built from wood, is a wonderful example of a mechanical system designed for heavy-duty use and simple maintenance and repair. Few things can go wrong and since all the components are out in the open, the problem is usually easy to spot. Common problems that might arise are:

1) **Wobbliness**. Be sure the frame is set firmly and squarely on the floor. Check for broken welds or loose connections of the frame components.

2) **Premature Slowing of the Wheel Head**. Make sure all the bearings and any contact of metal on metal are well lubricated according to the manufacturer's instructions. If the bearings are of the sealed type, they may need to be replaced.

3) **Uneven Rotation of the Wheel Head**. Wheel heads are designed for removal, so check for a firm connection between the wheel head and the shaft. Wheel heads are made of light alloy material that can become misshapen over time. The collar that connects the wheel head to the shaft may no longer fit tightly and the head may need to be replaced. Check the set screw (if there is one) that tightens the head to the shaft for a firm grip.

4) **Inefficient Transfer of Power from the Motor to the Flywheel**. Most motorized kick wheels operate on a system that depends on the shaft of the motor making contact with the edge of the flywheel through a small rubber bearing or drive wheel. Check the rubber wheel for wear and check the motor for correct mounting.

Electric wheels are subject to similar problems with the causes and solutions sometimes a bit different.

1) **Premature Slowing of the Wheel Head**. Generally caused by a worn drive belt, cone, or other drive mechanism. Tighten the connection or replace the belt.

2) **Jerky Rotation of the Wheel Head**. Usually because of either a worn drive belt or misalignment of the belt between the motor and the wheel head shaft.

3) **Poor Speed Control**. Electronically controlled motors usually have a foot pedal that is adjustable. Consult the literature that came with your wheel. Typically (but not always) there are high and low speed adjustment dials or screws that need to be calibrated for adequate slow and fast speed control of the wheel. These can easily fall out of adjustment.

## Mixers, Pug Mills, Extruders, Slab Rollers

The equipment used for clay preparation is the most industrial strength found in the studio. These items are the easiest to understand, yet can be the most difficult and frustrating to repair.

Mixers and pug mills are heavy, lumbering pieces of equipment that often require strength and can require special tools when repair or part replacement is necessary. Be sure to adhere to the maintenance schedule suggested by the manufacturer. That will most likely consist of cleaning, lubrication, and tightening of screws and bolts. When you get your mixer or pug mill, study the literature including the schematic diagram (if provided). Become familiar with the parts and their roles in making the machine work. You can often figure out what parts are likely to need replacement and you should have a replacement part or two on hand. If it's not evident, call the manufacturer and ask. Despite the seemingly indestructible nature of these tools, they can fail, usually because of overwork. Too much clay in the mixer or extruder can over stress the metal, hinges, mounting brackets, and other parts. Clay that is too stiff can cause premature wear of the blades and drive mechanism in a pug mill and can bend the dies and forms set up in an extruder. Parts of an extruder can be damaged if the plunging mechanism can be forced down onto the part of the die or die holder that is set inside the barrel. A slab roller can be damaged by rolling through a slab of clay in one pass, instead of two or three passes with the rollers set at subsequently lower heights. Although it is not common, motors on potter's wheels, mixers, extruders, pug mills, and other equipment, can burn out from regular use over a period of many years, but you can hasten the burnout by overloading the machine beyond its recommended capability.

# Kilns

Kiln maintenance and repair can be learned and performed by anyone! If you can't replace the elements, a switch, or a crushed brick in your electric kiln or replace some crumbling fiber, sagging brick, or corroded burner in your gas kiln, then you can literally be rendered frozen in time, unable to fire your kiln until you find someone to do the repair for you. My knowledge of electric kiln maintenance comes from hands-on experience driven by an interest in knowing how my equipment is designed and operates.

Few cities have kiln repair professionals at your service. At best, you may be able to coax an electrician or an appliance repairman to take a stab at your electric kiln or perhaps a plumber or industrial furnace company to look at your corroded burner or other malady in your gas kiln. Indeed, they could probably do an adequate job providing they are interested and resourceful in figuring out the best way to do a repair on a piece of equipment that they likely have had no experience repairing or using. Thanks, but no thanks, I'll do it myself!

Kiln maintenance, whether on a gas or electric kiln, consists mostly of periodic examination of the external and internal components and repairing or replacing parts as they wear out. Gas kilns have few moving or electrical parts to worry about and thus require less technical skill in their upkeep. If you are servicing a commercial kiln, you have the manufacturer as a resource for instructions, parts, and tips on maintenance. If your kiln is home built, you presumably were involved in the construction and thus already have a good sense of the kiln's components and repair.

Since the electric kiln is no doubt the most popular kiln in use today, I will focus on it rather than gas kiln repair.

Review the safety practices in the section on basic electrical installation and repair before attempting any work on your kiln. Never work on your kiln when it is plugged in unless you are performing a test that requires electrical power. Just shut off the circuit breaker, you say? Take the next safety step and unplug the thing before you stick your hand in it. If your kiln is directly wired, as all kilns that draw over 50 amps or so should be, make sure the power to the entire breaker panel is shut off, not just the breaker to the kiln. Test the circuit to be sure the power is off and then begin your work.

Often, the trickier part of doing a repair on an electric kiln is diagnosing the problem. The foundation to competent maintenance and diagnosis of problems is a reasonably thorough understanding of the workings of the kiln. This can be accomplished by making an overall examination of the condition of your kiln.

Cleanliness is next to godliness—keeping your kiln clean is very important and requires more than simply not spilling your hot chocolate on the lid. Dust, dirt, moisture, glaze drips, and other visible ugliness all contribute to an overall decline in your kiln's efficient operation. Cleaning is not just cosmetic maintenance! Regular inspection and cleaning should be part of your schedule. Vacuum out the interior as well as the top perimeter of the kiln. Check the entire inside for dripped glaze on the bricks or worse, on the coils. These drips should be chipped away as soon as they appear, for each successive firing will drive the glaze deeper into the brick and more permanently onto the coil. Often glaze that drips onto a coil can be carefully loosened and taken off with a long-nose plier. Heat up the coil first so it isn't brittle, but don't heat it to the point of real softness. Turn off the current before you work on it. If any coils pop out of their grooves, heat up the coil and carefully press them back in place. This time, heat up the coils until they are glowing and soft. Again, don't forget to turn off the current before you start working.

Open up the electrical boxes every ten firings or so and inspect for loose connections, frayed wires, and corroding parts. A common cause of kiln failure is loose connections. Electrical current vibrates, sometimes causing the connection between the element and terminal to come loose. This spot can then decay rapidly. Make sure no wires are touching the element tails that come through the wall of the kiln. Vacuum out these areas also. Be sure the element tails aren't coming in contact with the outside kiln jacket. There should be a porcelain insulator protecting the jacket from an accidental electrical connection. If your kiln is a multi-section one, there will be plugs, outlets, and sometimes electrical cord that connect sections. These components do wear out and must be periodically examined. If you find a plug that's darkened, misshapen, or in less than good condition, it must be replaced. Its corresponding receptacle will most likely need replacement also. Check the cord for complete integrity. Examine the cord, plug, and receptacle that connect the kiln to your electrical service for the same kinds of weaknesses. If the lid of your kiln is on a hinge, examine the entire hinge mechanism for corrosion, alignment, and security.

One of the most common causes of kiln deterioration is moisture. Proper ventilation—either with an individual ventilation system manufactured by Orton, Bailey or others, or having the kiln in a room that's adequately vented—will contribute much to its longevity and efficient operation. Proper ventilation will also keep you safe from the harmful effects of fumes.

To diagnose and repair problems, you must have some basic tools—pliers, hammer, screwdrivers, and other common tools that everyone should have around the studio. The one special-

ized tool that is an absolute necessity is a volt meter. Buy a model capable of the most basic functions. These are available in electronics stores, electrical supply stores, or a store like Radio Shack. The volt meter has a calibration switch or dial that allows you to set it for the voltage that it will be subjected to as well as a switch allowing you to set the meter to AC or DC voltage. Set it to AC.

Kiln problems can manifest themselves in many different ways. The most common is when your kiln will not reach temperature and you must

*Figure 5-6. The wiring box of a typical electric kiln is a myriad of wires, connectors, and switches that can be an intimidating sight. Before disconnecting anything, draw a simple diagram so you will be able to reconnect everything correctly. (Photo by Bethany Versoy)*

figure out why. At fault could be a coil (or two), a switch, the interbox plugs or outlets, the power cord, the fuse box, or any of the wiring in between. When trying to locate the source of the problem, it's best to work your way back from the recognizable symptom. Turn the kiln on high and observe whether all the coils glow with color. If one or more do not, you have a visible symptom. Just because a coil doesn't get red doesn't mean the coil isn't working, so do a simple test. Touch a piece of paper to any portion of the coil. If the paper burns, you know the coil is intact and getting power. If it doesn't burn, either the coil is broken or there is something preventing the coil from getting power. Touch the volt meter probes to each end of the coil as it enters the kiln. Does the meter register volts? If so, you know that electrical power is coming to the coil without causing the coil to heat up, so the coil must be broken. If there is no power, work your way back towards the fuse box to identify where the electrical connection is severed. Remember that you are now working with exposed connections and live current. Be extremely careful when touching the meter to connections. Many times the problem is not the coils at all and may be a faulty switch, loose electrical connection, or in larger more complicated kilns, a deteriorated electrical relay or some other component.

As complicated as a kiln may seem, there are only a limited number of things that can go wrong. By using the process of elimination you will soon become expert at pinning down those previously elusive mysteries.

Before tackling actual repair mechanisms, establish some basic benchmarks regarding the configuration of your kiln. First draw a wiring diagram. I don't mean one of those cryptic-looking complicated, "full of electrical symbols that only an electrical engineer would understand" type diagrams. I mean a simple drawing showing from where and to where each wire goes. Do not, under any circumstances, disconnect a wire without making a note of where it goes. The second thing you must know is the length of the coils. Although some kiln manufacturers or element suppliers deliver coils pre-stretched to their proper length, most coils will come to you unstretched. To determine the length, simply lay a string in the element's groove, marking the beginning and end on the string. (For your records, make a note of the length.) Stretching the coil to this length is a bit more complicated. Most important is that the coil be stretched evenly without sections of "tight" and "loose" winds of the material. The easiest way to insure an even stretch is to place the element end (the unwound part of the coil) in a vise. Measuring from the vice, mark the length on the floor, wall, bench top, or some other physical point. Hold the loose end of the coil and pull it evenly away from the vise in the direction of the distance mark. Pull it about 10% longer than your mark, then make a new mark. Slowly release the tension and you will see that the coil has not yet been stretched long enough. Repeat the procedure, each time pulling a bit further until the coil is stretched to its proper length. You now will have marked how far the coil must be stretched to achieve the correct length! Avoid stretching the coil too far. Compressing the length of a coil that has been over-stretched is a pain in the neck. Realize that although coils from different kilns may be the same length, unless they are made of the same gauge material, they will have to be stretched different distances to arrive at the same length.

Element replacement is without a doubt the most common "repair" procedure known to anyone who operates an electric kiln. Every potter who uses an electric kiln should know how to replace the elements. A common question regarding element replacement is whether or not to replace the entire set of coils when one coil fails. To answer this, you must have a good sense of how long the elements last and how old and used the present set of elements in the kiln is. If you determine that the set of elements is near the end of its usefulness, replace the whole set. If the remaining coils still have considerable life and energy left, replace only the damaged one. You are trying to avoid the creation of a "hot" spot in your kiln that can occur when a new full strength coil is added to a set of marginal ones. Remove the old coil by clipping its ends inside the kiln where they exit the kiln chamber. Remove the coil and carefully clean the groove in the brick of any debris, glaze melts, etc. Open the electrical box, exposing the element connections and make careful note of where each end of the coil attaches. Disconnect the old element ends (tails), feed one end of the new coil through the hole, lay the coil into the groove proceeding around the kiln, feed the other end through the kiln wall, and connect the ends to their appropriate posts or other means of connection. It sounds easy, and it is if you pay attention to what everything is supposed to look like—where the element tails connect, how the element end is bent (if it is bent), etc. Be sure all the connections are tight. Clip off any excess length of element and close up shop.

While on the subject of coils, here's a creative solution to the repair of a broken coil. Sometimes a coil will break not because it is old and worn out but because a glaze drip has eaten through it or it has been subjected to some other careless treatment. You can effectively "repair" a broken coil. While everything is cold, overlap the severed ends of the broken coil with a 2" to 3" section of a scrap coil. Press the scrap section over the ends like interlocking fingers. Be sure to clip off any foreign matter before effecting this repair. I have had repairs like this last for 20 or more firings!

Other common failures in electric kilns are switches, plugs, and receptacles. Simple. Just remove the old component and replace it with a new one. Again, be sure to make careful note of the exact, correct wire connections. You don't have to get the new switch, plug, or receptacle from the kiln manufacturer, but it may be the easiest and safest supply source. Electrical switches used in electric kilns are extremely common. Everyday electrical appliances such as ranges, ovens, toasters, and hot plates use them. With this in mind, it may be tempting to saunter into the local electrical supply or appliance parts and repair outlet and get yourself some switches. When you delve deeper into the switch maze you will find that the specifications of specific switches can be a bewildering network of befuddlement—15A/ 125V, 20A/250V, 20A/125V, etc. In addition, the meth-

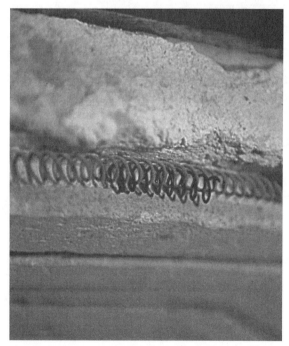

*Figure 5-7. This is what the temporary coil repair referred to in the text looks like. The repair section has been painted to make the photo clearer. (Photo by Bethany Versoy)*

# Chapter 6

## Business Practices

I can feel the fear, the withdrawal, the intimidation. I can hear the excuses. "I'm not a business person." "Record keeping was never my strong suit." "I'm no businesswoman, I'm an artist." I can also anticipate the reasons you think this chapter might not apply to you. You're not planning to sell your work. You're just doing this as a serious hobby. You're not going to be deducting any of your expenses on your taxes. Get it all out of your system because if there is one chapter that applies to everyone regardless of your "business" intentions, this is it.

Incorporating sound business practices is important to everybody and can make your pottery making activities more manageable and therefore more enjoyable. "Business practices" refers not only to those areas that apply to the actual establishment of a bona fide business entity (taxes, lawyers, accountants, employee/employer strategies), but equally to record keeping, bill paying, inventory management, utilities, and other essential areas of organization that apply to all of us. Obviously, as you read and begin to realize your own connection to all of this, you will pick and choose what in this mix is important and applicable. I urge you to become familiar with everything discussed here. It will come in handy, if not now, then sometime in your future.

Despite my belief in the importance of sound business practices, this chapter is by no means an end-all to the question of business and crafts. Fortunately, individuals with much more formal and technical training than I have written for the craftsperson and artist. There is no need for me to rewrite what has already been done far better than I could ever do it. What I have undertaken here is to make you aware of the business skills and areas of importance you should be familiar with. For greater detail and much more extensive study of business, I urge you to continue your reading with any number of titles in the Bibliography. Is this a cop out? a disclaimer? an excuse for being less than expert? Not by any means.

This is as good a time as any to give you some advice on knowledge. You cannot be expert in every area that you find yourself having to cope with and negotiate. Indeed, there is an indispensable aspect of knowledge that is often seen as a deficiency when it should be viewed as a strength—realizing and identifying those areas where you need to be knowledgeable, but accepting that you won't ever be an expert in that area. You must recognize your academic and intellectual black holes and learn how to overcome them, not fool yourself into believing that you can know it all. How do you do that? By learning how and where to find the information you need.

### Establishing Yourself as a Business

What is a business? You can call it anything you like, but for this discussion, a business is a duly registered and recognized commercial entity. A business takes money in and disburses money out. You sell objects or provide services or a combination of both. The items you sell may or may not be manufactured by you. Your business pays taxes and also uses the tax laws, along with other rules and regulations, to its advantage. A business is accountable and needs to keep rather copious records of its expenses and transactions. A business can be a pain in the neck but if managed properly can be very rewarding. Regardless of to what extent you want your pottery making activities to produce income or even profit, a series of organized business practices will help you keep focused on the task at hand.

Must you establish yourself as a bona fide business? The short answer is no but the short answer is also most inadequate and misleading. Not establishing yourself as a business can prove to be dangerous in the areas of personal and financial liability, both discussed in the section on insurance and legal issues.

Since this study is not designed to be an indepth treatise on business, I can safely and comfortably simplify the approach to business types, formats, and general business planning.

## Business Types

A **single proprietorship** is the most basic form of business organization. This is where a single individual owns and is financially responsible for all the business assets, liabilities, and responsibilities. Generally speaking, a single proprietorship is inexplicably linked to the owner's personal financial affairs. Your home, car, other income, and personal assets of any kind are all connected to your business and therein lies the greatest disadvantage of that form of business entity. A single proprietorship offers little insulation of your personal life in the unfortunate case of the business failing, or worse if some liability issue arises.

A **partnership** is essentially the same as a single proprietorship with the responsibilities, financial and otherwise, shared according to a predetermined percentage among the partners.

**Corporations**, though they sound large, complicated, and exclusive, are not limited to Fortune 500 companies. Indeed, they can be very similar functionally to single proprietorships while affording the owner separation and protection of personal assets, interests, and lives. There are many different types of corporate organizations, each offering different structures, tax responsibilities, and thus advantages and disadvantages for the craftsperson. The most popular corporate structure for the small business person is called a **subchapter S corporation**.

Another important category of corporate institutions are **nonprofits**. These are, for all intents and purposes, standard corporate structures in most ways with the added feature of important tax benefits available only to certain types of business enterprises. Common categories include educational, religious, and charitable institutions. Although we commonly assume all schools, art and craft centers, and museums (to name a few) are nonprofit, it is interesting to note that many are not nonprofit at all. Though the tax benefits afforded to nonprofits are great, along with that status comes added record keeping, governmental reporting, and tax filing responsibilities. Nonprofits generate much confusion and misunderstanding about exactly what they are and what they can and can't do. Through my experience as the president of a nonprofit educational institution (The Potters School) as well as the president of a profit-making S corporation (The Potters Shop), I have a good sense of the differences and similarities. I have experienced the frustrations caused by public misconceptions that surround the nonprofit label. A major misconception is the assumption that nonprofits are charity or community service endeavors. Nonprofit is not synonymous with charity nor does it necessarily have anything to do with community service or volunteerism. A charitable or community service organization can be nonprofit, but it doesn't have to be. The most common and serious misunderstanding about nonprofits revolves around the question of making money. Nonprofit does not mean you can't make money. That is a silly and seriously naive conception. Nonprofit does not mean the organization is staffed by volunteers who work tirelessly and endlessly for the good of the institution. In its simplest terms, when it comes to income, the "profits," or excess income after expenses, must be treated within certain guidelines as established by the federal government through the Internal Revenue Service (IRS) and each state through their commission of taxation. Included in an organization's expenses are salaries, benefits, perks, and other customary compensation to employees and corporate officers.

Nonprofits can be, and often are, just as ruthless as any Fortune 500 company. They can be just as environmentally unconscious as any irresponsible person out there and they can be as uncharitable as Scrooge was before his enlightenment. Nonprofits do pay their employees and clearly must operate in the black if they are to continue to exist. Staying in the black means, at the very least, taking in as much money as is paid out but often results in more income than expenses. This excess income must be turned back into the institution, not simply disbursed among the officers. Indeed, that is a primary difference between a nonprofit and any other standard business organization. How does that money go back into the institution? It can take many routes such as capital purchases of equipment or property, bonuses to its officers, and other means.

While I'm on the subject of expenses, salaries, as in the case of large museums, public broadcasting stations, large charitable organizations, and other institutions, can be big time, even unconscionably astronomical. The next time you hear the semiannual plea for membership and donations to your local public TV station, you may want to do some research before mailing your check. Wouldn't you like to know where your money is going? On a less cynical front, though, nonprofits are often places like pottery schools and craft centers where, if not for the tax and other benefits afforded them by nonprofit status, they wouldn't be able to exist.

The type of business entity you create depends on your goals, needs, and resources. You will need some help in deciding which way to go and ultimately how best to get there!

## Professional Assistance

Hear this: you cannot do it alone. You value your independence? You enjoy not having to rely on others? You relish your self-sufficiency? Fine. Do you farm all of your own food, refine your own oil, fashion all your own clothes, deliver your own mail? Are you a living CD-ROM of essential information? Let's face it, we all need the expertise of others to make a successful go of it. You can't be everything if you want to excel at anything.

First under the heading of professional assisters are to some the most unlikable. Indeed, lawyers, and to a lesser degree accountants, have developed a negative reputation to go along with an intimidating air. This seems to be especially true for those of us who consider ourselves as far removed from that segment of societal specialization as can be. It's time to break through the stereotypes and solicit the help and advice you need to establish, maintain, and further your career.

I readily admit that when I first started out I was sure I could do it all without any help and for a while I did just that. To be fair to myself, though, I was so naive I had no idea that consulting an attorney or accountant could be beneficial, much less invaluable and necessary. On the most basic level of business organization as a single proprietorship, you *can* do it alone. Conceptually it's simple, the forms are relatively easy to decipher and complete, and the tax filing is somewhat rudimentary. It is an especially simple task if your business is without a lot of deductions, equipment depreciation, investments, and the like. If you're willing to sacrifice some serious time and effort to the project, you can even forge ahead and form your own corporation and do your own IRS filing. There are certainly enough books, seminars, and tapes out there that purport to teach you how. I don't recommend it. There are too many nuances of interpretation of the laws and requirements as well as elementary questions that you might not even know to ask. Tax filing laws and requirements change year to year and as your own business grows you may be not only subject to additional aspects of the tax code, but you may be able to take advantage of others. There is no practical way for a layman to be well enough versed in the laws and codes to do an adequate job of tax and form filing. Even at the single proprietorship level, I suggest at least consulting an attorney.

Remember that every additional skill you learn and take on yourself, despite its relevance and importance to your craft, means time away from the actual making of craft objects. Always compare the relative value of your involvement in noncraft making activities to the time you have available to keep your hands in clay.

Attorneys and accountants can provide you with essential direction in very important areas that can be categorized in two broad based directions. They can monitor your activities to be certain you are doing everything to benefit your business interests, and they can help you do things in a correct and legal fashion. Some details of your business that will benefit from an objective professional eye are correct business structure, liability exposure, advantageous tax benefits, rentals, and leases. In addition, contracts, employee relations, banking and financial arrangements, tax filing, and a host of other areas will benefit from the insight of a trained professional. There are many more areas of expertise that one of these professionals can assist you with. Suffice it to say that while their help and advice won't come inexpensively, it will be well worth the expense.

Business consultants, in my view, can be considered almost as a sub specialty in the area of legal advice. They are, for the most part, not attorneys and thus cannot give legal advice. Business consultants can answer many questions about business startup, business plans, structure, etc. A business consultant may be a good first step on the road to establishing a business, especially since in many cities you can find this kind of advice offered free of charge through the local chamber of commerce, continuing education at local schools and colleges, and programs offered by the Small Business Administration.

Before securing the services of any professional, take a long serious pause to formulate a plan of your own. However general your plans and ideas may be at this early stage, getting established begins and ends with you. Help and advice occupies the middle. Bring at least a general idea of what you want to be when you grow up. Even the most ephemeral of plans will give you and your consultant a starting point.

So you've decided you're ready for some help and you want to find a lawyer or accountant. Where to look? Personal references and word of mouth should be your first sources. Ask your friends, neighbors, business associates, the proprietor of the local hardware store, etc. I firmly believe you should find a lawyer or accountant through some sort of personal referral. Indeed, if you go to great lengths to find the best clay supplier, plumber, electrician, and janitorial service through referrals, then you better be sure to expend at least the same effort and care when looking for a lawyer or accountant! After exhausting personal recommendations, consult local arts groups, craft associations, and the like. Often groups like this will have compiled lists of professionals who either specialize in arts and crafts law or have an interest in the arts.

Must you have an attorney or accountant that likes the arts? No, but it certainly helps. Not only are there many laws and regulations specific to artists and art groups, but having a professional who is experienced working with creative people helps tremendously in the areas of communication, organization, and a general meeting of the minds. Let's face it, creative people do tend to have some peculiarities, idiosyncrasies, and individual ways of doing things. We tend towards spontaneity and deadlines are often viewed as approximate. Note taking and record keeping are usually not our strengths and to most of us, a verbal promise or commitment is trusted. Working with a professional who can understand and perhaps even relate in a personal way to our values and styles can be comforting and allows for a better working relationship.

Hiring the services of a lawyer or accountant should follow similar guidelines to those you would use to hire an employee. You want this person to meet certain personality and professional standards that you will establish and identify. Ask questions, get into a conversation. Decide whether you think this person is someone you can work comfortably with. Once you determine that, ask about fees and billing procedures. Don't assume that what one lawyer charges is the going rate and you better be able to afford the fee! Fees are not only negotiable, but there may even be some sort of sliding scale already in place that you can simply plug into. Many attorneys and accountants have a special fee structure for nonprofit groups that may apply to craftspeople and artists. Of course, you may be a nonprofit group, in which case that fee structure is for you. You may even be able to interest the individual in an occasional trade of your work for theirs. Don't be too bashful or intimidated to ask.

Fees are usually charged on a per hour basis and can vary according to the type of work involved. If you hire someone to do a particular project such as a real estate transaction or business incorporation, you might get a quote for the completed work, forgoing the hourly charge. An attorney will most likely charge you an hourly rate not only for in person meetings and consultations, but for phone calls as well. An accountant or other financial professional will not usually charge for phone time.

Identifying and establishing a relationship with a lawyer and financial professional is important to do early in the establishment of your own professional activities. You will have a need for their assistance and expertise and you will be much more at ease and confident knowing you have someone to call when the situation presents itself, than having to scramble to find one when time is critical and your needs urgent.

## Rental Contracts

Many of you are either presently or will be sometime in the future, renting a space for your studio, shop, school, whatever. A common legal contract is the rental agreement or lease. It is not possible, nor is it practical or even necessary, to go into the details of the many different types of leases that exist or the myriad clauses and fine print associated with them. However, some basic knowledge and familiarity with rental agreements is necessary and extremely valuable.

A lease essentially spells out the details regarding your use of someone's space and herein lies the essential concept to understand from the onset: it is, in fact, someone else's space. No matter how lovely and personal you make it and to what degree you become attached, connected, enamored, or inseparable from it, you must always maintain a healthy degree of separation from your space.

The lease should clearly state your cost and what is included in that cost, the exact amount and definition of the space, the duration of the lease, and most importantly, exactly what you can and can't do with, in, and about the space. Never assume any inherent right to use the space in any way that hasn't been agreed to and entered in the lease. Additional clauses include who is responsible for maintenance of the grounds and common spaces and who is responsible for insuring what objects. A lease may include an escalation clause which may either predetermine the rate of rent increases or leave those increases contingent on the cost of building maintenance. Typical commercial leases are often offered on a "net" basis which means the monthly rent does not include electricity, heat, water, or real estate taxes. These expenses are calculated on a per square foot basis and shared among the tenants unless the utilities are available on a separate meter. In that more desirable situation, each tenant is responsible for the utilities in their own space. Be careful, commercial spaces are commonly quoted on a per square foot per year basis with the square foot figure including common space and otherwise unusable areas. In other words, you may be paying for space you cannot use. Makes sense doesn't it? Your lease may contain a clause dealing with subletting. If you intend to sublet now or in the future, be sure you have negotiated that option in your lease agreement.

Craftspeople are sometimes known to do things by the seat of their pants. But to our credit I am proud to say we tend towards warmth, friendliness, trust, and a personal touch in our dealings with people. That approach and attitude is one of the most fundamentally pleasant things I find in being a craftsperson and I would never advocate any attitude that decreases or deflates that personality. However, you cannot allow this friendly, trusting demeanor to undermine your best interests. Lease negotiations and agreements are a good example of a business forum where you can maintain your personal style while remaining businesslike and professional. Maintain a friendly air without overdoing it and perpetuate the positive stereotype of artists and craftspeople as warm and personable without being naïve innocents.

First and foremost, realize that there is nothing standard or automatic about a lease or a space. Everything (unless prohibited by law) is negotiable and landlords or rental agents expect you to negotiate. Don't be timid or hesitant to ask or even demand that a certain need or feature be part of the lease. Remember that a lease or contract of any kind is an agreement. Be sure you are comfortable with the terms and are satisfied that the entire deal will work for the term of the lease. A lease should be the kind of contract that you negotiate, sign, and put away. If you take an active part in the negotiations and understand the details and the terms, you shouldn't have to refer to it again.

Keep in mind that rental agreements do not pertain only to buildings and workspaces, but can apply to equipment, tools, vehicles, computers, and other items in your workspace. Approach the rental of these objects with the same careful style.

## Insurance

At its most elemental level, insurance isn't too difficult to understand, yet it's an intricate subject and can be somewhat mysterious and difficult to navigate. One thing is sure, though—insurance is absolutely necessary. It is not an option. You must not only have the correct insurance coverage, but you must have adequate insurance coverage in dollar amounts.

Basic insurance, the most fundamental and essential coverage, is relatively simple to understand. First you need to understand what insurance is and what you are insuring. Insurance products fall into several broad categories which you should be able to recognize and be at least minimally familiar with. These categories are health, life, property, auto, liability, and worker's compensation. Of these, the most relevant to you as a crafts producer and business person are property, liability, and depending on your circumstances and the state in which you conduct your business, worker's compensation. This is not to say that life, health, and auto insurance should be minimized or overlooked. On the contrary, these insurance products are as important as the others but, depending on your situation and needs, may apply more to personal types of exposure. The discussion that follows illustrates how these forms of insurance operate and how they may apply to you.

Insuring items or objects from damage or loss due to fire, theft, or other occurrence such as lightning or flood, is an example of property insurance. The insured objects can be your personal property, business-owned property, or can belong to others and held by you in some fashion such as real estate, equipment, tools, vehicles, supplies, finished and unfinished works. While I included loss due to flood, flood insurance is actually a bit more complicated and is not usually an automatic component of standard insurance packages. If the area of your studio or home is prone to floods or sewer backups, you should look into acquiring this type of insurance.

You can insure yourself from financial responsibility in cases of personal liability. For example, if someone has an accident in your studio or if a product that you produced somehow causes injury, your liability insurance policy guarantees financial compensation. A simpler example is the case of an automobile accident in which people are hurt and require medical care. Insurance will

cover the cost of that care. Although that exposure would be covered by the liability portion of your overall automobile policy, it still illustrates the general concept of liability insurance.

In addition to liability coverage, automobile insurance can protect you against theft, assorted damage to the vehicle, damage to other vehicles in the case of an accident, theft or loss of items in the vehicle, and other occurrences relating to the ownership and operation of the vehicle. If you own a vehicle, you probably have auto insurance. However, that particular insurance policy may not be applicable or appropriate if you are using the vehicle for business purposes. Those purposes can be something as innocent sounding as transporting some of your pots from your studio to your home or gallery.

As I mentioned earlier, you may be required to purchase worker's compensation insurance, depending on the state in which you are located and the type of legal format your business operates under (single proprietorship, corporation, etc.). Worker's compensation is a form of insurance that offers certain types of protection to those in your employ. This protection includes loss of wages and a blanket of medical coverage in the case of accidents. There are two critically important aspects of worker's compensation insurance to understand and consider. First is that the criterion for establishing whether an individual is an employee has little to do with how many hours they work or whether you pay them in money or materials. Second is that every state has worker's compensation insurance guidelines and has developed criteria for determining whether your business is required to have a worker's compensation policy in effect.

You can also insure less tangible things, those that may seem ephemeral in concept. A good example is insuring against loss of income. How's that you say? If you can establish a record of regular and consistent income from your business, if a situation arises that prevents you from earning this income, your insurance company will step in and pay you that amount. This is providing, of course, that you have previously elected to purchase that type of insurance. An example of this is the case of a fire shutting down your operation for some length of time.

While not specific or unique to craftspeople in any way, health and life insurance offer types of protection that are important and necessary to your overall well being and should never be overlooked or minimized.

The simplest function of insurance is to protect you against having to pay for the same object more than once should that object be stolen, damaged, or lost in a fire. If your wheel is insured for an adequate amount and its loss was due to a covered contingency, event, or circumstance, you may well be reimbursed by the insurance company for its value. Presumably you would then use that money to replace the wheel. This is property insurance at its most basic level, but one that clearly shows how insurance might work and what its value might be. You should realize, though, that insurance is hardly that elementary and involves much more in the way of comprehension, understanding, and decision making.

Buying insurance is often compared to making a wager. Think of fire and theft insurance as an example. You must decide how much you are willing to wager on whether or not you will lose any or all of your kilns, wheels, tools, and other furniture to fire or theft. If you have no insurance, you save the amount of the insurance premiums. However, in the case of a disaster you will have to purchase everything over again. Quite an outlay of money the second time around. Of course, there are ways to recover some or all the losses even if you aren't insured. For instance, if the cause of the fire can be declared the fault of the landlord or another tenant in the building, you might be able to recover some or all of your losses through their insurance company or from the individual directly through other legal means. In fact, that is just what your insurance company would do to recover their costs in paying your claim. However, by having your own insurance, you need only deal with your agent in completing the necessary forms to file a claim. This makes the process a relatively painless ordeal.

Insurance will even cover your losses (subject to a deductible amount) if the circumstance that caused the loss was your fault. The term deductible refers to an agreed upon amount that you, the insured, will pay up front for each and every claim (unless the loss can be clearly shown to be someone else's fault and that individual can be identified) before the insurance company contributes towards the settlement. Depending on the type of insurance, deductibles of different amounts are offered and can be chosen based on clear financial advantages and disadvantages. The higher the deductible, the lower the insurance premium. For example, the savings on a typical homeowner's policy with an annual premium of $500 carrying a $100 deductible compared to the same policy with a $500 deductible could be as much as 20% or $100! By comparing deductibles, premiums, and financial exposure, you can easily see the potential savings and pay back period.

The above example of an uninsured individual replacing their equipment out of their own pocket is a fairly simple one. Losses can be much more devastating, much more difficult (if not impossible) to indemnify yourself, and possibly career ending. For example, imagine that someone boils water in one of your teapots with the pot in direct contact with the flame of the range. Just as the water begins to boil, the pot shatters and the boiling water spills on their hands and arms, resulting in serious burns requiring a prolonged hospital stay and expenses. You are sued for your liability because of the inadequately designed and manufactured teapot and you are found to be negligent and at fault. Never mind that you clearly explained that the teapot shouldn't be used directly on a flame or burner. Never mind that ultimately, on appeal, the original court decision may be overturned and you may be found not at fault. The expenses to see you through this experience will be extremely high, and without adequate liability insurance, could wipe you out financially.

Another scenario involves you glazing a kiln load of ware late at night. You're getting tired and frustrated so you call it quits, forgetting to turn off the hot plate for melting wax. A fire ensues, causing great damage to not only your own belongings but to the building itself. You, being named as responsible for the damage, are liable for the subsequent costs.

While the chances of some devastating situation befalling you are small, they aren't nonexistent. In fact, I don't think there is a building owner alive who would rent you a space or a bank that would give you a mortgage without you having adequate (to their standards) insurance coverage. In deciding whether a particular insurance product or coverage is worthwhile, you need to weigh certain factors:

1) Your exposure. The dollar amount you would be liable for given a certain situation or circumstance.

2) How much money the insurance will cost you over a certain period of time.

3) The comparison between the cost of the insurance, the value of the coverage, and the financial benefit should a loss occur.

Clearly, there are many other types of insurance coverage and you may be in need of them. Now that you are somewhat familiar with types of insurance and the language of insurance, the next step towards purchasing an appropriate package is to get some advice in maneuvering your way through the insurance milieu. You must identify and choose an insurance company or agent. Not an easy task.

## Choosing an Insurer

You must understand the difference between an insurance company and an insurance agent. A company is the actual body that issues your policy and is responsible for coverage and payments to you or others as you may direct. Everybody who has insurance of any kind deals with and is connected to one or more insurance companies. You may deal directly with an insurance company, as millions of people do. An insurance agent is the individual you deal with who represents the insurance company.

There are agents who are exclusive to a single company and there are independent agents who may represent and sell the products of several different insurance companies. Which is better? Some people will extol the benefits of one over the other ad infinitum. In my experience with both situations, I've found that having the services of an independent insurance agent is indispensable. Conceptually, the biggest advantage of working with an independent is their ability to research, identify, and recommend the best company and policy for your needs. In fact, it is to their advantage to assemble the best looking package, lest you go elsewhere. An independent agent is not tied to the possibly limited products a single company may have to offer. In practice, the most significant advantage an independent agent has to offer is one-on-one, personal, and committed service. An independent agent is likely to be either a business owner like yourself or someone who works for one. They will often put in the added effort it takes to provide you with quality service.

Of course, the most critical area of this service isn't put to the test until you have a claim or problem and many people can go years or even entire careers without a claim. But it just takes one situation, one accident, loss, or claim of any kind for you to know if you made the right decision.

Another reason to consider an independent agent is that your needs as a craftsperson often fall outside of what may be considered the norm in comparison to more mainstream businesses. From the objects you make and how you market them to the type of exposure (in insurance terms) you exhibit, it often takes a special individual with more far reaching resources and knowledge to identify and provide adequate affordable insurance coverage. Your needs may not fall neatly into the corporate designed packages of a single company.

To be fair, I don't mean to paint all insurance agents in the same color, whether they represent one company or 100 companies. There are those from both varieties who are wonderful, compassionate, personal, well intended, and will go to whatever lengths are necessary to provide the correct product for your needs. Ultimately, you have to make the choice. Ask your friends and other craftspeople, inquire at a regional or local potter's or crafts guild or association. Attorneys and accountants can often recommend insurance agents. While it is not often thought of, there is nothing wrong with treating the first meeting you have with an insurance agent as an interview. You may not know much about insurance but you can certainly recognize, by asking pertinent questions, how much the agent knows or cares about your unique circumstance as a potter. Be resourceful and make an educated and wise choice.

If you find yourself totally bewildered or less than enthusiastic about investing time and energy in researching agents or companies, there is a rel-

atively simple alternative. Many craftspeople forego the insurance company or agent route altogether and opt for an insurance package offered through a craft association or guild. These policies are well designed for craftspeople, are usually simple and basic in their coverage, are generally very affordable, and are usually offered in the areas of fire and theft, liability, and personal health and accident insurance. They are, as a rule, excellent choices for individuals starting out who may have limited exposure, financial resources, and experience. These policies are affordable due to the buying power of the group. You can gain access to them by joining a group such as The American Craft Association or any number of other specialized art and craft associations. Some local and regional associations offer group policies as well.

Perhaps the greatest service these types of policies are able to provide is access to health insurance. Unless you are employed and have health insurance provided by your employer, you already understand the difficulty in obtaining quality personal and family health insurance. Though access to affordable health insurance is indeed difficult to come by and these craft/art association policies make it possible, they must be examined and analyzed with great care. Primarily, these policies tend towards the catastrophic variety and not the day-to-day health maintenance coverage that is just as important and critical. If so, they must not be looked at as long term solutions to your health insurance needs. Read the fine print and know what you're buying.

While these pre-packaged group policies generally provide good overall coverage in the most important areas, they are not the end-all in insurance packages and they do tend to fall short when compared to custom packages that an independent agent may be able to assemble for you. To make them affordable, the coverage is often limited in scope and the deductibles tend to be high. For instance, there may be a very low claim limit if your vehicle is broken into or if your wares are damaged or stolen in a location away from your studio. You may not be able to get coverage for work or equipment in your workspace that belongs to others. If you have a claim, the amount paid to you often reduces the value or the total amount of money that remains on the policy for future claims. For me, the most important deficiency of a group policy is that it is more than likely administered by an out of state company with no local agent or representative. Forget any notion of a one-to-one relationship. Claims can take a long time to resolve and can be very frustrating to negotiate. Questions or concerns about your personal situation will probably not be given the kind of consideration you need, and every time you contact the company, there will be a new voice on the other end of the line.

Despite the apparent deficiencies and disadvantages, you would be wise to investigate the availability of these insurance packages in your area. When I began my career, my knowledge of and experience with insurance was elementary and naive. I found the policies offered through The American Craft Association to be accessible, comprehensible, and affordable. I took advantage of the service and a policy with the craft association served me well for quite a few years. Though I never had any losses or claims, I always felt confident and at ease knowing that I had insurance in case something terrible happened. Peace of mind is a wonderful thing.

Regardless of the type of insurance you are thinking about purchasing or whether you are going to use the services of an independent agent or an insurance company directly, this is not an area to put off or take lightly. It's important to realize that your homeowner's policy may not cover your losses as a potter if the insurance company deems your pottery activity a profession, livelihood, or commercial enterprise. You can't carry on a professional pottery career and expect to be protected by instruments or devices designed for leisure or hobby indulgences. In short, you can't have your cake and eat it too. Insurance is not a very glamorous subject or one that you usually admire or display each day that you have it. You will pay serious money for something that sits in the background, hopefully never to be used. However, if and when the occasion arises, you will want to be adequately protected and you will be very happy that you are.

## Establishing Relationships with Suppliers

In the section on locating suppliers, I touched on the importance of developing solid relationships with the suppliers and vendors you regularly deal with. The advantages are numerous and apparent—quick on-time delivery, competitive pricing, notice of new materials and products as well as changes in the availability of products you rely on, and all the networking and goodwill that takes place between valuable and common allies. For business relationships of this type to grow, there has to be a mutual respect for, and reliance on, the parties involved.

You want the clay company to treat you like you are their most important customer. Fine. Do something for them in return. Everybody wants to buy at the lowest available price and although most clay companies have an established discount schedule based on the quantity of a material purchased, even this is often negotiable. If a supplier wants your business, they will do something special to get it and that might be to give you the next higher price break. For instance, if you buy 1,000 pounds of clay, they might charge you the 2,000 pound price. Or they might provide free shipping. At any rate, negotiate for a low price but don't nickel and dime them to death. In return, do as much business with a single supplier as possible and recommend them to your friends.

Don't just be a complainer. Communicate with them when they do something great as well as when they mess up. Expect them to show a reasonable degree of responsibility for the materials and products they sell. The exact characteristics of raw materials can change over time. The mine gets deeper, the location changes, impurities come and go, etc. That is simply the nature of natural raw materials. The responsible potter will mix up a test batch of glaze every time they use a new batch of raw material, eliminating the possibility of a bad glaze mix ruining a load of pots. If you choose not to take the responsible route, don't expect your clay supplier or even the mine to take up the slack for you. On the other hand, if a brand new kiln shelf cracks or warps in a firing for no apparent reason, it may not be unreasonable to hold the supplier and/or shelf manufacturer responsible for your loss. If a house clay you have used successfully for years with great and predictable results all of sudden fires a buff color instead of white, which drastically alters the fired work, be at the supplier's door or on the phone first thing in the morning.

As you gain experience, you will learn that there are certain costs to doing business, and those costs must be recoverable within your daily financial transactions. For instance, some companies will deal on a cash with order basis only—no credit. That doesn't mean they are bad or unreasonable. I do get irked, though, when a company doesn't offer their catalog for free or if they have a minimum order requirement that is too large. However, there are costs involved in writing up an invoice, posting it to your account, and billing you for a purchase. It is not unreasonable that there be a minimum purchase requirement in the neighborhood of $25 to charge a purchase to your account.

Returned items are another issue and it is wise to review a particular company's return policy before you have to return something. Paying a small fee to help cover administrative costs when making a return is not unreasonable, but when I see a 20% restocking charge, I hesitate a bit.

One of the most beneficial things you can do for yourself is to develop mutually beneficial relationships with your suppliers. They are the single direct connection you have to the materials, equipment, tools, and other supplies that are vital to your craft activities. Be fair and reasonable in your dealings and expectations and you will likely be treated with the kind of importance and respect you deserve.

## Utilities: Phone, Electric, Gas

I would say that having phone, electric, and gas services at your disposal is kind of necessary, wouldn't you? While you may think that everybody pays the same rates for electricity and gas, that is not necessarily the case. Your approach to getting the best deal is a bit different than when negotiating with a clay supplier, but you can often get a better deal. It is often a matter of finding out which category of user you fall in. Business rates for electricity are higher than those for residential service and it is usually your business location that locks you into a certain rate, not whether you are using the electricity for a business purpose. You may qualify for a certain rate based on the type of business or user you are.

Electric rates are charged per kilowatt hour—the amount of electricity in kilowatts used per hour. Rates charged for electricity vary widely in various parts of the country. Typical rates in the Boston area are in the neighborhood of $.05/kwh for residential service and $.15/kwh for commercial service. Often you can get a lower rate for electrical consumption during off peak hours or during early morning hours. While the availability of low rates during these times may not help you save money on your regular electrical use, you may be able to take advantage of them by scheduling your firings during these somewhat uncomfortable hours. Check it out, not only could the savings be substantial, but the increase in available voltage during these times could help you control your kilns and possibly shorten your firings.

If you use gas for heat, hot water, or kilns, there are savings to be had here as well. If you are a user of bottled gas, there may be several suppliers in your area to choose from. Each may offer a slightly different plan involving ownership of the equipment (tanks, gas lines). Investigate service contracts and the ultimate cost of the fuel itself. Natural gas service may offer pricing structures that are similar to your local electric company. Educate yourself on the available choices.

Phone service is a whole other ball of wax. There are more phone companies at your disposal than varieties of frits (and there are a lot of frits!). It used to be that making an intelligent choice when it came to picking a phone company was a matter of analyzing your calling patterns and finding a phone company with low rates to match those patterns. However, with the proliferation of local and regional companies, companies that specialize in interstate calling, those that specialize in intrastate rates, international plans, and now the introduction of long distance phone service via the Internet, choices are much more abundant and selecting a company is not such as easy task. As if comparing rates wasn't tricky enough, phone companies have added the feature of incentives to the mix. Sign up with Terry's Talk-to-Me and you get a 10% discount on UPS shipping rates. Let Alice's Telephone Taxi handle your long distance calling needs and for every tenth call to Siberia you get a free cupcake. Bob's

Fone Ferry offers bonus points that you can redeem at the end of the year for everything from free lunch to airline tickets. Don't overlook the savings that can be had in choosing the correct phone company.

# General Organizational Practices

## Record Keeping

Within the area of general organizational practices lies not only those that apply directly to the finances and health of your business and career, but equally to an overall ability to keep all of your daily materials, records, suppliers catalogs, photos of your work, press clippings, correspondence, archives, and other tangible items at your fingertips ready for use and review. Being able to pull out a photo of a particular piece for a newspaper article or finding a year-old letter from a happy customer without calling in the FBI's Crime Scene Investigative Task Force is a comfortable feeling.

Twenty-five years ago there were scant books available to the artist or craftsperson that offered instruction, help, and advice in the fine details of bookkeeping, accounting, and general record keeping. Today, there are volumes of information written for people with limited experience and skill in those areas, that focus on just those topics. I have no intention of breaking new ground in these territories, only to give some sound, practical advice.

Keep copious records of all your transactions—purchases, expenses, correspondence, inventory, etc. Some of the reasons for this are obvious, some not so evident. If you operate a legal registered business, you are responsible for either preparing your taxes yourself or providing your accountant with the necessary records to do it. Trying to gather up a year's worth of receipts, invoices, and other records can be an impossible task if not approached on a daily basis throughout the year. There are a multitude of ways to handle your own records and transactions and I urge you to consult any number of books and articles on the subject. In addition to books, there are several computer applications that make record keeping a cinch. These packages allow you to track inventory, expenses, and income, to generate purchase orders, invoices, and even checks. Too complicated? Too serious? Too advanced? You may be right! Record keeping can be a very personal experience and the bottom line is whatever works for you is probably okay, as long as you stick to it.

As my own record keeping needs have grown and developed over the years. I have found that record keeping can be classified into two main areas: appropriate and well designed forms to help you organize information; and the filing of these forms, receipts, and other pieces of paper or computer files.

While you will generate many different bits of information to keep track of, all this information, no matter how eclectic, can and must be classified into a finite number of categories. This is where sensible and logical filing systems are needed. Effective systems for filing must be designed and implemented in response to your own personality and idiosyncrasies. Basically, this means filing cabinets, closets, drawers, and shelves where file folders, envelopes, boxes, and other containers will hold your papers, photos, clippings, and other records. Keep things as simple as possible. Use title categories with logical, easily recognizable names and make as many different categories for filing as possible. Using the current year's expenses as an example, your filing drawer should be organized so each general category of expense is evident. Within each category, the individual suppliers or sources of your purchases should be grouped together so they can be searched independently of the others. You can use colored folders or labels to assist in this organizational detail.

Examples of expense categories for the current year are what you would expect—rent, phone, electricity, gas, postage, shipping, office supplies, clay, raw materials, and a whole host of other expenses that will make themselves clear to you. No matter what the title or category of expense, you want to be able to immediately identify what the contents of that file is. Be as logical as possible instead of trying to be creative. Use your own sense of associative recognition and recall when categorizing items. Of course, if your pottery activity is not organized as a business with the companion tax filing responsibilities and such, your approach to record keeping is likely to be more relaxed and spontaneous. However, keeping accurate records involves more than keeping track of what is necessary to compile and file your taxes. Record keeping also involves being able to find the supplier of your last batch of feldspar or where you got that great deal on packaging tape. It can be extremely frustrating trying to remember where you got those great cleanup sponges that are just the right shape, size, texture, and material. It is exactly these kinds of easily forgotten details that you have to get in the habit of recording and filing.

Other items that require organization include photos of your work, promotional material such as newspaper or magazine articles about you or your studio, exhibition reviews, past show and open studio announcements, and the many other materials you use in your activities as a potter. In the chapter on marketing, these and other pertinent items are presented in a more germane subject heading.

Ultimately, whether you are involved with pottery as an income producing business or as a serious avocation out of pure love of craft, some degree of sensible and proper bookkeeping, record keeping, and filing practices and systems will make your pottery making activities easier to manage, and allow you to carefully track, examine, and analyze not only your costs and income, but all the other bits of information that come in and go out of your studio. Of course, there is always the chance that you may not want to know what your pottery habit is costing you in dollars. The figures may frighten you!

## Business Forms

Forms are the items you will ultimately file away and refer to when necessary. Commercially designed and prepared business forms are available from national companies such as New England Business Systems and Rapid Forms. These companies have a variety of products that can be utilized by most any business. The forms are fairly generic, within certain categories. Often, the most popular forms are offered in more

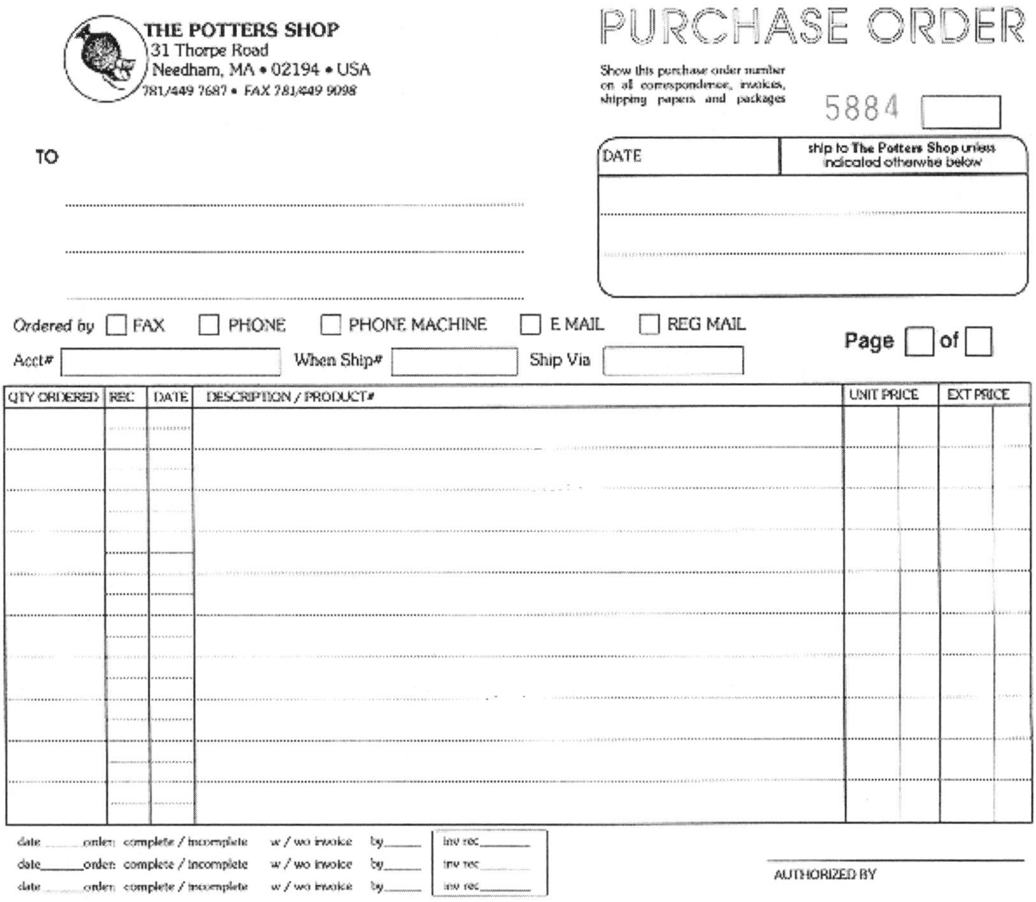

*Figure 6-1. The purchase order form is indispensable.*

specialized versions for use by specific types of businesses. Florists, gift shops, service stations, and repair services are usually served by these "custom generic forms." Purchase orders, sales receipts, monthly statements, bid forms, invoices, project proposals, order forms, packing lists, shipping forms, and other similar items are the staples of these companies. Check writing and bill paying systems and other more specific forms are also available. Stationery, envelopes, business cards, and promotional items are also offered by these and similar companies (more about these in the chapter on marketing). The forms are personalized with your business name,

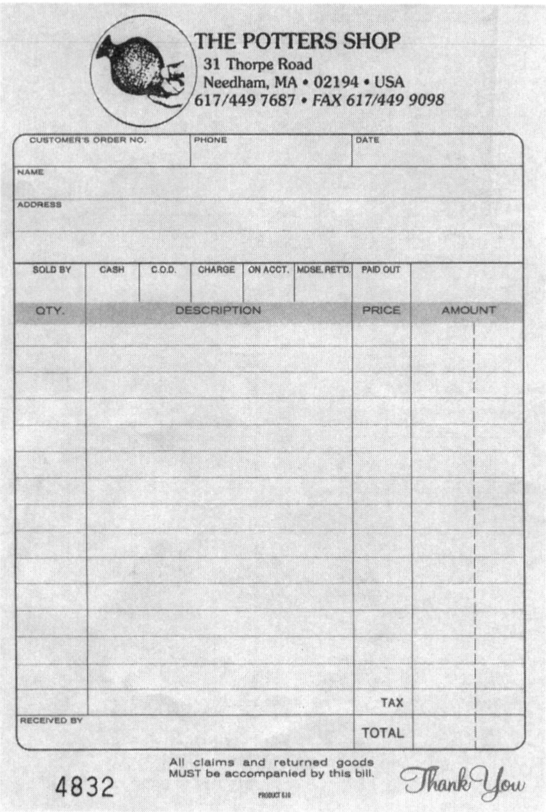
THE POTTERS SHOP
31 Thorpe Road
Needham, MA • 02194 • USA
617/449 7687 • FAX 617/449 9098

CUSTOMER'S ORDER NO. | PHONE | DATE
NAME
ADDRESS
SOLD BY | CASH | C.O.D. | CHARGE | ON ACCT. | MDSE. RET'D. | PAID OUT
QTY. | DESCRIPTION | PRICE | AMOUNT
TAX
RECEIVED BY | TOTAL

All claims and returned goods MUST be accompanied by this bill.
4832
Thank You

*Figure 6-2. A typical sales slip used by millions of businesses, large and small.*

address, phone, etc. and most companies will even slightly alter a form, do a complete reworking of an existing form, or help you custom design a brand new form for your specialized use.

You may be wondering why you shouldn't go to a local printer for help. You can, and your local printer may have the experience and capability to do this kind of work. Most likely, though, this area of printing will fall outside the competitive capabilities of your local printer. To begin with, consecutive numbering is a must when purchasing any of these forms and while that may seem like a simple thing for a printer to provide, it's not as simple as it sounds.

It is helpful to consult the form company's catalog to help you identify which forms may be useful to you at this stage of your business development. The basic commercial forms I recommend you use from the start are purchase orders, invoices, and sales receipts. The use of purchase orders is an absolutely vital aspect to clear and sensible record keeping and daily business organization and it is probably the one form I would not be without. Keeping track of and organizing your purchases and orders of materials and supplies is a task that can get very confusing without a simple method of doing so. By using a purchase order for all your ordering, you have a record of the purchase and all the details including date, ordering method (phone, fax, etc.), the exact items and quantities, shipping preference, and any other details that you will find helpful when placing the order and retrieving the order information afterwards. Fig. 6-1 shows a copy of the purchase order I designed and fine tuned from an existing form available through New England Business Services. I use purchase orders for all buying that is done from the shop. Only when I buy items from a store, in person, do I not use a purchase order. When the order arrives, I retrieve the purchase order and the arrival date and all the details are recorded including the condition of the items, whether an invoice was included, and whether the order has been received complete or if there are back ordered items that will be shipped later. What a boon to studio business organization!

Invoices, sales receipts, and the other available forms are just as useful as purchase orders and not only assist in keeping your records and transactions organized but add an important degree of professionalism to your daily business activities. In addition to forms that help track and record transactions, forms that aid in keeping track of daily activities are useful. Daily sales records, telephone calls, shipping records, inventory lists, production goals, custom order forms, kiln firing charts and sign up sheets, and employee work schedules need to be tracked, recorded, and filed in simple and sensible ways. As your professional activities grow and become more sophisticated, so will your need for additional means and methods of record keeping. As these needs present themselves, the type and style of record keeping will become clear and you will be able to design the appropriate form to meet those needs.

## Banking Practices

Here's a riveting subject that can't help but captivate your interest. What a bore. For me, the bank is a place where my money is held on a very temporary basis while it is waiting to be part of a payment to someone else. Seriously, sound banking practices, as well as understanding the role a bank can play, will go a long way in your effort to establish, maintain, and operate your business in a sound and reliable way.

Banks, like insurance companies and other service providers, are institutions that vary in the services they provide and the ways they provide them. On the most elementary level, banks provide you with checking and savings accounts,

credit cards, lines of credit, the opportunity to borrow funds, and other financial services. If you think about it, your personal banking needs are probably very different from your banking needs as a potter and you should use different criteria when selecting a bank to handle your business.

The most important banking action you must take as you begin your activities as a potter is to keep separate bank accounts for your craft activity, regardless of whether you earn income from it. Again, if you have or are going to establish a bona fide commercial enterprise, all sorts of banking decisions will have to be made and you will likely automatically realize the distinction between your personal financial affairs and those of your business. However, if your pottery involvement is less formal, a hobby, or whatever, you may overlook the importance and convenience of having a separate account. First of all, a dedicated checking account adds to the formality and seriousness of the endeavor. It makes keeping track of your expenses simple and it gives you the ability to quickly see just how costly clay work can be. As a learning experience, it may clarify the cost that goes into the wares you produce and give you an additional appreciation for your efforts. Who knows, you may not give those next pots away so quickly. At the very least, seeing the numbers may force you to be more careful about where you purchase supplies and the quantities you purchase. On the other hand, having clear records showing exactly what your pottery expenses are may surprise you, making it more difficult to justify it as an inexpensive relaxing diversion the next time your spouse or partner insists on taking up snowmobiling as a hobby!

In choosing a bank, what criteria do you need to consider? You have at least some experience in the role a bank plays in your everyday life. In choosing a bank for personal affairs, you might look for convenient locations, number of ATM

**CAROL TEMKIN**
**The Potters Shop**
**31 Thorpe Road**
**Needham, MA 02194**
**(617) 449-7687**

Order Date: _____
Requested By: _____
Invoice Date: _____
Shipping Date: _____ Via: _____
Terms: _____

Sold to: _____

Ship to: _____
(if different)

_____                    _____

_____                    _____

Terms: Minimum order $200.  First order C.O.D.  Subsequent orders Net 30.  Add 6% packing charge.

|    | Quantity | Item and Style | Size | Color | Wholesale Price | Amount |
|----|----------|----------------|------|-------|-----------------|--------|
| 1  |          |                |      |       |                 |        |
| 2  |          |                |      |       |                 |        |
| 3  |          |                |      |       |                 |        |
| 4  |          |                |      |       |                 |        |
| 5  |          |                |      |       |                 |        |
| 6  |          |                |      |       |                 |        |
| 7  |          |                |      |       |                 |        |
| 8  |          |                |      |       |                 |        |
| 9  |          |                |      |       |                 |        |
| 10 |          |                |      |       |                 |        |
| 11 |          |                |      |       |                 |        |
| 12 |          |                |      |       |                 |        |
| 13 |          |                |      |       |                 |        |
| 14 |          |                |      |       |                 |        |
| 15 |          |                |      |       |                 |        |
| 16 |          |                |      |       |                 |        |
| 17 |          |                |      |       |                 |        |
| 18 |          |                |      |       |                 |        |

Subtotal: _____

Packing (6%): _____

Shipping: _____

C.O.D. (First Order Only): _____

Total: _____

Ordered by: _____

*Figure 6-3. An order form/invoice designed by Carol Temkin. (Courtesy of Carol Temkin)*

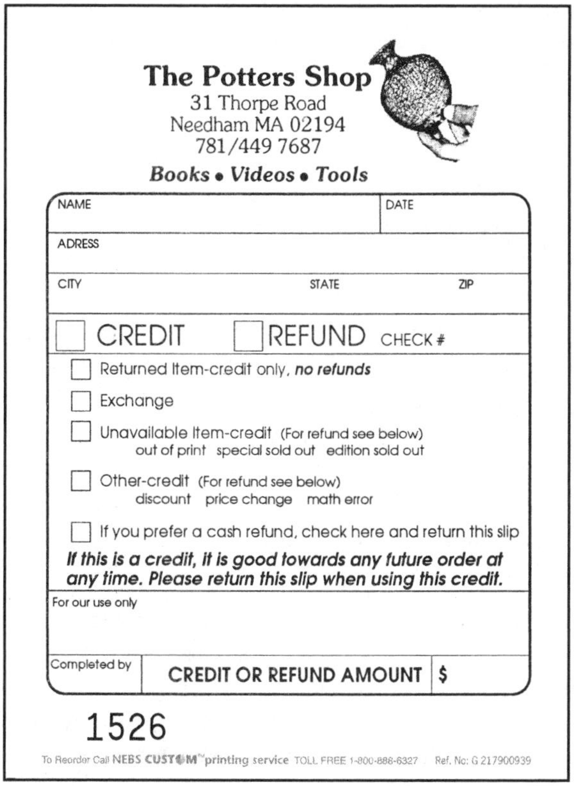

**The Potters Shop**
31 Thorpe Road
Needham MA 02194
781/449 7687

*Books • Videos • Tools*

| NAME | | DATE | |
|---|---|---|---|
| ADRESS | | | |
| CITY | STATE | | ZIP |

☐ CREDIT    ☐ REFUND   CHECK #

☐ Returned Item-credit only, *no refunds*

☐ Exchange

☐ Unavailable Item-credit (For refund see below)
     out of print   special sold out   edition sold out

☐ Other-credit (For refund see below)
     discount   price change   math error

☐ If you prefer a cash refund, check here and return this slip

*If this is a credit, it is good towards any future order at any time. Please return this slip when using this credit.*

For our use only

| Completed by | **CREDIT OR REFUND AMOUNT** | $ |
|---|---|---|

**1526**

To Reorder Call NEBS CUSTOM™ printing service TOLL FREE 1-800-888-6327   Ref. No: G 217900939

*Figure 6-4. A credit slip used in the book department of The Potters Shop. This form could easily be adapted for many other applications.*

machines, types of accounts available, safety deposit boxes, direct deposit options, other financial services offered, along with the costs for services. Depending on how and to what extent you plan to utilize a bank's services, you might consider the friendliness and personal nature in which they communicate, how important they make you feel, and how concerned they seem to be about your continued patronage.

In choosing a bank to fulfill your business needs, you might use the same criteria or you might focus on some specific factors, depending on how and to what extent you will utilize the bank's services. For instance, you may want to consolidate all your financial services and have a single institution handle your banking and credit card accounts. A line of credit may be useful for you, as would be the ability to take out a loan. Checking account overdraft protection offers peace of mind, especially when it may be inconvenient to get to the bank to make deposits. Perhaps you have foreign customers and need international banking services such as wire transfers, international bank checks, or other ways to accept foreign payments or make payments to foreign accounts. How about home banking from your computer? More and more banks are offering this convenience and it may interest you.

Most likely you will find yourself in a business situation where the services you require will be no more complicated or demanding than those for your personal banking. So consider the human qualities mentioned above. When I first started in business, I opened my banking accounts with the local branch of a large bank. It was the same bank I had used for my personal banking and I didn't give any thought to seeking out a different bank for my business. The reason I used that bank for my personal accounts was that it was convenient, my employer used it for direct deposit of my pay check, I had no special banking requirements, and they offered credit card accounts along with checking and savings. When ATM services were established, this bank was at the forefront and I knew I could use ATM machines from Boston to Bangkok. When it came time to open a bank account for my business, I naturally went there. Again, with no special banking requirements in mind, all I needed was a business checking account, a branch near the studio for convenience, and banking fees that were competitive with other banks. Bingo, all my criteria were met. After a few years, fees began to rise, additional fees were introduced, and my banking needs began to grow. Not that they couldn't handle my banking needs, but along with the rising fees, I began to realize the importance of friendly, personal, and caring service, which this bank sorely lacked, and I looked for another bank. Lo and behold, right next door was a local bank, not a branch of a mega institution. They were friendly, their fees were much lower, and they wanted my business. Imagine that, a little guy like me being wanted by a bank! What an important feeling.

I have since moved the studio from that location and none of the bank's three branches are particularly close to the studio or convenient to use. No matter. They have an ATM that is linked to thousands of banks, but I never use them. They offer banking at home from PC services but I never use that either. All I care about, and the main thing that has kept me doing business with them for over 15 years, is that they offer the services I need and use and every time I walk in, I get a friendly greeting. The bank president sits in an office adjacent to the main lobby and waves to me from his desk if he's not on the floor to say hello. If my account is going to be overdrawn (it happens to the best of us), I get a call warning me to get in with a deposit. If I have some special need or question, I don't have to go through an endless chain of voice mail prompts that end in a recording asking me to leave a message. My advice? If you are located somewhere with banking choices, take advantage of those choices and choose wisely. There may not be a need to settle for second best.

## Credit Card Services

Closely related to banking services are credit card services. Credit card services fall into two categories: having a credit card of your own and accepting credit cards in your business. Neither of these services or any aspect of credit card services need to be affiliated, associated, or originate with the bank where you do your regular business. In-

deed, the credit card industry is a totally separate entity whose services will integrate with any bank.

Having a credit card of your own is something I'm sure you have experience with. With solicitations arriving in your mailbox on a daily basis, securing a personal credit card, or ten credit cards for that matter, is easy to do. Getting a credit card in your business name is a little more difficult, but hardly insurmountable. Why have a credit card in your business name? For the same reasons that I advocate separate personal and business checking accounts. In addition to those reasons, having a business credit card is a good way to establish a record of credit worthiness for when you may need to apply for a loan or open a charge account with a supplier.

Accepting credit cards is another matter. It wasn't too long ago that I held steadfast to the belief that accepting payment by credit card was a customer convenience that would simply cost me money and not necessarily generate more business. After all, wasn't accepting checks just as good? I have changed my tune. I'm still not exactly sure what finally drove me to open a trial account, but almost from the day that I began to accept credit cards, the sales volume grew. Customers appreciate the convenience and they utilize the convenience by buying more stuff more often! But the advantage of accepting credit cards lies not only in the potential for additional sales due to the "impulse purchase" syndrome. When you set up a credit card account, you also initiate additional means of tracking and recording sales, along with what I have found to be an even better advantage—direct electronic deposit of the proceeds from credit card sales into your bank account on a daily basis. There is less cash and checks sitting in your cash box or cash register and fewer trips to the bank. If you are concerned about the legitimacy of checks, credit cards, with

## Credit Card Services and More

Though it is true that the competition between credit card service companies vying for a share of the small business market can be fierce, few of these companies have specific interests or experience working with craftspeople. When faced with the somewhat unique needs and styles of craftspeople, many companies will charge higher rates and fees, making their services impractical.

Arts & Crafts Business Solutions is one company that supports and serves only artists and craftspeople and has the interest, expertise, and demeanor to provide a quality and appropriate package of services. In addition to providing traditional credit card accounts with the necessary point of sale equipment, The Arts Group (the moniker they have been given by their members) has answers for potters who operate without storefronts, providing cellular terminals, equipment, and the associated support. They understand the unique business practices of craftspeople and have negotiated competitive rates for their group. Around the clock technical support is standard—especially important when you are at a craft fair on a Sunday and need some help. The Arts Group also offers group health, a prepaid legal plan, and other services useful to the small businessperson.

their automatic funds verification system, should make you sleep better. Don't think that credit cards are only for big businesses or "real" businesses. They are for business of all sizes, and you are a real business!

Choosing a credit card company can be confusing and time consuming but it is time well spent. All credit card companies offer the same or similar basic services. Where they begin to differ is in their fees and range of additional services available. More on that in a moment. The days of a merchant taking an impression of your credit card and phoning in your credit card number to get an authorization are all but gone. Your card may still be run through a manual machine for your signature, but an actual phone call from the merchant to the credit card company takes place only in unusual situations. A basic credit card acceptance system consists of a terminal connected to your phone line. You swipe the card through a slot in the terminal or you either automatically (through a computer system or electronic cash register system) or manually (on the terminal keypad itself) key in the account number. The system dials the clearinghouse phone number, connects, verifies your merchant identification number, checks the customer account number, and displays an authorization number. Once this authorization number is obtained, the sale is completed by pressing a key on the pad and having the customer sign a sales receipt. Using your terminal at the end of the day, you review the total sales for the day, check for accuracy, and electronically send them back to the credit card company for direct deposit to your bank account.

How does a credit card company make money? By charging you certain fees, the most obvious being a percentage of your total sales. This percentage varies, so when shopping for a company don't think that the fee is standard, regardless of what the representative might imply. A reasonable percentage might be in the 3% to 5% range, though you may be able to negotiate or find a company offering a rate in the 1% to 2% range. Other fees might include a monthly service charge, fees based on whether you electronically enter your customer account numbers by swiping the card or if you manually key in the numbers, fees for accepting cards originating from foreign countries, and other so-called nonqualifying fees. The basic system requires a no frills terminal and you can expand to include a printing device to print each transaction for your customer's signature, an interface with your computer system, and other more sophisticated pieces of equipment. Depending on the complexity of the system, you decide what meets your demands.

Monthly rental or leasing fees for the equipment must be considered on top of the fees already mentioned. Be sure all applicable fees and charges are disclosed and that you understand them. Be certain you understand just how the deposits and fees will appear on your bank statement and how quickly they will be posted there. Understand what the company's statements will look like, what will appear on them, and whether they will be generated on a weekly, monthly, or other basis.

All in all, I have found the total charges for a basic system to be money well spent and I can't even imagine not having the capability to accept credit cards in my business. Credit card companies are abundant and they are all looking for your business. Many professional associations have agreements with credit card companies offering reduced rates for members, so when you do your investigation don't neglect an opportunity that might be right before your eyes. Shop wisely.

## Staff

At some point in your pottery career you will require additional help in the studio. Perhaps someone to clean, mix clay or glazes, teach a class, answer the phone, or help keep your showroom open while you are at the wheel. Your decision to do this will be based on your needs at the time and what you determine to be the best use of your own time in the operation of your business.

Hiring staff need not be a difficult or stressful undertaking but there are procedures and guidelines that will help make the process sensible and help to insure that you not only hire the most qualified individuals but that all the other facets of taking on employees run smoothly and efficiently.

Help in the studio can fall under a variety of categories. You can call them assistants, apprentices, helpers, staff members, work/study, or what have you. Anyone who works for you on a regular basis in your studio with somewhat regular hours is considered an employee. You may also hire individuals to come in and perform services such as cleaning or teaching a class or hire temporary help to complete a specific project, do inventory, or move the studio. These individuals may be considered independent contractors. The distinction between employees and independent contractors is important when it comes to understanding your responsibilities as an employer in the area of payroll, taxes, and other legal filing. But before your heart rate rises and you get palpitations, let's go over the practical considerations and responsibilities of having help in the shop.

The most common form of employment in small craft studios is when you have an assistant or helper come in certain hours to do certain jobs in exchange for their use of the studio and perhaps materials and instruction. Often, the assistant is a student or young person who is happy to have access to the shop and you are happy to have her work. There is no money exchanged and the situation may be temporary or open ended. In fact, a form of money is being exchanged—the goods and services you are providing in exchange for the work being done. Is it really necessary to jump through the hoops of payroll, deductions, taxes, withholding forms, and the like? Technically, the answer is yes, but on a practical level, don't bother. You may be the only one who does it.

Once your needs advance beyond the work exchange arrangement, you get into actual payment for services rendered. Here is where recognizing the distinctions between regular employees and independent contractors is important. In simple terms, a regular employee works for you in your location on a regular basis and you control and set their hours, pay, and other compensation. Working for you may or may not be their primary occupation, but it is regular, nonseasonal, and not subject to weekly or monthly changes or major adjustments. Regular employees are subject to withholding taxes, unemployment tax, social security deductions and payments. You are responsible for the employer's contribution of social security and unemployment taxes as well as for making the necessary deductions from the employee's pay check and sending those payments into the IRS and state tax division or wherever they go. Remember when I discussed the value of having an accountant on call? Pick up the phone and schedule a meeting.

Do you have to comply with all of this official stuff? As in many questions, there is the short answer and the long one. In short, most likely no one will be the wiser if you simply pay your assistant and forego the tax thing, but it's not that simple and this leads right into the long answer. Having an individual in your employ has implications beyond simple compensation and these implications are all intertwined. To recognize these implications shows a comprehension of the serious nature of operating a business. If you pay your assistant in cash, taking no business deduction for the expense, and your assistant chooses not to declare this income on their income taxes, you have probably sufficiently clouded any paper trail leading back to you that would result in back taxes, fines, or other unpleasantries. I am

not advocating this practice. If an employee earns less than $600 a year, you most likely don't have to make payments or adjust for deductions, but for employees who earn more than that, I suggest you act in a responsible and legal manner by making the appropriate social security and unemployment tax contributions along with the correct withholding. Yes, it will cost you a bit more but you will be doing things in the correct fashion, taking the fair business expense deductions of your own, and sleeping better at night knowing that the IRS isn't about to barge into your living room.

In the confusion of W-4s, W-2s, 1099s, and a host of other forms, as well as correctly identifying workers as regular employees or independent contractors, an accountant will be able to advise you as to the extent to which you need to be compliant. You can decide whether figuring the payroll is something you want to do yourself or whether you feel it necessary to retain the services of a payroll company. A payroll company will, after you report the correct earnings for each individual for a given pay period, make all the calculations and deductions, generate payroll checks, do the appropriate tax filing, make the tax payments, and provide you with enough paper records to choke your office efficiency to death! I have been using a payroll company for several years and find it well worth the expense. Don't minimize the importance of understanding the implications of, and complying with, the necessary and appropriate rules and regulations when it comes to employees and payroll.

Once it appears that you might need some help in the shop, you need to go through some organizational thinking and plan your strategy. Below are the steps to follow when hiring.

1) **Identify Your Needs**. What do you need help with? Studio maintenance, production, clay or glaze mixing, office work?

2) **Define the Job(s)**. What exactly do you want an assistant to do? What do you not want them to do? How many hours a week do you expect the work to take? What are the work days and hours?

3) **Decide on a Compensation Package**. Consider salary, studio benefits, instruction, or a combination.

4) **Advertise the Job**. Word of mouth, newspaper, professional journal, or magazine.

5) **Collect and Review Applications**. How much experience and what level of skill is necessary to perform the job? How much training are you prepared or interested in doing? Is this part of the compensation package?

6) **Interview Candidates**. What qualities are you looking for in a candidate? Prepare questions, set your expectations, and decide how selective you plan to be.

7) **Check References**. After you talk with a promising candidate, call their references for confirmation and support of their qualifications and personal characteristics.

8) **Offer the Position**. Be prepared to negotiate.

Too serious a process to hire a pottery assistant? Too time consuming? You just want to trust your judgment? Throughout this book, I have advocated and encouraged you to treat the craft and whatever you wish to make of it with a serious and professional approach. The act of hiring a helper, assistant, or studio manager must not be treated with a cavalier attitude. In fact, it should be one of the most careful things you do. In effect, you are inviting a stranger to work with you side-by-side and that should be done with care and an eye towards a positive, rewarding, and comfortable relationship.

Regarding the compensation you offer, most likely some sort of studio use will be part of it. Before you make that part of the package, be sure you have resolved any issues you might have about someone sharing your workspace. You might want to review the section on small group studios earlier in the book. The chapter on teaching is also pertinent to dealing with employees.

Going through the job description and hiring process is only half of what it takes to manage employees and to be a good boss. Effective communication is the single most important skill necessary in making the work environment comfortable and the success of the experience likely. This communication begins with the interview and must continue throughout the relationship. Positive reinforcement as well as appropriate criticism are necessary components, along with regular evaluations of job performance. Rewarding your assistant with a raise is nice but the nature and volume of your business may not make it possible for you to do. Other forms of appreciation can be equally satisfying but be certain that either the possibility or the impossibility of a pay raise has been discussed and is out in the open. If studio use, materials, firing, and other benefits are part of or possibly the entire compensation package, be sure you have carefully explained this to the potential assistant and that they understand exactly what they are getting in return for their work. I have seen many situations where the initial excitement and even gratitude over having access to a facility, materials, and firing gives way to disappointment and a feeling of exploitation when the individual perceives an apparent imbalance between the amount or kind of work they are doing and the benefit of having studio use. For an exchange like this to be successful, the employer must present the work situation in all of its brutal honesty and reality. You have to be convinced that this person understands the nature of the work and will have time in their schedule to take advantage of the availability of the studio and what you have to offer as a mentor. They have to feel that not only is the compensation fair and equitable, but that they are getting the better deal!

It is very likely that the kind of work you have available is suitable for only novice potters or those in certain stages of their own careers, and once they have mastered the skills necessary to perform the work and have gained an additional measure of experience from working in your shop, they will be ready to move on. It's important that both you and your helper recognize this possibility and when the time comes, one of you makes it happen. You also have to recognize that the possibility exists for the whole experience to be a failure from one perspective or another. If this is the case, either you as the employer have to ask the individual to leave or the employee has to announce their resignation. No hard feelings.

The issues and decisions surrounding staff matters are undeniable elements of business and studio management that require competence, resolve, and diplomacy, as well as empathy, thoughtfulness, and understanding.

# Chapter 7

## Sales, Marketing, and Self-Promotion

For many, the sale of work is the most exciting and exhilarating, and yet the most difficult and intimidating aspect of their craft practice. The idea of somebody liking your pots enough to pay money for them is very satisfying and rewarding. The two greatest compliments I receive as an artist are when my work is either bought or copied! I prefer the former. If sales are crucial to you, then that concern is undeniable. Yet it is not uniformly pertinent, for not all craft makers are interested in selling their work or at least making sales on a formal basis. However, it is important to recognize that if you are to survive as a potter, there must be some means of financially supporting your expenses.

For those who don't make pots for a living, pottery expenses are budgeted and supported like any other personal entertainment or household expense would be. For others, the family or personal financial situation is not a problem and whatever it costs to do pottery is easily covered. And for others, sales, though not eminently vital, are an important part of their pottery activity and contribute either to supporting their pottery involvement or to the household income. Whatever your situation, there is much to be learned about clay work and crafts making from a study of marketing and promotion.

Marketing, or sales, is another area where craft making exists on a slightly alternative plane than other occupations where the sale of manufactured objects is critical. This is not to say that merchandising crafts is any less serious or formal than the marketing strategies and procedures of other items destined for retail or wholesale audiences. However, the successful making of craft objects must be emotionally and creatively driven, with the sale as the end result. The sale must not be the driving force that inspires the manufacture. For many craftspeople, the creative process is not complete until the work is sold and being used or enjoyed by someone else. The sale of the item invokes an emotional response. This is how I feel about the sale of my own work—completing the piece may be the climax, but the sale is the conclusion.

As you will see, there are many different aspects to selling your work and you would think there would be a logical, systematic order to addressing them. In fact, it's more like the question of what came first—the chicken or the egg? You need to be concerned about developing your production line, locating sales outlets, identifying your customer, promotional tools, pricing, sales contracts, retail, wholesale, advertising, and other issues relevant to marketing. As you attempt to figure out what to do first, second, and third, you begin to see how each of these concerns both defines the next step and is reliant upon it. For instance, you must price your work before you approach a sales outlet, but until you investigate and approach the sales outlet, you don't really have all the information you need to effectively price your work. Another critical step is to determine the demand for the type of work you do, but until you actually attempt some sales, this assessment may be quite difficult. So, while you do have to make some sense out of all this and address each phase of sales intelligently and completely, you must make your marketing attempts along the way. Marketing can best be viewed as a collection of activities, each requiring its own degree of expertise. You'll investigate and learn about the various aspects and piece them together like a puzzle. As your experience and fluency increase, the result is a clearer overall picture.

## Defining Your Production / Identifying Your Market

Assuming that successful and meaningful sales are going to be the result of excellent production, you need to decide what you want to produce to sell. "Everything I make," may be your response and that approach may be valid but more likely there will be a line or segment of your wares that you feel are best suited for sales. Perhaps you only want to sell the most expertly done work or the most easily produced items. Perhaps the wares that are the most developed and sophisticated aesthetically are the most saleable. Whatever the criterion, decide what you will produce for sale and stick to it. As your work progresses, you may want to add other products to the sales line. The reason for this approach is to force you to maintain quality control over your wares by establishing a routine of self-criticism and evaluation. Examine your pots periodically and don't allow sales and marketing to obscure careful and dedicated quality production.

Once you establish a line of work, examine the marketplace and identify your market. Who will be interested in your work and who are you interested in selling your work to? Get out into the marketplace and look around, investigate, observe, and take note of what kind of work is being produced, who is buying, and where the sales are taking place. Imagine your work in these various settings and try to picture how it would fit in. Of course, the type of work you do will have a lot to do with who will be interested in buying it. Functional, decorative, small, large, brightly decorated, earth tones, etc. Are you aiming at a kind of common ground buyer who would rather use a

handmade mug than a mass produced one as long as it is not too expensive? Faced with the task of buying a gift for someone, the same person might head to the craft shop for a handmade decorative object before going to the department store. Or are you looking for the very discriminating craft collector who buys only the absolute finest examples of handmade craft?

Sales and marketing is a gradual process where increasing success and rewards come from your evolution and growth as a marketer. Increased sales will result from continuing analysis and examination of your marketing style and strategies. Question sales figures and try to understand what factors are either driving sales up or causing a de-

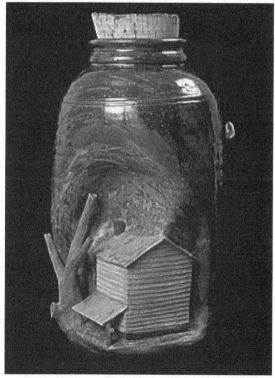

*Figure 7-1.* **Dan Finch**. *Barn Pot. 1998. 13" H, wheel-thrown and handbuilt, cone 10 reduction fired. This is one of Dan's sought after signature pots in his production line. This piece is also shown in the color section. (Photo by Spectrum Multi Media)*

cline. Has your work changed? Does a particular gallery or shop not attract the appropriate client for your work? Does your work appeal on a seasonal basis or have a regional attraction due to a particular motif?

Regular criticism and evaluation of your own work should be part of your continuing efforts to be the best craft maker possible. Higher quality work will generally result in better sales. I say generally because the discriminatory ability of some of the buying population will reach a level beyond which higher quality work won't attract any more attention or result in greater sales. As a matter of fact, assuming the higher quality work is more expensive, it may even generate fewer sales. When faced with this situation, your choices are clear—lower your price, limit the line of work you sell in this market to that which is appropriate and cost effective, reduce the care and quality of your work in order to charge a lower price, or find a new outlet that will respond to your work and the price you need to charge.

Finding your market can be a challenge but with a creative approach to problem solving you can uncover it. Think beyond the general craft shop, gallery, and gift shop and direct your attention to specialty outlets or opportunities. Expanding on the idea of motif, perhaps your functional work is bright and joyful and appeals to sunny cookouts on the deck. Look for sales outlets in beach communities with seasonal residences. Do you specialize in animal designs or decorations? If so, perhaps the zoo or aquarium gift shop would be a suitable place for your work. I am reminded of museum gift shops, nature stores, and other shops that appeal to a particular interest, sensibility, and thus, customer. If you investigate the museum shop avenue, make note of the characteristics of the museum and the shop. Do the items for sale relate to the museum's collection? Are your prices in line with other items in the shop? Do you have something new to offer the shop that will be unique and yet harmonize with the current selection and their interests?

Don't neglect noncraft oriented stores. Kitchen and cooking shops like Williams Sonoma or The Kitchen Store, often located in upscale malls, can be untapped outlets for your work. Often, special events such as dog shows, automobile rallies, or flower extravaganzas are opportunities to ply your wares. Sounds funny? Not if the motifs, themes, or subjects of your work correspond to the interests of the attendees. Even if the promoters haven't thought of inviting craftspeople, make the proposal yourself. You may have a lock on the market (at least the first time).

## Types of Sales Outlets

Locating appropriate sales outlets can be a frustrating and time consuming effort. In addition to the suggestions above, a variety of venues exist for craftspeople to sell their wares.

### Your Studio as a Sales Gallery

For many, the ultimate goal is to have a workspace of their own where they can sell their work. If you presently have a studio space or place to work where sales are inappropriate, impossible, or impractical, this section may not hold any immediate value for you. However, you may be building or searching for a studio or have one where a salesroom could be incorporated. If that's the case, sales out of your studio may be an appealing notion.

Selling work directly from your studio may be glamorous and has the potential to be the most financially rewarding of all the marketing methods, but it's not as simple as it sounds. Many things factor into whether sales from your studio will be successful. Issues such as the location and accessibility of your studio will have much to do with attracting and maintaining customers.

*Figure 7-2. A partial view of Dick Lehman's showroom. Dinnerware is displayed in a typical setting, helping the customer visualize the ware in use. The display units, designed by Dick, are handcrafted out of cherry and have built-in lighting. (Photo by Ryan Miller)*

To effectively market from the studio, you must have a dedicated display or sales space separate from your work area. It's not necessarily that you don't want people in your workspace, but you do want to control access to that space. You also want to try and keep your finished wares dust free and displayed in a fashion that will encourage serious sales consideration.

Of course, there are some advantages to opening your studio to the public. The people who choose to come to your studio over a shop or gallery will be looking for a different kind of experience. They will appreciate the idea of visiting the place where the wares are made and getting a glimpse into the life and lifestyle of the potter, if you will. You can tap into this kind of emotional desire by staging special events such as kiln openings or the unveiling of a new line of work. Be careful when you use the term "sale," though, because you don't want to give the impression that you are discounting the price of your work.

*Figure 7-3. A partial view of the gallery/showroom at The Potters Shop. Work in the gallery is made by staff or studio members exclusively. (Photo by Marna Kennedy)*

Obviously, by selling from your studio you avoid having to pay a sales commission to a gallery or shop, but there is more to the financial angle than that. As I will discuss in greater detail in the next section, the commission you pay to a shop covers the costs of promoting and selling your work. By taking on these responsibilities yourself, you will be taking time and financial resources away from your other activities as a potter. You must be prepared to stop your clay work to accommodate a customer and if you perceive this as a disturbance or bother rather than an opportunity, it's a good indication that sales from your studio may not be for you. Of course, you can set up any operating guidelines you like and

if customer visits are more infrequent, you can arrange the studio so you can see or hear the showroom and continue to work as people visit and browse. Don't be a hermit though, if you don't greet your visitors and make the experience inviting and comfortable, it's not going to be a success. Another method is to limit the weekly salesroom hours and plan to sit, do paperwork, or relax during those hours. You can also have the studio open only during the summer, leaving the rest of the year for production. Another strategy is to hire a salesperson to run the gallery while you are in the studio working. This way, you can meet visitors and invite them into your workspace without taking substantial time away from your production. Yet another way is to host one or two studio openings a year. Some potters have built up such a loyal customer base in this way that their customers wait for the open house and make all their gift purchases for the entire year in one day!

Realize that while your studio as a sales gallery may be an appealing notion and may be exactly the kind of operation that fulfills your dreams as a producing craftsperson, there are sacrifices and adjustments that will need to be made and only you can determine whether those adjustments are worth the possible rewards.

## Craft Fairs

Years ago, the craft fair was the primary (if not the only) means for craftspeople to sell their wares. Craft shops weren't invented yet and galleries that handled crafts or understood or appreciated crafts as special objects were nonexistent. As craft marketing has become more mainstream and sophisticated, many more outlets have become available to the potter. However, the craft fair as a marketing, sales, and promotional tool remains a staple for many craftspeople regardless of their sales level. In fact, while the old-fashioned craft fair still proliferates (to the tune of thousands of fairs each year throughout the country), the Craft Fair has given way to Buyer's Markets, Artisan's Festivals, Handcraft Expositions, and more.

Regardless of what they are called or who they cater to, the general style of a craft fair remains the same. It is a collection of craftspeople in one place at the same time. It can be indoors or out and last anywhere from a day to two or three days or longer. Each participant or exhibitor is responsible for setting up, staffing, maintaining, and dismantling their display space or booth. Craft fairs range from informal, local community organized affairs to highly sophisticated productions that ri-

val the finest and most complex marketing and sales opportunities of any industry.

What has changed is the advent of the "wholesale only show" where buyers representing retail outlets such as galleries, craft shops, and even department stores, scan the various booths looking for work to fill their display space. Each exhibitor shows a representative sample of their production line and does their best to interest those buyers in making serious commitments to purchase their work. At a wholesale show, no actual pieces are sold, rather orders are written for an agreed upon delivery date, allowing the potter to plan his production and work schedule for the coming months. (More on the details of managing wholesale orders later.)

Don't underestimate the viability of a local production. Even the so-called church or community fair can be planned and presented very professionally. The type of fair you choose will depend on several factors including your degree of experience in both marketing and production and the description of the fair itself. Never enter a fair blindly regardless of what you may have heard about it or what you think you know about it. Do some research and try to figure out whether the fair is appropriate for you and your work at this time in your career.

The single best way to investigate a particular fair and at the same time become familiar with how fairs operate and function is to visit it with an eye to participating next year. Of course, this is not always practical or necessary, especially in the case of smaller local fairs. But in the case of larger, well established markets, it is strongly, no it is *really strongly* suggested. Beyond the value of visiting a particular fair as a scouting mission, you can learn a lot from visiting fairs in general. Planning to "do" a fair without having some experience as an observer is surely to head for doom and disaster. Regardless of what you read and

# Ginsu and Raku

During one phase of my career, I found myself testing the craft fair waters. Beginning with local fairs, I was having some credible sales success though I found the fair scene not exactly to my liking. While I did enjoy meeting and interacting with the public and potential buyers, I got easily frustrated during slow periods in my booth and wished I was back in the studio at my wheel. After being solicited by the promoter, but against my better judgment, I contracted to do what promised to be a major retail fair called the Home Interiors and Decorating Show. I say against my better judgment not because I had grave misgivings about the show, but because I really wasn't interested in doing craft fairs anymore. Evidently, this show had a successful history but the promoters thought it would be even better with the addition of fine crafts. The terms of the show were generous in order to attract fine crafts to an otherwise untested show.

While I was not a veteran of the fair scene, I had visited numerous fairs of all types and was experienced enough in other aspects of sales to know the questions that needed to be asked. Since this was not a crafts only show, I was very concerned about the other craftspeople who would participate and about the noncrafts exhibits. The list of exhibitors was impressive—among them were high-end furniture showrooms, interior designers and decorators, marble and tile flooring showrooms, and others of very elegant, stylish, and refined aesthetics. The list of participating craftspeople was equally impressive, with many highly recognizable names.

In addition to the chance for some major retail sales, it was brought to my attention that another reason for the addition of crafts was that the other exhibitors had expressed personal interest from a wholesale point of view. Not only would retail customers be flooding my booth, but the exhibit hall would be filled with potential wholesale accounts for the duration of the show!

Well, I can be going in only one direction here. From the long impressive list of craftspeople, only a handful actually contracted to exhibit and while there were quite a number of impressive home furnishing presentations, I found myself in a hell that only Danté could have designed. In the booth to my right was the original pot and pan man whose wares are indestructible and cook with no water added! You've seen him on late night TV. Every 20 minutes (with a 10 minute break between) came the clanging of his pots and the hawking of his wares. As if this wasn't enough, in the booth to my left was, you guessed it, the Ginsu knife man whose knife can cut through a tin can and never need sharpening. Home interiors and decorating took on a whole new meaning for me. Attendance was so light it looked like the show wasn't open. Five people came into my booth, not one expressing any interest in my work.

The show was a bomb, not only for me but for the handful of other craftspeople who were there. In this sea of kitsch, it wasn't difficult for us to find each other. After the first day of the three-day show, two of us approached the promoters and demanded the return of our money. After a serious hesitation, he agreed to refund our booth fees under the condition that we stay for the duration of the show. I told him we were leaving immediately and we would do him a favor and not sue him for misrepresentation and fraud. I was packed and in my truck in record time. Just so it wouldn't be total loss, a few of us did some trading and, in exchange for a few of my larger pieces, I got a walnut and teak bed for my son learn from colleagues about the fair experience, nothing can take the place of walking the aisles, observing the interchange, noting the design of booths, and witnessing the entire milieu. There is much you can discover about the fair by asking pertinent questions of the promoters. Some large fairs with more regional or national orientation and recognition send out extensive prospectus, press releases, and application forms that are very descriptive.

Here are some key areas that will yield the most revealing information about a particular fair.

1) **Category, Type of Work, Style of Show**. What kinds of crafts will be displayed and to what degree is "handmade" a determining factor? For example, many small unsophisticated fairs allow items to be sold that are made from kits or commercially mass-produced in part. Stay clear of these types of productions. Is there a theme (contemporary, traditional, etc.) for the show?

2) **Selection Process**. Is the fair open to all applicants or is it juried? To what degree and standard is the jurying? Is it by resumé, reviewing the work, or a combination? Who is the jury and what are their qualifications?

3) **Selectivity**. How many applications were received for the show last year and how many were accepted? How many repeat exhibitors are there from last year?

4) **Attendance**. What was the total attendance last year? What is projected for this year?

5) **Display Areas and Signage**. Will all exhibitors be expected to conform to established aesthetic or technical standards? Is any display equipment (tables, chairs, drapes) supplied? What is the lighting situation? Are identification signs provided by the organizers or does each exhibitor supply their own?

6) **Costs**. Are there additional costs beyond the booth fee such as electricity, parking, equipment rental, or advertising?

7) **Business Certification**. Are there any documents such as resale certificates required in order to exhibit? A yes answer indicates a more professional production.

8) **Entrance Fee**. Are attendees charged an entry fee and/or parking fee?

There are many other questions to ask and you will have no problem adding to the list after visiting some fairs on your own.

Despite my tale of woe, craft fairs are a very valuable and vital marketing opportunity. Many potters have built entire careers around the sales and contacts they make by attending only a few major fairs each year.

## Shops and Galleries

Unquestionably, craft shops and galleries account for the major volume of crafts sales in this country and you should be a part of that. Differentiating between the craft shop and gallery used to be simple, but today the line is blurred. Not only has it become hard to tell by looking (there are plenty of elegant looking craft shops with lots of floor space), but the marketing and sales styles of these two types of establishments have become similar. Many so-called crafts shops have adopted exhibition, sales, and marketing styles that traditionally belonged to galleries, while many galleries have altered their retail styles to reflect a more aggressive approach.

Traditionally, the primary differences between shops and galleries is that shops tend to be tighter in space allocation, while galleries are more open. Shops have a wide ranging stock of wares that is constantly in flux. As items are sold off the floor, new stock is added. Galleries generally present exhibitions of an individual's work or a group reflecting a theme for a limited number of weeks. Objects are sold, but left on exhibit until the show has ended. In addition to an exhibition schedule, it's common for galleries to display the work of a number of artists/craftsmen on a regular basis in a space adjacent to the exhibition area. This is what used to be referred to as the gallery's "stable" of artists. Shops tend towards buying a craftperson's work outright, while galleries will usually exhibit an artist's work on consignment. Galleries tend to attract a more affluent, discerning collector, while shops appear to attract the everyday buying public. Galleries ring of exclusivity, while shops lean towards more popular trends.

Despite the established and traditional contrasts between galleries and shops, in reality there are more similarities than differences. Only visits and research will reveal the truth and help make clear which outlets are more appropriate for you and your work.

Approaching shops and galleries requires patience and a somewhat formal business-like style. If you are nervous about the prospect, you are not alone. Most craftspeople anticipate this to be an uncomfortable confrontation rather than a positive experience. At the very least, you can learn something about marketing and your own work. Shops and galleries always have their eyes open for new work and you just may find yourself in the right place at the right time. It's time to get beyond the fear of being rejected. Rejection is a fact of life for the artist or craftsperson and if you can't take rejection for what it's worth, successful sales and marketing will forever be unobtainable. Above all else, don't take rejection personally. It's about your wares and that particular shop. If your work is rejected, try to get the gallery to offer more than just the obligatory "nice work, but it doesn't quite fit with our theme" response. Ask for a more descriptive and helpful analysis and if they accommodate you, listen to what they say about your work and take the criticism positively.

I speak from experience when I say that you really can learn something and make your work better. After my work had been rejected by a major Boston area crafts gallery, I asked the owner to give me some feedback. He pointed out some unresolved aesthetic issues in my work and asked me to come back again in a year. I was skeptical but back to the studio and to my career I went. My sales didn't stop over the course of the year, but as I continued to make pots, I kept his critical remarks in mind and experimented with some of his suggestions. A year later I was back, this time making my first delivery of work to his gallery.

Unless you are prevented from doing so by distance, your strategy should begin with a visit to the prospective shop so you can informally and leisurely examine the place, the kind of wares it sells, the style of the sales staff, the people who come in to buy, and the overall appearance of the displays. In fact, almost everything you need to know can be discovered in the guise of a customer! If a visit isn't possible, find out as much as you can through the mail and recommendations by friends and colleagues.

Once you select a shop, contact the owner and introduce yourself as a potter who feels that your work would be a good fit for the shop. Ask how you should go about presenting your work. Do not, under any circumstances, enter a gallery or shop with slides or work in hand and expect a meeting and review. It's true that often the squeaky wheel gets the grease, but one that grinds, screeches, annoys, and is in-your-face gets the dump! Most galleries will ask you to send slides with some supporting material such as a resumé and artist's statement. When you send in your packet, send it to the attention of the owner or buyer. In your cover letter, introduce yourself again and make reference to your previous conversation. Any connection you can make between yourself and the gallery will help elevate your slides to the top of the pile. After they review your work, you'll be notified with an answer. Keep in mind that popular galleries may get as many as ten or more packets of slides and materials from artists each week, making timely replies difficult. There is nothing wrong with calling the gallery after they have had your materials in hand for a week or so, especially if you sent your slides in response to a conversation.

A better strategy than mailing your material is to make an appointment to bring in your work for review. Most craft shops and some galleries prefer to examine new wares in this way. When you arrive *on time* for your appointment, be professional and business-like. Dress neatly in a way that reflects how you do business and how you want to be treated. Don't wear a suit unless it's your everyday attire, but don't wear your clay working jeans either. Treat the meeting as much as your opportunity to interview the gallery and decide whether this is a place you want to do business as it is a chance for the gallery or shop to see you and your work.

If you presently enjoy any degree of name recognition or if your work is large or otherwise difficult to transport, you may be able to interest the gallery or shop to visit you in the studio to review your work. This is not as far fetched as it may seem—many buyers and owners welcome the opportunity to get out of the shop and into the artist's studio. If you are successful in arranging a meeting in your workplace, you can be a little more relaxed about your dress because your visitor will expect to see you in working attire. Offer your visitor a beverage or snack and begin with a short introduction and tour of your studio. This will relax both of you. The advantages of having a buyer come to your place are numerous. They will see all you have to offer, thereby reducing the chance that the work you selected to bring in may have been on the wrong track. You will likely feel more comfortable in your own space and there will be less chance of your visitor being distracted by the daily goings-on in their gallery. On the other hand, be prepared to talk about anything in plain view because unless you arranged the space in some special way, what you see is what you get!

An experienced gallery owner will expect some disorder and disarray in a studio setting, but not having a place to adequately show the work is unacceptable. A formal display space isn't necessary, but be prepared with at least a clean table, an uncluttered background, and good lighting. If you have prices stickers or other indications on your work, be sure they are what you want your visitor to see. Remember that your studio is dusty and even though you may be vigilant in keeping the studio clean, unless you have a formal display area where your work is kept clean on a regular basis, there will be a film of clay dust on the ware. Clean up before the visit.

In an effort to establish relationships with shops and galleries, many craftspeople send unsolicited packets of slides and material in the hopes that a particular gallery will be open to reviewing material in this way. While there is nothing wrong or incorrect about doing this, realize that a timely reply is unlikely or you may never get a reply to your mailing. You can increase the chances of a reply or at least a return of your slides by enclosing a self-addressed stamped envelope.

## Craft Competitions

Entering craft competitions cannot be looked at as a sales opportunity, but rather as a means of gaining recognition for your work and yourself as a potter. This is not to say that sales don't happen, it's just not a viable way to sell your work. If the fear of rejection looms heavy over your head, sending in your slides and entry fee to a competition is akin to lying on the railroad tracks and waiting for the 6:05 to come rumbling through town. Rejection is inevitable. Craft competitions are always juried affairs and, by their very nature, are not objective. In fact, the level of subjectivity in judging a competition is the highest possible. While even a gallery with the highest level of excellence imaginable selects work that goes beyond the likes and dislikes of the owner and looks for work that will be attractive to its clientele, the jury of a craft competition selects work based on any number of arbitrary standards, including its own personal biases. Juries can be a small group of three or four people or can be a single individual. Work is usually judged by slides but sometimes by the actual work itself. Often there will be a note in the prospectus warning that once your work is accepted, if the work submitted varies in quality from what was viewed in the slide, it will be rejected.

A bone of contention among craftspeople is the entry fee charged by craft competitions. Why should you have to pay a fee to have your work reviewed? The costs of organizing and mounting a major exhibition are substantial and reasonable entry fees are a legitimate means for the organizers and hosting institution to help defray those costs. A reasonable fee might be in the neighborhood of $5 per slide or perhaps a flat $20. Of course, you must be the final judge. When deciding whether to enter a show, do some research to determine that the show is legitimate and then enter as many items as you have the energy to do.

## Seasonal Cooperative Outlets

A popular marketing venue is the so-called cooperative seasonal shop—a temporary space rented by a group to sell their work during the holiday season and share in the operation of the shop. The founding members usually establish the procedures, terms, commissions, and sales policies as well as oversee the jurying of new members. Due

## Secrets

Secrets is a well established sales cooperative located in the Boston area that started 25 years ago with a small group of craftspeople who got together to assist each other in the sales of their work. Their idea to have a cooperative sale in the home of one of the group members was exciting, but they were a little uneasy about doing retail sales in a residential neighborhood. They decided to try it, keeping it low key by inviting their friends and others by word of mouth. Thus the name "Christmas Secrets" was born, reflecting the quiet, clandestine nature of the operation. Needless to say, Christmas Secrets was a success and after a few years, the group expanded the idea by inviting other craftspeople to join and by holding the sale in a more formal, publicly accessible space. They went from utilizing a local gallery to searching out vacant retail spaces they could rent on a short term basis. A good deal for both the owner who had an empty space and the group who needed a visible location that would attract walk-in customers.

Today, the name Christmas Secrets has given way to Secrets and the group has about 50 members representing a multitude of crafts with annual sales of between $90,000 and $100,000. It is organized as an unincorporated cooperative to the seasonal nature of the arrangement, it's likely that a different location will need to be found each year, though this isn't always the case. Once the members for the coming year are chosen, a series of meetings are held to fix the hours of operation and assign duties. As a cooperative, the duties will include setup, advertising and promotion, and staffing the shop. Seasonal coops are extremely viable ways to sell your work at retail during the height of gift buying for the year.

## Designers and Decorators

Sales opportunities beyond the obvious include decorators, designers, architects, art consultants, and department stores. Department stores can be viable outlets for your work, though dealing with one can be a trying and frustrating experience. Department stores have buyers for each department and they alone are responsible for what ends up on the floor. There is fierce competition in the business, which can work to the your advantage when the unique individuality of your handmade items is exactly what a gift department is looking for to set them apart from the rest.

Your approach to getting your work seen by a buyer is the same as it is with a gallery owner. Keep in mind that a department store buyer may be thinking in terms of one store or 20 and may be looking for a one-time purchase or an ongoing relationship. Due to fads and trends in commercial sales, the one-time purchase is not unusual, although this may not be clear when you make that initial sale. Only time will tell. I once made a very large sale to Neiman Marcus and from everything I was able to find out after the work had been delivered and placed in the stores, it was received enthusiastically by customers and sold quickly. Despite the success, I was never contacted again. I later found out this is a common practice and since they are able to achieve equal success with other potters doing different work, there is no reason to stick with the same craftspeople year after year. Change is good for business.

Designers, decorators, art consultants, and architects represent yet another avenue to market your wares. While each represents a different segment of the design profession, the circumstances and manner in which they might buy crafts is sim-

with all members as equal partners. After being juried into the group on the basis of the quality of their craft, members are required to put in 60 hours (or the established equivalent) serving on one of the many committees or doing sales work in the shop. Every three years, members must assume the responsibilities of a committee head and it is those heads that constitute the executive committee, or decision-making body. Committees include site search, jury, sales, publicity, display, setup, and others. Within the executive group, there are two organizers (the equivalent of president or CEO) and a bookkeeper, both paid positions. While the coop is most active between the months of September and January, much of the work to keep the group together, organized, and poised for the next season is year round.

Susan Tornheim is a felt maker who has been a member of Secrets since 1985. For Susan, two critical aspects of participation in the coop stand out: the opportunity to work closely with other craftspeople, networking and sharing information and resources; and the opportunity for an intense period of public interaction where reaction to her work is immediate and is often worthwhile and helpful. "Joining Secrets was a turning point in my career, an affirmation of my commitment to being a professional craftsperson," Susan says.

ilar. Essentially, they are looking for art or crafts to fill a specific need in a particular project. Design professionals usually represent corporate or commercial clients but they also do art placements for residential customers. A typical commercial project might be a law firm office renovation or relocation with a need for decorative art or crafts, or a commercial building looking for art to enhance public spaces. A residential client might be looking for one piece or a collection of work encompassing decorative and functional ware. Since anyone can call themselves a designer, a business card as a form of identification doesn't tell you anything about their qualifications or legitimacy. If you are approached by a designer, ask for credentials in the form of ASID (American Society of Interior Designers), IBD (International Board of Design), AIA (American Institute of Architects), or other professional association membership. Art consultants are like gallery and craft shop owners in that the industry is unregulated and there are no identifiable professional organizations that would lend credibility to their name. Use your good judgment in establishing a relationship.

Working with a designer may be as simple as providing work from your regular stock and production line or might involve complex negotiations and efforts for special order and commission work. Designers and consultants generally keep active slide files of artists and craftspeople to recommend to their clients as a particular need arises. Keep these professionals up-to-date on your current work, pricing, and professional projects as they are more likely to make an effort to place your work if they have a comfortable and reliable relationship with you.

## Commissions

A commission sale is one in which a client works with you or an agent (gallery, art consult-ant, sales rep), to produce a piece or series of pieces especially for them. There is no question that selling work from your regular production line and stock is more convenient, easier to plan, carries lower production costs, and is far less stressful than doing work on commission. There is so much room for miscommunication, misinterpretation, and disappointment that, for many, taking on commission work is simply not worth the effort.

Commissions can involve different degrees of "specialness," ranging from a regular piece of your work created anew for an individual and not sold off the shelf, to something totally out of the ordinary. Regardless of the nature of the piece, a successful commission depends on a meeting of the minds—often an impossibility. Assuming the customer knows exactly what they want, they must communicate that to you and you must produce the piece that is in the customer's mind's eye. Often, the customer only *thinks* they know what they want or may even admit that they don't know quite what they want. This can be a real problem. If you take on a commission through an intermediary (art consultant, etc.), don't allow them to hinder direct communication between you and the client.

My general advice is to only take on a commission if you feel comfortable with the request. Through experience I have learned to turn down a commission if I get the feeling the client is more interested in seeing their design and aesthetic come to life than having me do something for them. If the client is a frustrated potter looking for someone else's hands to do their work, it will be very difficult for you to produce a piece that will satisfy them.

If you are doing the work through an agent, their percentage should not exceed 25% and should be in the neighborhood of 15% to 20%. This sale requires no capital investment on their part, takes up no floor space in their shop or showroom, and involves very little actual work because the responsibility falls primarily on you. A contract that includes the price, delivery date, and commission paid to the agent must be prepared. The remaining contractual points have to do with the actual piece. Details regarding the exact nature, including shape, color, clay, glaze, and other pertinent factors, must be clearly spelled out for you and the client to agree on. If a piece is supposed to be 18" tall on completion, there should be some agreement stating an acceptable range of heights. Do not, under any circumstances, leave anything to the imagination or make assumptions.

Keeping all this in mind, there are two approaches to commissions. You can go through the negotiations and discussions, draw up the proposal in a contract, and assume responsibility for completing the work. If you choose to proceed in this way, I strongly suggest that you include a payment schedule where you receive partial payment as the work proceeds that is nonrefundable. This will insure at least partial compensation in the event the commission is not completed, the client changes their mind, or the work is capriciously rejected by the client.

My approach to commissions is quite a bit different. I am not interested in getting into a stressful situation where one of the parties can be disappointed, resulting in bad feelings all around and I am equally not interested in doing work I don't feel comfortable doing. I listen to a client's wishes and as long as I feel the work is within the limits of my interests, I will agree to do some work which I feel will satisfy them. I state what the finished piece will cost and I explain that I am doing the piece for them and if it meets with their approval, they can buy it. If not, no bad feelings. I write up no contract and take no money. By doing this, I retain complete control over my work and if the piece is rejected, I know I have done

something that I very well might have done anyway.

If you are serious about trying to make the sale, you have to treat the situation with seriousness and a degree of exclusivity. One of the attractions of commission work is the customer's desire to own something one-of-a-kind and specially created. If the way you present yourself and attitude undermines that feeling, you have defeated the uniqueness of it all and will alienate the client.

## Catalog Sales

Selling your work through a catalog can also be a viable way to market your wares, though individual craftspeople often think of catalog sales as beyond their realm. Some think their work is unsuitable or that catalog companies aren't interested in small time potters. There's often the fear of not being able to meet the required production levels. Of these, only the last has some merit. Being involved in catalog sales does present special considerations including possible concern for copyright protection and a call to your attorney is advisable.

If production pottery interests you, investigate catalog sales as an option. In fact, national catalogs are always looking for unique, innovative products to bring to their customers and you may be making that item as we speak. John Jensen was. (See "Houses: Painting and Toads" on page 174.)

## Sales Representatives

I have placed this manner of sales and marketing last on the hit parade not because it is the least popular (though it might be) or viable, but because it can encompass all of the previously discussed methods. As I first mentioned in considering sales from your studio, one of the difficult aspects of marketing and sales is the time it takes away from your actual production. A way around this is to contract the services of a sales rep or agent. Essentially, an agent will represent you and present your work to a list of clients, be it shops, galleries, designers, decorators, or others. For a fee that usually amounts to around 10% of the sale, they will do their best to get your work placed in appropriate sales outlets.

Exactly what, in addition to placing your work, an agent may do for you is variable. An agent may negotiate the terms of a sale, check the credit rating and payment frequency of a gallery, and even handle all the financial transactions for you. As the agent takes no fee up front, you have nothing to lose in experimenting with an arrangement like this. That the rep does the work doesn't absolve you from some of the responsibility though. Interview the rep to be sure they understand your craft, your sales terms, production capabilities and schedule, and anything else that is particular about your work. Ask about the places they are thinking about showing your work. Provide them with whatever promotional materials would be helpful. Keep in contact on a regular basis with updates on your work. The more interest you demonstrate, the more aggressive they will likely be in showing your work.

## Houses: Painting and Toads

*John Jensen started his clay career like many of us. An early interest led to his own pottery education and eventual pursuit of clay on a more dedicated basis. Soon he was faced with the question of how to move on to the next level.*

I had long wanted to be able to pursue a pottery career but the investment in space and equipment, along with the uncertainty of the market prevented me from doing so. Painting houses was my bread and butter while I worked at my pottery at a local community arts center. Soon I began to teach some classes there and found the additional income sufficient to begin to build an economic base for a possible pottery business. Slowly, over the course of the next five years, I sold my work in local shops, out of my studio, and at craft fairs, working out of my converted garage. I began to feel that I might be on the verge of letting go my house painting and teaching for a pottery making career but was still uncertain.

A local shop owner suggested that I approach The Plow and Hearth Co., a national catalog, with one of my items, a fanciful toad house. Hopeful, I sent them a photo and in short order I received an order for two dozen that they would try out by selling in their retail store! Nice, but not yet a career. I continued along with my usual work load. About a year later, the company called with bigger plans. We discussed my production capability, pricing, delivery dates, and other details. Evidentially, the toad houses were a hit. After negotiations, they gave me an initial order for 200 toad houses to be delivered in six weeks and I have yet to look back.

Now, about two years later, I have completely gone to mass production with a staff of five part-time potters in a fine-tuned studio efficiently arranged to produce this one item at the rate of about 200 per week. Despite the production load, I have made it a priority to maintain the integrity in my design. The toad house is completely handmade with no molded parts (except for the hand-stamped letters) and in fact, the more we make, the better the item gets.

Not only has this been a great boon to my career as a potter, but it has proved to be a great opportunity to develop my throwing skills, similar to how an apprentice in the eastern pottery tradition would be made to produce piece after piece as a means of discipline and education. Who knows how long this

## Shipping

No discussion of sales would be complete without at least a mention of packing and shipping. Even if you sell your work exclusively from your studio, there will be occasion to pack your work for a customer to take home or to ship a piece for a client. Packing is the art of protecting the piece as it travels from one place to another. Shipping is the method of getting that piece from one place to another and will range from you transporting the work yourself to a customer leaving your studio with the ware in hand, to your use of United Parcel Service (UPS) or another common carrier.

If you pack work to transport yourself or for a customer to take with them, let common sense prevail. My exclusive method is to wrap my pots in towels and either place them in corrugated boxes in the bed of my pickup truck or load them in the extended cab without boxes. You can do the same with any vehicle. I have never had a piece break. For a customer leaving your studio, don't simply leave them to their own devices. Pack the ware with newspaper or bubble wrap and if space in their vehicle permits, use a box.

UPS is by far the most popular method of shipping among craftspeople. UPS is affordable, convenient, reliable, reasonably safe, and if you follow all the rules, easy to collect from if your work is damaged in transport. When packing for

will last, but whatever happens, I consider myself one of the luckiest guys in the world. As I work at this, new ideas are always coming up and I'm sure they'll be life after the toad house.

*Figure 7-4. **John Jensen**. Toad House. 1998. 5" H, stoneware. Attached is his descriptive card which serves as a sales and marketing tool. This piece is also shown in the color section. (Photo by the artist)*

# A Packaging System

*Jonathan Kaplan is a potter, teacher, and entrepreneur. He offers the following advice.*

My feeling is that if one spends a lot of time on their work, with clients and delivery dates that are important, why wouldn't the same effort that goes into making your work carry over into proper packing? I have used the same packaging system for as long as I have been making and selling pots, which is well over 25 years and the system works. Yes, it may cost a bit more, but I have better things to do with my time than deal with shipping damage and claims through endless phone calls from customers and doing the UPS paperwork. The key is to double box everything that leaves your shop. Here's the system.

1) Find two sizes of stock boxes that have a 2" differential on all sides, top, and bottom. For example, the combination of a 22" cube exterior box and an 18" cube interior box.

2) The 2" void around the inner box is taken up by "Grey Filler Flats" which are used in the egg industry. These are 12" by 12" by 2" egg holders. Grey filler flats are available from Atlas Paper Company (800) 264-5765.

3) Place a layer of these on the bottom inside of the outer box. Tape, staple, or glue a layer on each side of the inner box and insert the box into the outer one.

4) Pack the inner box. Items are wrapped in bubble wrap and items are grouped into modules and taped together. Use corrugated shims and flats where necessary to isolate the work from each other. Overfill the interior box with Styrofoam and shake rattle and roll to fill all voids. Seal the inner box.

5) Place a layer of filler flats on top of the inner box and seal the outer box. Clearly label the box FRAGILE to inform UPS of the nature of the contents and to also help substantiate a claim for damage if there is to be one.

This constructs a bomb-proof system that not only isolates the work in the inner box from its neighbors, but also isolates the inner box from the outer box. And for all who are recycle conscious, we collect and reuse the loads of otherwise discarded peanuts and bubble wrap from other businesses in town. My best advice is not to skimp on your packing. If you do, it is usually returned to you in broken useless shards.

UPS is by far the most popular method of shipping among craftspeople. UPS is affordable, convenient, reliable, reasonably safe, and if you follow all the rules, easy to collect from if your work is damaged in transport. When packing for shipping via a commercial carrier, you must first know the expectations and requirements of that carrier. For instance, UPS has a size limit of 130" in combined length and girth and a weight limit of 150 pounds as well as an unwritten assumption that the contents of a package will not be damaged if dropped from a height of two feet. If the contents of a package are damaged, a representative will inspect the damage as well as the packaging and if it appears the packaging was adequate, will approve the claim. I often joke that UPS is the largest collector of my work! The truth is that over the years I have lost work to UPS, yet I have never had a claim for damage turned down. I make it a point to over-pack my work, not so my claim will be approved but so the work will arrive unscathed.

## Selling Methods

You can't actually make a sale without coming to terms with the details of pricing structure, discounts, and commissions. There are three main ways you will sell your work and fix prices, each with advantages and disadvantages.

**Retail** sales are when you, as the maker of the ware, sell that ware to the buyer at full price. This can take place out of your studio, at a retail craft fair, or in some other informal situation. Selling your work at retail gives you the highest rate of return for your creative efforts—a distinct advantage. The clear sacrifice here is that in order to earn that full price, you have to put in the time and effort to make the sales, thus reducing the time you have for production. Take a quick look back at the section on your studio as a sales gallery. Is your time better spent as a potter or as a shop owner or salesperson? Either way, someone has to facilitate the sale and whoever that person is will be earning a commission on the sale. Confused? Think about it. If you are the one making the sale, the time you spend away from production means less work produced, less work available for sale, and less income. However, by selling at retail, you have effectively paid yourself the additional money you would have otherwise paid to a shop to sell the work for you. Whether that amount is sufficient to cover your time and effort is something only you can decide.

**Consignment** is when a shop or gallery displays your work and pays you only after an actual sale is made. A predetermined percentage of the retail price will go to the potter and the balance will be retained by the gallery. A shop will typically adhere to a fixed payment schedule where, for instance, checks are sent to craftspeople on a monthly basis. The commission you pay the shop is their fee for marketing and selling your work. However, since the shop hasn't invested any money in your work, their risk is minimized. This usually (though not always) translates into a commission in favor of the craftsperson. A fair consignment arrangement is 60/40 with 60% of the sale price to the potter and 40% to the shop. Many shops and galleries do business with a 50/50 arrangement, especially if they are located in high

rent, upscale locations where operating costs can be extremely high.

Critical to the consignment arrangement is that all dollar amounts are figured from a fixed retail price agreed upon by the shop and the potter. (Contrast this with the method galleries use to arrive at retail prices in wholesale purchasing arrangements below.) Consignment arrangements are often a craftsperson's introduction to marketing their wares through shops and galleries, since a shop is more likely to take a chance on a new line of work or a young craftsperson if their risk is minimal. On the other hand, a consignment policy also makes it easier for a new shop to get off the ground, since no money needs to be tied up in inventory.

Clear and substantial bookkeeping is required by both parties to keep track of work on premises, work sold and paid for, work sold and not paid for, work not sold, work returned, new work delivered, etc. Sales progress and the state of your wares can be very difficult to monitor if you have pots at several shops, all covered by consignment agreements. For these and other reasons, consignment situations are best entered into with galleries and shops within your geographical region. It can be difficult enough working with a local shop if things aren't going according to your liking. Having to deal from a distance by phone, letter, and UPS can be a nightmare. This is not to say you should avoid consigning to galleries outside your area. There are many fine galleries that will do you and your work justice and do business honestly and promptly, regardless of their proximity to your studio.

Successful consignment arrangements depend on a clear understanding of the terms of the agreement which must be spelled out in a formal contract. Any reputable shop or gallery will present a standard consignment contract indicating:

1) List of the works involved.
2) Retail prices.
3) Length of time the work will be in the shop.
4) Commission paid to the craftsperson.
5) When payment will be made.
6) Insurance coverage against loss or damage of the work.
7) Statement indicating ownership belonging to the potter.

Additional stipulations may include an exclusivity agreement based on a certain geographical area, whether the artist can remove their work from the shop and how much notice must be given to do so, how much of the artist's work will be on open display at a given time, and other variations. If the shop doesn't offer a consignment contract, you can certainly present one of your own but I would be very wary. A contract is as much for the shop as it is for the potter and a shop that overlooks or minimizes this important aspect of sales strategy, to me, is suspect.

My advice? Avoid consignment whenever possible. The record keeping and tracking of your wares is a bother and why should you bear the brunt of the financial risk? A reasonable compromise would be to agree to consign as you begin a relationship with a new shop but switch to wholesale as soon as your sales show growth and promise.

**Wholesale** is when a shop buys your work outright on speculation that it will eventually sell the work. Full financial risk is assumed by the gallery because they become the owners of your work if it doesn't sell. Wholesale arrangements are neat and clean with no loose ends. The gallery places an order, you deliver the work, send an invoice, receive the check, and it's done. Nothing to keep track of except the next order coming in and going out.

Unlike consignment arrangements, when you make a sale to a gallery, a contract is unnecessary. There is an understanding between the gallery and the potter that centers around responsibility and professional obligations regarding delivery time, accuracy of the order, payment terms, and the like, but these are mostly common business practices and not issues that would be spelled out in a contract. For these reasons and the fact that the gallery can earn more money from the sale of your work when they buy it outright, wholesale purchasing is the preferred method of doing business by the vast majority of shops and galleries.

Expect to be paid 50% of the usual retail price of your work, although retail pricing rarely has anything to do with wholesale arrangements. When a gallery is considering your work, they will take your wholesale price, add an amount to cover shipping and handling, tack on their own administrative fee, and arrive at a retail price that might be in the neighborhood of 210% to 250% of what they paid you, well over a 100% markup. For instance, a vessel I would retail out of my studio for $300 carries a wholesale price of $150 to a gallery. After they add their markup and fees, the retail price becomes $337.50, $37.50 more than I would sell it for myself. This pricing may strike you as unfair, but that attitude is narrow-minded and shortsighted. Galleries serve a very important role in the marketing of our wares and they have to make a profit to stay in business. If you view the gallery and craftsperson as adversaries, you are missing the boat. We need each other, and the best galleries and most astute craftspeople work together to make each other successful.

If galleries and shops are reluctant to buy your work outright, there are a few strategies you can try to help make a sale easier to accept. As suggested above, you can agree to begin with a consignment arrangement with a switch to outright purchasing when your sales reach a certain level of consistency. Another suggestion is to agree to an outright purchase with the understanding that you will exchange work that has not sold after an agreed upon length of time, say six months. This arrangement reduces some of the risk, giving the gallery a bit more confidence in their decision to buy your work. Yet another arrangement would be to agree to consign a certain number of pieces if an equal number are purchased.

Just as a gallery might be reluctant to buy your work outright, you must exercise good judgment when making a sale to a gallery for the first time. Check credit references, especially other crafts-people they buy from. Find out how promptly they pay their bills and how easy they are to do business with. Regardless of the credit report, your first order should either be cash on delivery (COD) where you are paid immediately when your work in delivered, or via a pro-forma invoice where you send an invoice for an order that is pre-pared for delivery. Upon receipt of payment, the order is shipped. Many galleries find COD terms difficult to deal with, which is understandable since receiving a COD delivery can disrupt the daily activities of a busy shop. A pro-forma invoice can be examined and if any questions or concerns arise, they can be dealt with in a relaxed fashion.

## Pricing

Here it is, the bane of most craftspeople. To many, pricing work is either an almost arbitrary act or one that occupies so much time, effort, analysis, and intellect that they forget what their goal is and who they are! Arriving at fair values for your work is a vital aspect of marketing and sales, but is not something that should bog you down in a corporate mentality where spreadsheets and expense reports make bedtime reading.

Many books and business manuals offer de-tailed cost analysis equations that will result in painfully accurate prices for the items you make. However, where does that leave you if your equa-tion for coffee mugs results in a retail price of $32 or $4? There is a certain degree of adjustment that must be made when fixing prices to reflect the re-ality of the marketplace. All methods of "correct" pricing are figured upwards from analyzing your costs to arrive at a price that recovers those costs and generates a profit. Yet the science of pricing warns that there are generally accepted price ceil-ings and when an item exceeds it, it meets with re-sistance. So, another way to arrive at a reasonable pricing structure is to examine the market, com-pare prices of similar work, and try to price your work in the same general zone. If that means making adjustments in your production style to reduce your costs, then make it happen. When pricing, keep in mind that the discerning public will pay more for an item with impeccable crafts-manship, consistent captivating design, or unique function, so don't automatically reduce your pric-es if they seem a little higher than the established norm.

Costing and pricing are two terms that need ex-planation and although they are intimately relat-ed, should be kept separate. Costing is the analysis of what your expenses are to produce an item and will include the following:

1) Production costs—the isolated costs of making a single item (clay, glazes, other materials, firing, and labor).

2) Overhead, or the fixed costs of operating your studio—expenses that are not produc-tion dependent. That is, they remain rela-tively constant regardless of how much clay you are throwing. Among these costs are rent, utilities, phone, advertising, insurance, taxes, office supplies, postage, travel, etc.

3) Selling costs—additional expenses that are directly related to the sale of your work but are not reflected in the cost of materials. These expenses include booth fees and trav-el (if you exhibit at shows), packing and shipping, advertising, additional labor, de-livery time (if you make your own deliver-

ies), bank or credit card fees as they relate to sales transactions, among others.

By analyzing these costs and expenses, you can begin to see the actual dollars involved in each item you make.

Pricing is the next step and involves taking your costing figures for an item, adding to it a reasonable profit, and arriving at a wholesale price for that item. It's important to make the distinction between profit and wages or salary. Many craftspeople make the mistake of equating the two, when they are actually two different components of the same equation. Profit is above and beyond what you might pay in labor costs to have a product manufactured. It makes no difference if that labor is supplied by you or others in your employ—labor is a cost of production. Many craftspeople forget to include a salary for themselves as a part of regular operating expenses!

Profit is a reasonable additional amount that gives the business funds for a financial cushion. This money might be used to invest in additional equipment or other means of growth and to reward the efforts of the person who founded the company or who assumes the primary financial risk of operating the business. Profit is an established aspect of the business financial picture and must not be omitted.

One of the components in analyzing selling costs—shipping and packing—are often undercharged, which results in a failure to recover the actual expense involved. Since these are costs unique to individual orders and shipments, it is best to arrive at a formula for assessing these charges. A common method is to charge the actual shipping fee plus a percentage (in the range of 2% to 5%) of the wholesale value of the order. This additional fee helps to recover the cost of packing materials and labor.

Your pricing equation must result in a wholesale price, as that is the price you will be forced to sell the item for unless you sell at retail out of your studio or at retail craft fairs. The standard means of arriving at the retail price is to double the wholesale price. Since you have already figured in the cost of selling, you might look at the difference between the wholesale price and retail price as a bonus of sorts. This difference is the amount that allows a shop or gallery to market your wares for you, cover their expenses, and make a profit. As mentioned above, some galleries more than double your wholesale price to cover expenses or maintain a higher profit margin.

These examples of cost and pricing analysis are fine for production type items, but what if your work is one-of-a-kind, limited-edition, exhibition-type wares made more slowly and more reflective of aesthetic attraction and appreciation than everyday decorative wares? Similar costing must be done to understand your overall expenses, but pricing your wares will undoubtedly be figured by comparing it to wares of similar size, style, and other less tangible factors such as the name of the artist, their established following, and all that contributes to being a well known and recognizable personality in your craft.

Prices must reflect consistency and logic and cannot be affected by subjective standards. A series of vases of similar size and technique should be priced the same or very near the same. Never modify the prices of your work according to your likes and dislikes. Earlier I talked extensively about aesthetic and technical standards and how anything you put out for display or sale must meet a minimum standard you have established for yourself. Once you have done this, your work must be judged on its aesthetic merits without any additional input from you. While you may like one piece more than another, setting prices in this way will appear arbitrary and make no sense to anyone else. Your customers may be very sophisticated, but they can only react to what is put before them and they can only judge an item according to their own reflection and common sense. Likewise, when I am asked by a client or customer which piece I like the best, I try to answer in a way that reflects the personal nature of choosing a craft object, thereby taking the responsibility off me and putting it back on them. I assure them that if they buy what they like, it will be the right decision.

Novices to marketing are often so concerned with setting the absolute correct price that they become frozen with no price at all. There is no advantage to setting prices that are too low. Indeed, low prices can sometimes work against sales by communicating a false sense that the work isn't worth as much as a similar piece by another potter and must be defective or less desirable in some way. On the other hand, prices that are too high

---

## Earnings, Time, and Weight!

*Bob Kavanagh is a potter and the dean of White Mountain Academy of the Arts in Elliot Lake, Ontario. He is passionate about working with clay and his desire to simplify his approach is illustrated in his unusual method of pricing.*

Several years ago, I established a rule of thumb for pricing my work. A friend of mine who was a jeweler had reduced all his pricing concerns to one variable and it seemed like a simple guide. I chose weight as the variable because it was easy to measure. There are quite a few assumptions in what I do, not the least of which is that my dollars are Canadian. Simply put, I multiply the amount of wet clay for an object by a given retail dollar value, most recently set at $22 a pound. A coffee mug is a pound of moist clay, handle included; I retail my mugs at $22 and wholesale them at $11. When I established this rule I had factored in several matters, including:

1) Market ceiling for work comparable to mine.
2) The amount of money I needed to generate as profit or net income as an individual apart from my business.
3) The percentage of my overall sales from the previous few years that was "cost" and what was "net income."
4) My sales distribution at the time was 75%

wholesale, a small percentage retail out of my shop, and the rest at craft fairs.
5) My production capacity and how much weight I could throw in a given time period.
6) I always factored in my favorite pots in any given production cycle.
7) I try to push my prices up whenever I can and this ends up getting reflected in the formula and other issues of this sort.

At first, I always checked my calculations and felt a little silly figuring out price from wet pounds, but after a while it became natural. When I throw bowls, large plates, or big vases that are not my usual production line, forms for the first time, or if I get confused and simply forget to weigh my clay, I can still price by weight using a reverse calculation. Taking into account trimming, drying, and weight loss due to firings, the wet clay is about 1.6 times the weight of the fired pot.

I still allow myself a personal intervention in pricing when I feel it necessary. Occasionally, a pot that I really like to make or that I am trying to find a market for just won't sell at the price my rule says, and I might have to lower it. I will also adjust prices upwards to reflect a more difficult or time consuming process or technique (teapots for instance), and occasionally I still price a pot very high just because I like it so much that I figure someone will have to pay a fair amount of money if they want to take it away from me.

can communicate arrogance and a degree of exclusivity that may be way beyond reason.

Once you have come to terms with at least a general price range for your work, there is nothing wrong with asking the shop or gallery owner for some advice and guidance. Contrary to what you might hear from some craftspeople, a gallery has nothing to gain by having work on display that is priced too low or too high. Every item has its optimum price and there is no one better qualified than the owner of the shop to help you set that price.

Keep in mind that if your work is priced fairly and sells well, prices can easily be raised to more accurately reflect its true value and the forces of supply and demand. Customers will recognize this, and as long as those prices remain logical and within reason, there is no reason your work won't continue to sell. However, if your work is not selling because your prices are too high, lowering prices will most likely not result in increased interest in your work. Lowered prices communicate sale, clearance, liquidate, vacate, depart, and evaporate! Customers will notice the change but will have already conditioned themselves to pass by your work. It will be back to square one with new work in a new shop.

Another aspect of pricing is maintaining consistency in the selling prices of your work when it appears in different venues and areas of the country. Often, the craftsperson will assume that large cities boast a higher standard of living, people who are more sophisticated, and markets that will bear higher prices than smaller less cosmopolitan cities. This may be true, but the intrinsic value of your work remains the same regardless of where it is on exhibit. In fact, it may actually cost you more, thereby reducing your profit, to get your work to a more out of the way place where the market may be less receptive. Regional pricing is condescending to those in smaller cities and pe-

nalizes your clients in the areas you feel can support higher prices.

Keeping pricing consistent is an indication of fairness, confidence, and professionalism. There is, however, only so much you can do to maintain authority over the ultimate pricing of your work once it's delivered to a shop. Unless there is an issue of dishonesty or miscommunication between yourself and the shop, your prices will remain as you marked them in consignment situations. When a gallery buys your work outright, there is an implied freedom on their part to price your work as they see fit. Most galleries do their best to keep your work priced as close to the recommended retail price as possible. Don't allow a shop to persuade you to lower your prices to match the local market.

How about the issue of discounting your work when you sell it out of your studio? Big no no. Many customers feel they deserve a discount for purchasing directly from the potter. After all, they realize you are paying a commission of some kind when you sell through a shop so why not pass that on to the customer who seeks you out to buy direct? Here are just a few reasons why this is a major mistake. First, if I have communicated anything at all about pricing, it should be that your work has a certain value at a certain time in the marketplace. This value is the same regardless of the actual dollars you may receive for it—less for a wholesale purchase, a bit more in a consignment situation, full value at a retail fair or out of your studio. By discounting your work, you are in effect saying that yes, the piece would be $500 in a gallery but it's really only worth $300, so go ahead, do me a favor and buy it. Don't feel guilty about charging full price. You deserve the occasional "bonus." Take the opportunity to educate the public about the value of your pots. The second reason is one that impacts the entire field of crafts and art. Whether you sell out of your studio or not, at some point you will need a gallery or shop to sell your work. Even if you never use the services of a gallery, your fellow potters do, and by selling your work directly at a discount, you undermine the effort and the very existence of those shops in business to sell your work.

As in most situations, there is room for small adjustments and incentives. You may feel you want to reward customers who collect or purchase your work from you on a regular basis, or perhaps you feel you can afford to offer a small discount for a purchase of several pieces. Keep the discounts small, say 10% or so. Use your good judgment and formulate a plan before the situation presents itself and you are caught off guard.

Arriving at prices for commission work requires some additional considerations. Generally speaking, a commission can legitimately command a slightly higher price than your regular line of work. The higher price reflects a departure from your usual production schedule, any techniques or processes that might be out of the ordinary for you, as well as the simple fact that this is a "special" project. Prices should be thought out carefully and presented only after you have had a chance to review them at your leisure. Never feel pressured to state a price spontaneously because once you do, you will be forced to live with it.

Pricing is an issue that confronts us all at some point. Take your time to examine all the factors that contribute to the fair and equitable sale of your work. Anticipate and come up with a sensible approach, doing your best to get it right the first time.

## Promotional Tools

If you were to rank the most important aspects of being a craftsperson, you would most likely first think of your commitment to your craft and the objects you make—two private and solitary

elements to crafts making. However, if you have aspirations of going beyond the confines of your studio and into the marketplace, you will have to begin thinking about a third element of craftmaking—your image. The way you present yourself precedes and helps to influence any impression your work may have on a client, gallery owner, or anyone you may have the occasion to do business with.

### Printed Materials

Your image is a composite of two sides of the same coin: your personal appearance, eloquence, and sincerity; and the printed material in the form of cards, brochures, photographs, announcements, letterhead, advertisements, resume, and more that represents you and your work. You cannot afford to be careless or to skimp on the effort to develop a personal style that is warm, honest, and appealing while remaining professional and businesslike. At the same time, an equal effort must go into the design, use, and distribution of printed materials to promote and advertise your work.

Business stationary, envelopes, note cards, and business cards are basic to any collection of promotional materials and are often not even thought

*Figure 7-5. Logos of The Potters Shop and The Potters School. A logo can represent your identity and serve to harmonize all your promotional tools. Designed by the author.*

*Figure 7-6. Carol Temkin's business card is well designed and communicates elegance. The teapot is her unifying logo, appearing on all her printed material. (Courtesy of Carol Temkin)*

of as image setting instruments. These items are absolutely necessary tools for running your business. After all, are you really going to consider writing letters on plain white paper stuffed in a plain white envelope? When you meet someone and wish to exchange phone numbers, are you going to fumble for a scrap piece of paper or are you going to hand them a distinctive looking business card? I'm not going to discuss graphic design, but a consultation with a professional who designs logos and business image solutions would be a worthwhile move. And by the way, this would be a fertile opportunity to barter your work as a potter for their work as a designer!

Depending on the nature of what you do and your goals and intentions in the area of marketing and promotion, your battery of printed tools may include a brochure, catalog, descriptive product tag, resume, biography, personal statement, and more, in addition to the items mentioned above. A graphic designer can not only help you come up with an appropriate look and feel for your promotional tools, but will design them as a package where all the components coordinate. Your logo

will usually be the unifying feature. It can be in the form of an identifiable icon, symbol, signature, or some other distinct graphic detail. As skilled and competent as you may be in graphics and design, it is important to include outside input in the design of your promotional package. The images you think represent you most advantageously may be way off base.

Just as useful as promotional and marketing tools are copies of articles, reviews, interviews, letters, and other media items. These are integral to promotional packages and should be stored in a systematic fashion for easy retrieval and distribution.

## Photography

Perhaps the most important promotional tools at your disposal are visual images of your work. You will need current photos and slides on an ongoing basis and should keep those files organized and arranged chronologically. Images should be labeled with name, date, technique, and dimensions, with additional information as may be requested by a jury or gallery. My system of slide organization utilizes a loose leaf binder and transparent slide pages. Original slides are numbered and inserted in the pages chronologically. Opposite each slide page is a sheet with a record of the sale or other fate of each piece. Duplicates of each slide are stored in metal slide file boxes and those are the only slides that are ever sent out. Never violate that rule by removing a slide from your binder! If you do, you may be left without an image of a piece. Since I make one-of-a-kind exhibition pieces, the foundation of my slide/photo record system is that I photograph every piece, without exception. If you do multiple works or production pottery, photos of a sample of each type of ware you make is adequate. Any time I need a slide of my work, I look in the binder, select the piece, and pick out a copy from the slide file box. No bumbling, fumbling, or delay!

When you send slides with an application to a craft fair or competition, the prospectus will usually state that slides will be returned only if a self-addressed stamped envelope (SASE) is included. In this case, you can be reasonably certain your slides will be returned. However, when I send slides to a gallery or shop, whether solicited or unsolicited, I assume that I will never see the slides again and this is a wise attitude. It further goes to the advice of never sending out original slides.

As you might suspect, photography can be an expensive proposition if you have to hire a photographer. Not to worry, any craftsperson can learn to take competent slides of their own work and there is ample literature available to teach you how to do this. Books and articles on photographing art and craft work will guide you step-by-step through choosing equipment, selecting film, setup, lighting, processing options, and more. Take the time to learn the techniques and purchase quality equipment. It is an investment of time and money well spent. Although I can take quite adequate photos, I hire a photographer in certain cases and for special projects when I feel the requirements and standards of the photo are beyond my capabilities. It pays to know your limits!

## Advertising

Promoting yourself and your work is a two-part effort. First, you respond to inquiries, solicitations, and existing opportunities and situations as you find them (the announcement of a craft fair or a gallery with a classified ad looking for new work, for example). Second is creating such op-portunities and this is what can be called advertising.

Print media advertising is a very underutilized method of generating sales among potters, mostly because other avenues of promotion and sales are more natural and available. However, more and more craftspeople are using the media to promote their wares. A glance in an issue of *The Crafts Report* reveals many ads of different styles, each calling attention to a specific craft or item. Advertising can take the form of small, relatively inexpensive classified ads or more visible and distinctive display advertising. Paramount to successful classified ads is being descriptive and brief in your copy. Add visually appealing when considering display ads. You may advertise a product or series of items or your ad may be designed to generate interest in your catalog or other extensive listing of the wares you produce. You may be interested in attracting the retail customer or the wholesale buyer. The graphics professional you consult for designing promotional material can help you form an advertising strategy.

If advertising your wares in the media doesn't interest you right now, don't dismiss it altogether—it may be relevant at a later time. It's important to realize that any situation where you show your stuff is advertising. When folks come into your booth at a fair or visit a gallery and see your work, you are advertising. If marketing and sales are to take place, you must embrace the notion of advertising in one way or another!

Don't let the prospect of sales and marketing intimidate you into a frozen state of inaction. You can enter this phase of your career slowly, with care and caution, gradually picking up speed as you gain experience and confidence. And while most any mistake you make along the way can be corrected, you might as well make an effort to do it right the first time.

# Chapter 8

## Teaching

### On Teaching

*Then said a teacher, Speak to us of Teaching.*
*And he said:*
*No man can reveal to you aught but that which already likes half asleep in the dawning of your knowledge.*
*The teacher who walks in the shadow of the temple, among his followers, gives not of his wisdom but rather of his faith and his lovingness.*
*If he is indeed wise he does not bid you enter the house of his wisdom, but rather leads you to the threshold of your own mind.*
*The astronomer may speak to you of his understanding of space, but he cannot give you his understanding.*
*The musician may sing to you of the rhythm which is in all space, but he cannot give you the ear which arrests the rhythm nor the voice that echoes it.*
*And he who is versed in the science of numbers can tell of the regions of weight and measure, but he cannot conduct you thither,*
*For the vision of one man lends not its wings to another man.*
*And even as each one of you stands alone in God's knowledge, so must each one of you be alone in his knowledge of God and in his understanding of the earth.*

--from "The Prophet" by Kahlil Gibran

Perhaps you find Gibran's words a bit too ponderous, formidable, pensive, and profound. Indeed you are probably surprised to see them here in the first place. Are all these powerful principles necessary if all you want to do is teach a few pottery classes? In a word, yes. For teaching—whether it be pottery, philosophy, history, or literature—is not an activity to be taken lightly.

Teaching for me is an activity I do with joy, love, and dedication, and the personal rewards that I've reaped are numerous. To witness the exhilaration and satisfaction on the face of a student who, for the first time, succeeds at a task, masters a skill, or realizes a concept, is a reward unlike any other. I always admired my teachers and from an early age felt drawn to teaching as a possible profession.

However, after reflecting on my own experiences as a teacher and how I would present them in this book, I couldn't help but be reminded of all the assumptions and generalizations that are often made with regard to craftspeople or artists teaching. You've heard them too, I'm sure. "Those who can't do, teach" is a popular cliché that transcends the craft world and is supposed to apply to any trained professional who chooses to teach instead of practicing that profession. Another prevailing attitude is that a craft maker or artist only resorts to teaching when they can't support themselves through the sale of their work. Teaching is presented as an inferior occupation, taking a back seat to the more noble activity of producing and selling craft objects. So I was faced with a dilemma: will a section on the virtues and craft of teaching be viewed with skepticism and as a sort of career decision cop-out, explaining what to do if the professional pottery thing doesn't work out? I know that many craftspeople—whether they support themselves from the sale of their work or not—take a dim view of craft and art teachers. Frankly, it's a senseless attitude. After all, how did they learn their craft?

The "teachers can't be real potters" view sometimes evolves from craftspeople who find it difficult to support themselves solely from the sale of their work and turn to teaching to make financial ends meet. This can sometimes lead to teachers who are less than skilled and far from as committed and passionate about teaching as they are about making pots. At worst, this results in teachers who compromise and demean not only the craft through poor teaching, but themselves as creative, purposeful, and honest individuals.

Many of you are either currently teaching or are considering being a teacher. Understand that what I have to say here is not the final word, nor is it the complete story. I do hope, however, that it is enough to help guide you towards being a good teacher—one who is prepared for and engaged in teaching for the right reasons.

## Does Teaching Fit Into Your Scheme?

First you must consider the question of whether teaching fits into your overall scheme. Ask yourself and honestly answer a few basic questions to help unravel the uncertainties you may be feeling.

1) Why does teaching appeal to you?

2) Is teaching something you are drawn to?

3) What strengths do you have to offer as a teacher?

4) Who do you want to teach?

5) Are there opportunities, institutions, and venues for you to plug into, or will you teach in your studio?

6) Will teaching be a sacrifice, taking valuable time away from clay making or will it be an integrated and important component in your career as a creative individual?

7) Will teaching be at the forefront of your professional activities?

Much to the surprise of many, being a teacher and a serious maker of craft objects are not mutually exclusive. The two disciplines can coexist, though it does take a special effort requiring powerful energy, interest, and driving dedication. Just as you have a passion for your craft, you must have a passion for teaching. Can you be passionate about both the *making* of craft objects and *teaching* the making of craft objects? Only you can answer the question and to be fair, you probably can't answer it now. Put it in the back of your mind, but realize that to be the best at what you do, you'll have to answer it at some point.

Despite any uncertainty you feel now about your interest in teaching, resist the impulse to teach out of necessity. That's not the way to get involved in a profession as vital and influential as teaching can be. Yes, success stories abound about artists and craft makers who are thrust into teaching, but these are the exceptions and not the norm. Indeed, many of those stories have sad endings. Consider teaching only because you want to do it and are confident you can be good at it.

## The Art of Teaching

*If you teach, you perform a sacred duty and just as one teaches with spirit one learns with spirit.*

-Robert Piepenburg from
"Treasures of the Creative Spirit"

Teaching is a craft, an art, and a skill. Teaching is academic, intellectual, and emotional. All your personal reasons for becoming a craftsperson—passion, drive, desire, need, and the other inner forces that direct your energy and interest—apply to becoming a teacher. To be a good teacher and excel at that difficult task, you must possess intimate knowledge of the subject matter and have the ability to share that knowledge with your students. Sounds logical? The notion that any moderate degree of proficiency in a field is adequate

*Figure 8-1. Children as young as age five learn to make pots both on and off the wheel at The Potters School. (Photo by the author)*

as long as it is one step beyond that of the students is at best, naive and simpleminded, and at worst, a detriment to the student's education. The teaching profession is filled with individuals who lack expertise in their field of study and are trained more in the discipline of how to teach rather than what to teach. I admit that my standards are high and to some, unreasonably so. Too bad. Indeed, it doesn't take an master thrower to teach the basics of centering and throwing simple forms, just like it doesn't take a mathematician with a Phd. to present an inspiring unit of Algebra I. So what defines "intimate knowledge of the subject matter?" It is a fluid ability and comfort with the subject. It is a fluency that has been mastered through failure and repetition. It is ease, and freedom, and an effortlessness with the vocabulary. It is confidence and skill.

Does intimate knowledge of the subject matter make you the don, maestro, guru, sensei, or singular expert? No. Does it mean you know everything there is to know about the subject matter you teach? No. Because what you also must possess is humility and the realization that you can't possibly know everything. There must always be room for you to be questioned and for you to question. There must always be more for you to learn and you must always be active in that learning.

Admittedly, this whole idea sounds most broadminded and modest—which are two important personal characteristics for a teacher to have. But you'll need to be a bit more precise in your self-evaluation of knowledge. Along with admitting that you don't know everything, you must also be able to identify your strengths and weaknesses. You're a master at hand forming techniques, but not very experienced on the wheel. You can mix glaze recipes and know all the steps and procedures in that process but have limited knowledge of glaze chemistry or technology. Plug yourself into the equation. Realizing and acing your weaknesses is the first phase, doing something about them is the next.

A good teacher must have as much interest in the areas they don't know or understand as in the areas they are expert in. There are teachers who exist only within their academic comfort zone. For them, nothing belongs in the classroom or studio beyond their experience and expertise and they operate within a very limited scope. Within this scope, knowledge turns to familiarity, which degrades to routine. Not likely to lead to inspiration in the classroom.

Don't try to teach something you don't know. It sounds obvious, but as a teacher, it is easy to get caught in the frenzy of being surrounded by students looking to you for inspiration and knowledge. The best teachers recognize that their knowledge and experience is only part of the picture and they freely admit this by saying the words, "I don't know" when faced with a question they can't answer. Instead they encourage and help their students to find out more. Hey, you can learn at the same time! The most important thing a teacher can do to benefit their students is inspire a thirst and a curiosity for knowledge. A good teacher needs to communicate their love of the craft through an equal degree of love and passion for the act of teaching.

## Teacher Training

Teaching must be learned and practiced. The particular teaching environment, student population, and skills to be taught determine what qualifications are necessary to teach in that environment. Teaching a basic high school pottery course within the context of a larger art department is very different than presenting a course with similar content to a class of adult education students at the local art center. Considerations of detail, depth, style of presentation, and even the choice of words are very different. The comparison between a basic first ceramics course to majors in a liberal arts college and one taught in a professional art school can be equally distinct despite the apparent similarity in the students. Even with the best of intentions, you cannot enter into a teaching situation and hope to be effective without training, practice, and a high level of commitment.

Quality teacher training can take many forms and it need not require a college degree in education. That is not the end-all in preparation, though it certainly can provide a solid foundation. If you are contemplating an undergraduate degree in art education, read the fine print and carefully investigate the program before you send in your check. Traditionally, art education programs exist to provide teacher certification to meet the standards of the state where the college is located. Teacher certification will generally result in the granting of a state teacher's license, giving the holder the necessary credentials to teach in public schools. (Conveniently, teacher certificates issued in one state are often valid in other states.) To achieve this end, the curriculums of art education programs consist mostly of courses that teach more educational theory, philosophy, and general teaching methods than you ever imagined. Much less emphasis is placed on achieving a degree of knowledge or expertise in a chosen studio area. Realize that there is a serious sacrifice to be made here, resulting in a rather forbidding irony—giving up time in the studio actively learning about the practice of your craft to spend time in the classroom learning how to teach a subject you don't quite know enough about!

Frankly, I don't generally think highly of undergraduate art teacher education programs. That is not to say the content of these programs is bogus. On the contrary, they offer some very valuable and irreplaceable components, one of which is the opportunity to practice or student teach. The value of the student teaching experience depends on the following factors that are often out of your control: the school you are assigned, the style and quality of its art program, your supervising teacher, and the caliber of the students. All practice teaching experiences have value and will impart important skills, impressions, and understanding, but the ultimate value and usefulness of the experience and what you, as a developing teacher, may gain and be able to put to use is unknown when you begin. At best, you can hope for a practice teaching experience that will give you the confidence and ease to go into the classroom or studio with minimal nervousness, an ability to prepare for your teaching day, maintain focus and concentration, and be able to apply the managerial skills necessary to preside over a class and the facilities. If that sounds like a tall order, you're right, it is! If you haven't yet thought about those aspects of teaching, you are taking some of the most vital teaching skills for granted.

As a novice, regardless of the teaching venue, you will make mistakes. Learn from your mistakes and don't make the same ones twice. Like any other craft, teaching is one you grow with, and if your heart is in it, teaching grows within you.

An effective teacher treats the classroom and contact with students as a dialogue. You have knowledge and information to pass on, but your knowledge is not without limitations, gaps, and holes. Believe it or not, some of these holes will be filled through a conversation with a student or other teaching/learning exchange that results in a discovery for you. The sooner you understand that teaching doesn't move in a single direction and that teaching is dynamic, moving in many directions between student and teacher, the sooner you will find yourself on the path to continued growth and maturity in the teaching profession.

The best teachers generally develop in schools that offer periodic evaluations, criticism, and encouragement. Many grade schools, high schools, and colleges provide mentoring programs that pair young teachers with experienced ones. This can be a wonderful experience for both participants. Young teachers are helped towards mastering solid skills and style while the experienced teachers are faced with a mirror in which to view themselves.

When it comes right down to it, though, teaching, like the crafting of objects, requires practice and an attitude that welcomes constant learning, growth, flexibility, and fluidity.

## Teaching in Your Studio

Assuming that you are trained and ready to teach, a tempting notion may be to do some teaching out of your studio. Kids or adult classes or private instruction are realistic possibilities. Teaching may also take the form of offering an apprenticeship or work-study arrangement.

First to consider when contemplating any of these scenarios is your own working style and how suitable that style and your space is now or how it might be altered to accommodate other people. How important is your privacy? Are you prepared to share your space, even on a limited scale? How will the dual utilization of your workspace as both studio and classroom affect your work habits and comfort? These are essential questions to consider and they must not be taken lightly. If you rationalize that "It's only one class a week," or "It's only five students," you are being dangerously unrealistic and doing a serious disservice to yourself. A teaching space involves not only the time the class is in session, but all the peripheral support that goes along with the class, including storing work in progress, bisque ware, kiln space and firing time, tools for class use, increased burden on clay containment systems and clay recycling, and more. Will the students use your glazes, risking contamination? As the students take their place in your studio, consider the safety of your own works in progress. How fussy are you if you find a tool or other object out of place, or worse, lost?

Throughout this discussion, I have made the assumption that you are an individual potter in a space of your own, but the same considerations apply equally to any existing workspace, whether it be two people sharing a studio or a large group. Again, imagine the impact on your present situation by the addition of just one more person, say an apprentice, helper, or equal studio member. What would their role be? Where would they work? Where would they store their wares? As you ponder the addition of a single person, you can begin to imagine the effect a class might have. This is not intended to discourage you from teaching out of your studio. It is meant to make you aware of the special considerations to be addressed when you plan to use your workspace as a classroom.

On a more encouraging note, even the smallest and modest of spaces can be arranged to accommodate more than one person. Keep in mind that the key factors are your own work style and idiosyncrasies and the number of additional people you can realistically accommodate. Think it through, being responsible to yourself and each other and if you can see solutions to the issues that will present themselves, then by all means, go for it!

In the face of all of this concern, possible inconvenience, and reservations you might have, can there be any positive aspects to having others share your workspace? Absolutely yes. I have thoroughly enjoyed having a studio within a larger community of potters. I enjoy the contact and interaction with others on a multitude of levels. I find reward and satisfaction in being able to offer my help and advice to others and I have equally benefited from the experiences and personalities that others bring to the studio. Having a space with others, either studio mates or students, keeps you from being isolated. In many ways, it forces you to confront your work and reasons for doing what you do in a kind of public forum on a semi-regular, if not more frequent, basis. This is a very good thing.

My studio, The Potters Shop and School, is a multi-functioning space. It is large by some standards (over 2,500 sq. ft.) and has several dedicated areas: lounge/library, gallery, kiln room, glaze and materials room, storage spaces, main workspace, and most significant to this discussion, my own workspace. I readily admit that I have the best of both worlds. I work in a studio of my own design and control that services over 150 people each week through classes, studio members, retail customers, and staff, and I can interact with any number of them at any time. I can also retreat into the privacy of my space and talk to no one!

The bottom line? Weigh all the factors, positive and negative. Don't fear the uncertainty, but be realistic and honest with yourself. Trust your instincts. Of course, you won't really know all the ramifications until you open your studio to others. For me and for many others, it has been a decision that held wonderful benefits for all involved.

## Organizing a School and Providing Services

Teaching classes and ostensibly offering other services out of your studio involves more than just deciding what classes and services to offer, scheduling and organizing the space, and placing advertisements in the local paper. Presumably, at this point you have some knowledge about what you are about to get yourself into. Be sure you do, because the success of this effort will be governed in a major way by the degree of interest you have in making it work, along with the realization of the impact that developing a school and teaching situation will have on your clay career. Go in with your eyes wide open.

You've got your space organized into a teaching environment and have decided on the general class offerings. As an example, assume you want to teach two or three adult classes a week. Are the classes going to be arranged by ability—beginner, intermediate, advanced—or are they going to be mixed groups? Are you going to offer a variety of clay working instruction or limit your teaching to the wheel? Are you going to make the studio available to the students before or after class for independent practice time? The answers to all these questions hold ramifications beyond the immediate resolutions.

You have to be sensitive to the market in which you are operating. Perhaps the population in your area won't support specialized classes and the only way to fill the classes is to offer a general curriculum of hand building and wheel throwing to a group of individuals with a range of abilities. Most classes of this sort meet once a week, but that is certainly not set in stone. Some adults would rather take a class in the evening, while others would be more apt to register for a morning class. When dealing with children's classes, many variables that pertain to adults are moot. For instance, the children's

*Figure 8-2. With proper instructions and safety measures, children can do raku. A class of 6-9 year olds at The Potters School. (Photo by Marna Kennedy)*

classes are most likely going to meet after school or Saturday mornings and they should be organized by age groups rather than experience, interest, or ability. For kids, the goal is social comfort, not a high level of accomplishment in the craft.

Of course, the more choices you offer in scheduling, the more success you are going to have in filling your classes. If you can, offer classes that are age specific as well as a class that allows kids of all ages to attend. For example, you can have classes for ages 5-8 and 9-12 as well as a class for 5-12 year-olds, giving parents the choice of two classes. While the idea of a class spanning such a wide age range may give you pause, my experience at The Potters Shop has shown that that there are always enough kids in each age bracket to make the social aspect work successfully.

The next consideration should be the length of the session. Since adult schedules and activities tend to be more stable, adult class sessions can be in the 8-12 week range. At The Potters School, we find that 10-12 week sessions offer enough time to become comfortable and at least somewhat successful at manipulating clay and learning the basic technical skills necessary for a student to be sufficiently satisfied. That amount of time is also short enough to keep the student's interest fresh without boring even those who are only marginally interested. You want your students to come back for more! Again, when it comes to children, the considerations are different. Their activity schedules and interests tend to be much more diverse and thus place greater demands on scheduling. Pottery class is competing with soccer, baseball, ballet, music lessons, religious school, and a thousand other things on the typical ten-year-old's plate. We schedule children's and teen classes in six week sessions and have found that time frame to fit conveniently with the other activities.

How long should the classes be? Again, children's and adult classes offer different challenges. Our adult classes are two and a half hours, with an additional hour set aside for independent practice and work. Students are free to come into the studio and work on their own for an hour before their scheduled class (morning students have the hour after the class ends). This gives the students an opportunity to take advantage of the facilities in a totally nonstructured way and allows for more hands-on time if they want it. We also offer additional studio time on a pay-as-you-go basis by the hour or by the month. Children's classes meet in two-hour time blocks with no additional studio or work time available. To some parents, two hours seems too long, but even for the youngest kindergarten students, two hours is an optimum length. There is enough time to get set up and do some work with adequate time left for cleanup, and they are still raring to go at the end of two hours!

## Fees

The enthusiasm and excitement you feel in the beginning stages of organizing a teaching environment can be powerful and have almost a life of their own. However, once you tackle and begin to resolve the issues discussed above, one thing that often brings you back to reality is the totally perplexing problem of what to charge for the classes and for your services. Indeed, I have been asked more questions during workshops, presentations, and through correspondence regarding how to arrive at fees and charges than about any other aspect of setting up a studio, school, or business. I've already discussed pricing in the context of your work, and while some of the same considerations can be applied here, class fees, firing fees, and the like are a different kettle of fish and can be examined in a much more logical and systematic fashion.

A simple analysis of the costs involved in offering a pottery class will illustrate the factors that need to go into arriving at the actual class fee. I love lists as a means of organizing my thinking, so let's make one. By the way, lists, outlines, plans, notes, and other means of personal mental organization are for you to be able to decipher and understand. Make them in any format you like and title them in any way that makes sense to you. Forget about what others may think if they should look at them!

Costs in offering a class:

1) Clay
2) Glazes
3) Firing

There you have it. Short, sweet, and simple? Not so fast. This is exactly what happens when you take something you think you understand for granted without spending the time and effort to really look at the factors and costs involved.

Here's a more complete list of costs:

1) Fixed studio costs

   a. rent
   b. insurance
   c. utilities

2) Teacher salary

3) Additional staff (studio assistant, apprentice, helper)

4) Expendable materials

   a. clay
   b. raw materials for glazes and slips
   c. commercial glazes, slips, etc.

5) Supplies to be purchased and periodically replaced

   a. potter's tools
   b. sponges
   c. pails, buckets, etc.
   d. bats, ware boards

6) Firing fees
7) Printed materials

   a. registration forms
   b. brochures

8) Postage for mailing above
9) Advertising
10) Profit to the studio/school

You can see that after a more careful look at what it takes to put a class in place, there are many more costs to consider when deciding on a fee. To be fair, not all these costs can be realistically analyzed, broken down, and figured into a fee for a six-week kids pottery class, but they all must be considered. Costs such as rent, utilities, insurance, etc. will be supported by the fees you collect for classes and services but cannot easily be figured into the fee structure directly. These costs are among those that are more easily viewed when examining summaries of your expenses and income from your services and sales. At that point, you can adjust fees if it appears these expenses are not being recovered.

You can, though, identify some of the major costs and considerations and figure those into your fee. Assume you already have the necessary supplies and tools on hand and no immediate expenditure is necessary. Using your experience as a potter and former pottery student, estimate the amount of clay one student might use in one class. Then estimate how much of that clay will end up in a finished piece that will actually be fired. Multiply that by the number of students in the class and then by the number of classes and you have an idea of how much clay will be used during each session. Remember that it is really only the fired clay you are concerned about, since the rest of the clay used will presumably be recycled and used again.

One way to simplify this aspect of class fees is to not include clay in the fee and, as an alternative, have the students buy clay in 25 pound increments. You can easily decide on a price for clay based on what it costs you and the current retail price. A good tack on would be 25% to 50%. This allows for the money you have to lay out each time you have a large shipment of clay delivered, the storage of the clay, and a small profit. By having the students pay separately for clay, you simplify your fee structure and at the same time make the student's fee more equitable since they only pay for the amount of clay they use. Students who use less clay will not be subsidizing those who use a lot. There are problems with this kind of arrangement though. You will need to resolve the issue of each student storing and recycling their own clay, which could take up more space than you have to offer. As a solution, you could offer a lower price on the clay if they allow you to do the recycling and keep the end product. If a student chooses not to bother recycling, you can have quite a bit of clay slop to dispose of. And are you really going to have kids buying and recycling their own clay? I don't think so. It is for these reasons and others that at The Potters School we include clay in the class fee. By doing so, the entire issue of clay storage, recycling, and supply is the school's responsibility. Less space is required and we have complete control over the process.

Raw materials for glazes can be analyzed in a similar fashion. Arrive at a dollar amount for the amount of glaze that will be used by a single class and multiply it by the number of classes you have. You will see that this is a relatively low cost item.

Firing fees, on the other hand, can be substantial and require a more careful analysis. I recommend that you not include firing in the class fee, but charge students for the work they actually fire. Firing is an aspect of pottery making best kept as equitable as possible because the students who are either the most proficient or the least discriminating will fire the most work. If the firing fees are included in the class fee, students who are the least productive and the most critical will be seriously subsidizing the others. To arrive at a fair fee for firing, you need to do an analysis of your firing costs. You can perform this analysis for both electric and fuel fired kilns, but I use electric kilns as an example since they are in far wider use. The following analysis assumes that you are prepared to do your own kiln maintenance and repair. If you are not capable of troubleshooting kiln problems, replacing your own elements, switches, and wiring, and doing other regular kiln repair, then the costs involved in operating your kiln will be substantially higher because you will have to pay someone else to perform all those chores and services.

Starting with the obvious, you have the cost of electricity. Look at your electric bill or call your local provider to find out your kilowatt/hour charge. Often, your actual charge will be a combination of two or more factors so be sure you include everything. Here in Massachusetts, electrical costs are a combination of the kilowatt/hour and a demand fee. This demand fee is essentially a surcharge based on the time of the day the power is used. Power is more costly during peak demand times and the electric company figures that in to your cost. Looking at the specifications of your kiln, note the entry under wattage. My old Skutt 231 kiln (24" diameter by 27" tall, 7 cubic feet) draws 11,250 watts per hour when the switches are set to high. Divide that number by 1,000 and you get 11.25 kilowatts. When you multiply this by my electric charge of .15/KWH you can see that it's costing me $1.70 per hour to fire my kiln when all switches are on high. To be more accurate, you can compute the cost to reflect low, medium, or infinitely variable heat settings, but for the purposes of understanding firing costs, by assuming the highest setting you build in a small financial cushion.

With your electrical costs in hand, you are well on the way to arriving at the total cost for firing the kiln but as I'm sure you've guessed by now, it's not quite that simple! In addition to electrical costs, you have a variety of other costs to consider. There is the initial investment in the kiln, its installation, and kiln furniture. There is regular and ordinary maintenance of the kiln such as cleaning, washing kiln shelves, and minor repairs. Periodically, switches, elements, wires, and other hardware will fail and need to be replaced. Kiln furniture doesn't last forever and in fact, when student work is being fired, those surprise glaze disasters will inevitably shorten the life of your shelves. And, on top of it all is the labor it takes, whether yours or an employee's, to stack, fire, unstack, and perform maintenance chores. Whether you can accurately compute all these costs down to a single firing is not only questionable, but probably an unnecessary chore. I have found that utilizing only the major costs in the analysis simplifies the equation and serves my purpose perfectly well.

1) Electric costs as discussed above.

2) Elements. Estimate the life of a set of elements to be 100 firings. The cost of a set of elements not only varies from kiln to kiln, but from supplier to supplier. A set of elements for that old Skutt of mine costs $175.

3) Switches. Switches can last hundreds of firings but can also burn out at any time. Figure in the cost of two switches every 100 firings. Cost $50.

4) Kiln Furniture. The life of shelves, posts, and setters is more variable and with good care, these items can last quite a long time. Figure having to replace a couple of kiln shelves every 50 firings or so. Cost $50.

5) General Maintenance. Replacing a hinge, brick, burnt out wire or connector, or other relatively minor part will have to be done

once and a while. Figure the cost of a switch ($25) every 50 firings.

6) Labor. If you're experienced and efficient, you can probably do a good stacking job in an hour or so. Unstacking in maybe 30 minutes. The actual time you spend tending an eight hour firing is about one hour. Figure in the cost of your labor or the amount you pay your assistant or studio employee. For this exercise, figure $10 per hour.

If you break down the figures above to arrive at a cost per eight hour firing, you get the following cost per eight hour firing for Skutt Model #231:

| | |
|---|---|
| Electricity | $13.60 |
| Elements | 1.75 |
| Switches | .50 |
| Kiln furniture | 1.00 |
| General maintenance | .50 |
| Labor | 25.00 |
| Total | $42.35 |

You can see that it actually costs me over $42 each time I fire this kiln. Of course, this doesn't include the initial cost of the kiln, any of the peripheral support services that the studio provides, or the kiln's fair share of rent, phone, insurance, or any of the other costs incurred to maintain the studio and workspace. At any rate, this $42 figure gives you a pretty good place to start when trying to come up with firing fees. To this $42, you must add a fair markup as a profit for the studio.

Don't confuse labor costs with profit. This was previously discussed in the chapter on marketing your work, but a little reminder is warranted. Labor is a cost, an expense. Granted, you may be providing the labor yourself, and if so, you can reap double rewards, but salary or labor costs are not profit. Only after you determine all your costs including labor can you add on a markup for profit. Profit is an amount above and beyond your costs and it is how a business makes money! For argument's sake, add a $10 markup for profit, bringing the total cost of the firing to $52. In this case, to cover the costs and make money on each firing you need to collect a total of $52 from every kiln load.

There are a few ways you can make sure this happens. Some studios have been able to arrive at a per cubic inch charge by determining how many actual cubic inches of stacking space there is in the kiln and then assessing this charge after measuring each piece either as it goes into the kiln or as it comes out. A little too time consuming and detailed for me. Others have somehow come up with a charge based on the weight of each piece. How they arrived at that I'll never know! Here's a much more personal and humane approach to pricing firings. Taking the above figure as a guide, you can arrive at a per hour charge for the use your kiln. In this way, an individual who wants to fire faster will pay a bit less. If someone wants to extend the length of their firing, they are free to do so and will pay a bit more. The actual temperature or cone that the kiln gets fired to is irrelevant. All that matters is how long the firing lasts. If more than one person shares the kiln load, they divide the charge according to how much space in the kiln their respective work occupied: 50%, 25%, 10%, and so on.

When charging for single or a small number of pieces, as would be the case in firing the work of a class, I have come up with a unit of measurement called the "mug." A mug is an amount of space taken up in the kiln. It is easily recognized by the staff members who load the kilns, as well as by the students, and by looking at the wares and determining the mug equivalent of each, they can assess the firing charges! No measuring, weighing, or other time consuming maneuvers—just the simple mug. I charge $1 for each mug fired.

The teacher's salary is an important component of your costs and will be decided by a combination of your good sense and judgment and the current market rate for teachers in your area. Figure approximately $20 per hour as a teacher's fee.

The remaining costs and expenses will be difficult to figure in directly. You must research similar classes in your area and see what the current fees are. While you need to be able to meet your expenses and make a profit, you also must be competitive. At The Potters School, our current fees of $126 for a six week children's class (materials and firing included) and $225 for a ten week adult class (materials included, firing additional) are competitive with the other venues offering similar classes in the Boston area. To help pay for the administrative costs incurred in operating the class, we charge a $10 annual registration fee for all students. We operate classes on an academic schedule that essentially follows the school calendar from September through June. Once this fee is paid, it is not assessed again until the following school year.

After you have designed your scheduling, class format and basic content, and fees, you are ready to think a bit more about exactly what and how you will teach in those classes. Adult classes can be presented in a somewhat relaxed and spontaneous fashion, but this spontaneity must have a firm foundation in an organized syllabus. Designing a plan, outline, or lesson plans, will greatly help you organize your presentation as a teacher. You must know what is next on the hit parade! Kid's classes, on the other hand, cannot be left to chance or to spontaneity. Each class must be planned within the context of the students' ages, abilities, the length of the class and of the session, and the number of classes that still remain. A great idea is to design projects to be presented each class and that can be continued from one week to the next. The older the children, the more

ful this kind of approach will be. For the
r ones, each class is treated more like a
single experience with a project seen through to
completion. Skills and techniques are the things
that span from one week to the next. For both
children and adults, plan it so the students can
complete any projects in one session. Don't assume they will sign up for the next session. Students who will be continuing need not be
restricted by the calendar.

Adult classes simply require good use of time
and an awareness of how much time is left. At the
Potters School, our approach with the kids is
quite a bit different. We plan the last class of each
session as the glazing class. All the work done
during the session is bisque fired and ready for
glazing during that last class. To be able to have
the kids producing work on the second to last
class and still have that work bisque fired for the
following week, we present a project called min-
iatures. Mini pots or sculptures based on certain
themes are made and because of the size, can be
dried and fired in the short time left.

In designing both adult and children's classes
there are many other details of organization and
policy that you will need to identify and resolve.
There's registration, pre-registration, and re-reg-
istration policies, procedures and forms, drop off

## Claymobile

Exactly as the name suggests, the Claymobile
is a clay studio on wheels. Rolling the streets of
Philadelphia and surrounding communities since
1994, the unique vehicle garages itself at the Clay
Studio, a well known ceramic arts facility that includes a school, galleries, studio space, lecture series, and outreach programs. The idea for the van
came out of an interest in expanding clay programs to parts of the city that were distant or in-
conveniently located from the studio, making it

*Figure 8-3. The Claymobile. (Courtesy of The
Clay Studio)*

difficult for families to get their children there.

The Claymobile travels to schools, community
and cultural centers, senior programs, social service shelters, as well as public and parochial
schools.

Classes are not held in the van. Rather, the van
serves as the transport vehicle for the teacher, clay,
tools, glazes, and everything needed to conduct a
class. The host institution provides a space to conduct the class and a staff representative or teacher
who remains with the class throughout the program. Since the hosts do not have ceramics facilities, the students' work is transported to the clay
studio for firing. Classes are held once a week for
six to 12 week sessions and are funded by a combination of Clay Studio membership fees, the participating sites, and local institutions offering
grants and donations. This allows the program to
visit hosts that otherwise couldn't afford the costs.

The purpose and impact of the Claymobile
transcends pottery and has become an integral part
of the children's art and cultural education with
accolades coming from all those who participate
in its programs. "The Claymobile is the greatest
thing. I can't even put it into words," says one
teacher at a local elementary school.

*Figure 8-4. Instructor Janice Strawder conducting a Claymobile class at Camp St. Vincent, Germantown, Penn. (Photo by Heeseung Lee)*

and dismissal rules for the children, cancellation and makeup class policies, school vacation schedules, and more. The particular design and structure of your school as well as your personality and teaching and administrative style will dictate these and other issues. Let common sense rule and deal with them as they arise.

## Teaching Outside Your Studio

The first part of this chapter touched on different types of teaching venues: grade school, high school, college, art schools, etc. These are generally contracted full or part-time positions. The contract defines the position and the responsibilities that go along with it, salary, benefits, and the term or length of your commitment to the position and the school's commitment to you. There are, however, many other opportunities for teaching that can be much more informal, offer shorter term commitments, and can be just as rewarding and professional. These include pottery studios that offer classes, community art centers, adult education programs administered by local school boards, college and university adult education programs, and others.

Facilities you will encounter will range from studios that are exceedingly well equipped to those that are barely marginal. Sometimes, as in the case of some community school and adult education programs, the administration would be thrilled to offer a course in pottery if they had a place to hold it. Here is where you come in to take advantage of a unique opportunity. You can not only offer your services as a teacher, but you can also offer your studio as a classroom. If you are presently unaware of these types of offerings in your area, look into it. Inquire with the local school board or with the local elementary school as these types of programs are often designed, implemented, and administered by the parents' association as part of an arts or cultural enrichment curriculum. If your investigation turns up nothing, step up and make a proposal. You could find yourself a pioneer!

A significant component of our educational programs at The Potters School is one developed and nurtured by our education director, Carol Temkin, and has its origins in a class she taught at the elementary school her children were attending. When word got around that she was a potter, Carol was asked to present a pottery class as part of an after school arts program. She was young in her pottery career and it seemed like this would be a good opportunity to extend her clay time and generate some income. Since the school had no pottery facilities, Carol brought in clay and tools and fired the work in the studio where she worked.

Several years later, Carol joined me at The Potters Shop and began to teach classes here. Word of the uniqueness and success of the after school class had spread and inquiries from other schools began to be more and more frequent. Carol then incorporated that single after school class that she had continued to teach into our class offerings,

providing these schools with one of our staff members to teach a similar class under similar conditions. Today, that single class has grown to as many as 20 classes in that many different schools per week. Over the years, we have continued to refine the curriculum and the result is a well designed, self contained program. Each session lasts approximately six to ten weeks depending on the school schedule and is usually held in a local elementary school, often as part of that school's after school enrichment program.

Other places we present these classes include recreation centers, day care, and after school facilities. We charge the school a flat fee and they have the responsibility of handling the registration and collecting the money. Classes are strictly limited in size to ten children and the projects are chosen appropriate to the age group. The teacher must be able to keep the children occupied every minute of the one hour class. The teacher is a mobile pottery program. She travels to the school with a toolbox and box of clay and teaches the class in an available classroom or other designated area. These classes have been held in cafeterias, gyms, hallways, and closets! Since there is no storage space in the school for the works in progress, they are transported back and forth from the school to the studio. Since each class must involve creative activity with no down time and all finished pieces must ready to take home on the last class day, incorporating the glazing and firing of the work has been a challenge. Of course, the glazing step can be eliminated altogether but it is important to give the children a well rounded exposure to clay and the processes involved in the making of ware, and glazing is certainly an integral part of that. In a typical six week class, the first four classes are spent making the clay projects. A selection of these pieces are bisque fired and brought back to the fifth class for glazing. The remaining pieces are fired to maturity with the glazed ware and the last class is spent painting these pots with acrylic paint. We have found our approach to be a viable way to bring a clay program to a school that has no facilities.

The Clay Studio in Philadelphia has a similar program that travels the city, bringing clay where it has never been before.

So what might teaching hold for you? Rick Malmgren sums up the interest and vitality that teaching commands for him very well.

"Teaching has broadened my view of pottery, craft, and my own work in clay. It has also added a happy balance to the physical demands and social isolation of full-time studio work. Students are interested in all sorts of things. I see my job as a little bit of leading and a lot of running to the front of the parade to find and negotiate the few areas where our intuition leads us astray. To do that, I spend a good bit of time learning techniques I would not otherwise have been moved to try. In order to respond to student work, I am also pushed to consider what makes pottery "good." The issues go far beyond my own interests or what moves well in the market. The issues are more fundamental and to me, now more important. Years of experience selling gave me tremendous respect for the clarity of the marketplace, but it also narrowed my vision. That narrowing did not enhance my work. Teaching widens my view. It is tremendously rewarding to see the insights and skills developed over the years enthusiastically absorbed by students."

Are you interested in a teaching opportunity? There are many more possibilities than the usual mainstream educational paths. Use your imagination and make that interest a reality. Teaching can augment an already satisfying experience with clay or it can be the beginning of one. Teaching can be central to your profession or exist on the fringe. For Rick, me, and for many others, teaching is a rewarding and absolutely integral part of our professional craft careers and without it, there would be something missing!

# Chapter 9

## The Fruits of Your Efforts

*The challenge is to do the thing you have to do because you're in love with it and can't do anything else. Not because you want to become famous or rich, but because you will be unhappy if you can't do it. It is not something you can turn on and off.*

--Warren McKenzie

One of the essential themes in this book and in my life has to do with forging an existence founded on honesty, integrity, and the interests that are fundamental to one's spirit. Warren MacKenzie expresses that theme with inspiring simplicity and eloquence.

As you begin to tie up this whole package of the professional potter, you will likely have found that the discussions and issues raised have done as much to stimulate more questions and concerns as to answer them. That is a good thing. Answers should forever be leading to questions. If I have been successful in my presentation, you also have begun to build a foundation of confidence and knowledge, as well as a collection of resource material to help you deal with these new questions, and to confront the challenges that lie ahead.

### Measuring Success

One of the nagging questions you will continually face during your career as a craftsperson is that of success and how to gauge and measure it. To be fair to yourself, you must first measure success in relation to the goals and objectives you set for yourself. As these goals are met and objectives conquered, new visions are formed and more challenging ambitions set out. As you proceed along this evolution of personal growth, maturity, and professional expectations, your ideals,

concepts, judgments, and measurements of success must evolve as well. Recognize that success isn't a rigid target set off in the distance. It is perhaps more like a threshold that can be crossed and an area that can be entered.

The attainment of success is not an identifiable, finite moment in your career or activity as much as it is like the quest for your ultimate pot. You get closer and closer, but getting there is always at least one step away. Success should never be measured according to someone else's standards. Success must be measured according to the yardstick you set out for yourself and the amount of satisfaction and reward that you enjoy from your career and involvement with clay.

Perhaps you have conflicting right-brain/left-brain interpretations and thus, standards of success. On one side, there's the touchy feely, sensual feeling-of-clay-in-your-hands, do-what-you-love measure of success and on the other, the apparent diametrically opposed view that success means being able to afford the material pleasures such as the car, house, education, vacations, big screen TV, etc. Without a doubt, the tensions between these different aspects of success are difficult to reconcile. When you then place them in the same boat with the likely modest financial reapings of the average potter, the stresses becomes even more apparent. The truth is that as an individual studio potter, your earning power will be

*Figure 9-1.* **Author**. *Vase. 1998. 15" H, wheel-thrown with inlaid colored glass, raku fired. This piece is also shown in the color section. (Photo by the author)*

less than that of many other professions—professions you could be engaged in if you choose. It is a rare craft maker who is without the ability, education, and drive to have a career in a higher paying, more financially rewarding activity.

Measuring and reconciling financial success has always been a somewhat uncomfortable confrontation for me. Make no mistake, I love what I do and I am exceedingly proud of the career I have crafted and the accomplishments I have achieved. Despite the complete satisfaction I have with all of that, there exists for me a "parallel success measurement line" that is often dotted with frustration and sometimes even anger over the amount of money I earn at what I do and the hours and effort it takes me to do it. Where do I find the basis for reconciliation? Simple. I find my love for the craft and all that goes with it outweighs the dissatisfaction I feel towards my lack of compensation. Now, let's be honest. To put this in perspective, I am not singing the blues. My spouse has a career of her own as well as working for me in the studio as my office manager. My personal income is a combination of my teaching salary, sale of my work, writing and consulting fees, author's royalty fees, salary from The Potters Shop, workshop presentation fees, and the few other things I do. Yes, I have a close relationship with my accountant! Ellen and I, and my children, have a nice house in suburban Boston, we take a few vacations during the year and honestly don't want for too much. So where is the dissatisfaction? It is felt when I compare my professional training, expertise, and efforts to others who share a similar level of accomplishment but in a different profession, and I discover my income to be at the bottom of the list. So, what to do about it? Remember the advice the doctor gives the patient who feels pain when he walks. "Then don't

walk," the doctor suggests. Well, "don't walk" may be a bit facetious, but the basis of the advice is sound. Avoid making those unrealistic comparisons that are likely to make you feel disappointed and dissatisfied. On the other hand, if you find that making those comparisons is unavoidable, perhaps you are in the wrong profession.

Earlier I related the anecdote of how my college friends used to introduce me to others as "their friend majoring in hobbies." At the time, their remarks were taken as lighthearted and good-natured and I'm sure they were. But their references really illustrated their lack of understanding and ability to connect with and take seriously the interests and concerns I was developing as a student and person. I still have close friends from those college days and, guess what, they're not the ones who thought of me as a hobbies major! There is no question that your friends and their sensibilities and sensitivities contribute to your feelings about yourself. Don't overlook the significance of the influence your friends may be having on you and the way you feel about your craft activities and profession. Again, it comes down to self-confidence, personal honesty and integrity, clarity of vision, commitment, and the comfort you feel with yourself and your choice of career. Focus on these aspects and measurements of your "success" above any others.

In the face of your idealistic vision of what draws you to making things and what it means to be a craftsperson, there must be a degree of pragmatism in your plan. At the most basic and perhaps low end of the scale, you must at least be able to financially support your craft making activities. At the other end of the scale sits a full fledged career where your clay activities anchor your income and financial independence. You must identify where you presently lie on that

*Figure 9-2.* ***Warren MacKenzie***. *Teapot. 1997. 8" H with handle, wheel-thrown, faceted surface, reduction fired. This piece is also shown in the color section. (Photo by Peter Lee)*

grand line, where you wish to lie, and how you are going to get to that comfortable destination. You will be measuring, dissecting, examining, and otherwise grading your success in that effort for as long as you engage in clay. Get used to it and learn how to make it a constructive part of your day to day work with clay and evaluation of your comfort and success.

The ability and desire to evaluate success is not universal. You may be wondering why you should engage in this aspect of careerism at all. Indeed, for you it may be a totally unnecessary exercise. For many, the attainment of success doesn't exist as a separate objective. Rather, it is

an ambiguous image that is integral to their everyday struggle to be the best they can be at whatever they do. Success is left for others to decipher, decide, and reward. I will tell you that no matter what your view of success is, success itself cannot be the goal that you set out for yourself. Success is more like a kind of relief. It is the achievements and conquering your personal tangible goals that lead to overall success.

## Keeping Your Interest in Clay Alive

I have been making pots and involved with clay since 1971, 28 years as of this writing. The question I hear most frequently from high school students and young potters at workshops is something like, "How can you still be interested in making pots after so long? Isn't it boring? How do you come up with new ideas?" In the interest of time and simplicity, my answer usually reflects on my love of, and dedication to clay and making vessels. And while that is the basis for my apparent limitless connection to, and engagement with clay, there clearly has to be more to it than that. One of the most intimidating factors about making a commitment to a career based on creativity is the question of ideas and how to generate them. That question rings loud and clear in the minds of most young craftspeople. New ideas? I don't remember where, from whom, or in what context I first heard it said that there are no new ideas, only new combinations and reshuffling things that have been done before, but it has been part of my modus operandi to craft making for many, many years. The concept touches me on an emotional level and makes sense to me intellectually. I no longer have to remind myself of it on a regular basis, for I believe it in my heart. Embracing this notion can be a relief and help dispel some fears and apprehension.

As in most jobs and professions, the threat of burnout is real. You enter a job with boundless energy, enthusiasm, ideas, and objectives and your approach is often one that unknowingly compresses much of this power and interest into a huge burst of activity. This explosion usually produces a significant body of work over a relatively short period of time, then can forever scatter your interest and enthusiasm, not to mention your creativity and ideas. As these particles of yourself drift further and further away, the result is what is often called burnout. There is nothing left—no energy, interest, enthusiasm, or desire to continue. Activities that once were riveting have become routine as your job performance becomes second nature and automatic. In fact, your output

(daily workplace production) becomes greater than what your input (thought, contemplation, ideas, expectations) contributes to it. If only physicists could harness that energy equation! The advantage the craft maker has over others is that you are, whether you realize it or not, the controller and master of your continued enthusiasm and interest in what you do. Unlike other situations where employees work to meet the goals and expectations of their employer, a crafter of creative objects sets their own goals and expectations and it is up to them to keep those goals fresh, vibrant, challenging, and exciting. How you go about doing this is really very simple in concept, but a bit more difficult to carry out. The strategy is to be constantly in tune with your emotional connection to the craft. Change directions and refocus when your present course turns less exciting. Open your eyes and look outside your immediate environment for ideas, influences, and inspiration. If you lose touch and wait until it turns unexciting it may be too late. Easier said than done? Yes, for some for sure. But for others, it makes perfect sense and is only a case of recognizing the cure and acting on it.

My career has been shaped by trial and error with a significant amount of luck and serendipity thrown in. Early on, I was sure I wanted to be a production potter of sorts and make pots for a living. After just a year or so of success, I began to feel a lack of drive, interest, and desire to go to the studio. Success consisted of regular sales of my work at shops and fairs and I was beginning to see a financial future in production pottery. I realized, though, that this was coming at a price. My wares were regular, repetitive, and they lacked excitement and spontaneity, the very qualities that first attracted me to clay. In the face of a fairly good income from pottery sales, I changed directions and decided that I would have a career in clay, but not one that depended on the sale of my work.

# Twenty Questions

*Jack Troy is a well-known potter, teacher, and writer. Having taught well over 150 workshops all over the world, he knows something about techniques of generating ideas and encouraging contemplation and self inspection. His "Twenty Questions" below can serve to remind you of what it is about clay that attracted you to it in the first place.*

Recently I taught a workshop at Arrowmont School of Crafts in Gatlinburg, Tennessee. Before I left home, I made a list of 20 questions, and it was my intention to cut up the list and insert each question in a little greenware clay "fortune cookie," which participants would open, read aloud, and respond to spontaneously, as a way of introducing themselves.

1. If you learned you had six months to live, would your work in clay change? If it would, why would it take a death sentence to make this happen?
2. Can you describe a single unforgettable pot that you have encountered at some point in your life?
3. Can you share with us any of the ways you measure success in what you make?
4. What was your life like before you began to work in clay?
5. Of all the words you have heard or read about ceramics, is there a single phrase or sentence that stands out in your memory as being especially meaningful?
6. Do you believe a pot can change the course of a human life? If so, how? If not, why not? How are you sure?
7. Aren't there already enough pots?
8. What is the difference in encountering a pot that you **like** and being **inspired** by a pot?
9. Some work we encounter reinforces what we already know, and other work challenges what we already know. Can you describe the work of two contemporary ceramists that has those effects on you?
10. Can you describe a pot you have lived with for more than five years, and share with us why it is important to you?
11. Why, in our culture, do more women than men buy pots?
12. If any pot in the world could be yours, which one would you choose and why?
13. Why can a pot never be successfully photographed?
14. To what degree are you curious about the materials you use?
15. If you judge a pot you have made to be awful and someone whose opinion you respect believes it to be wonderful, do you try to resolve the difference? If so, how?
16. Can you recall any comments about your work by another person that influenced what you have come to make?
17. If you could work with clay at any other period of time, what era would you choose and why?
18. If you had to choose one piece that you have made as being "the best" you have **ever** made, could you do so?
19. How do you gain confidence in knowing what direction your work should take?
20. Can you describe a broken pot whose memory you carry, and which has meaning for you?

Clay as a medium of expression and creativity was too important to me. At that moment, I decided that I would no longer make pots to sell but rather I would sell the pots that I made. Bold? Perhaps. But that shift in focus and direction became the foundation of my career.

It may be difficult and disappointing to face, but for many, taking almost childlike and intrinsic enjoyment and love of making things and "improving" that into a profession or job results in a metamorphosis of grave consequences. For some, the marriage of clay working and business is a recipe for failure. If that's the case, choose to preserve your love of craft by keeping it free from and unencumbered by the pressures of sales, income, and cash flow. Do it out of love entirely.

## Balancing the Act

My life, and perhaps yours, is a juggling act where the object is to keep all the balls in the air for as long a stretch as possible. A well-used metaphor but so apropos to our story. The balls are flying and you're catching them. Occasionally one flies a bit too high, occupying more of your attention while the others just seem to float on their own. Every so often, another ball or two gets added while another gets dropped. How you decide which balls to add and which to drop, along with how comfortable and proficient you are in keeping the whole thing in the air is the struggle.

I juggle a multi-faceted career consisting of teaching, making pots, marketing them, traveling to present workshops and demonstrations, writing, and running a business with several components to it. I am also devoted to my family and the time we spend doing things together as well as my own personal interests in sports, entertainment, and community service. You must set priorities, and while these priorities can be flexible and vary in their relative importance and critical nature depending on circumstances, you must respond to the priorities as they exist at each given moment. My priorities? Family and personal interests first, everything else second. Of course, this doesn't mean I wake in the morning and decide not to show up at school because I feel like going skiing. (Now a powder day, that would be another story.) Within the establishment of your priorities, you must be responsible for your commitments, promises, deadlines, projects, and dependents. Your priorities? It doesn't really matter. I am making no value judgments here. But to have any measure of success, identifying and setting your priorities is essential. Don't neglect yourself when setting your priorities. Make time for your interests and activities as a scheduled part of the day. It can be difficult to do and you may be suffering from the "everything else is more critical" syndrome—your child needs to be picked up at school, grocery shopping needs to be done, bills need to be paid, and on and on. These are critically important things to tend to, but you must break away and come to the realization that you, your interests, and your life are just as critical and important—your child needs to be picked up at school, grocery shopping needs to be done, pots need to be made, bills need to be paid...

Make life as simple as possible while you go about discovering what you love to do. As you try things, your familiarity with your own abilities and interests becomes more confident and you get better at not only unearthing your interests, but judging just what you can and can't do within your current mix of activities and responsibilities.

There are those who say you can't do everything. I say that you can, just not all at once.

Have fun with clay.

*Figure 9-3.* **Jack Troy**. *Pitcher. 1998. 14" H, wheel-thrown, natural ash glaze, anagama fired, cone 10. This piece is also shown in the color section. (Photo by Hubert Gentry)*

*Figure 9-4. **Author**. Vase. 1998. 16" H, wheel-thrown, textured and altered surface, raku fired. This piece is also shown in the color section. (Photo by the author)*

# About the Author

Steven Branfman enjoys an international reputation as a potter, writer, and teacher. He is the founder of The Potters Shop and School—a gallery, school, workshop, book store, and studio—in Needham, Mass. Steven's raku ware has appeared in more than 150 group and one-person exhibitions around the United States.

He is the author of *Raku: A Practical Approach* and writes frequently for international craft and pottery magazines. He has been the subject of and has authored many articles on clay which have appeared in *Ceramics Monthly, The Crafts Report, Clay Times, Boston Globe, Studio Potter,* and *Pottery Making Illustrated.*

Steven currently teaches at Thayer Academy in Braintree, Mass., and has taught in several public school systems and at the college level. He also travels the country presenting guest workshops of his pottery forming, glazing, and firing techniques.

Steven lives in Newton, Mass., with his wife Ellen and sons Jared and Adam.

# Addendum

## Bibliography and Suggested Reading

*The Potter's Professional Handbook* is the result of my education, reading, experiences, and research. The following list of books is by no means meant to represent an all-encompassing bibliography of books on pottery and ceramics. Rather, it is a compilation of those titles I have found useful, educational, enlightening, or otherwise interesting in my development and growth, and that pertain to the themes discussed in this book. Some of these books are out of print and very difficult to obtain, though they should be available in major libraries. These are indicated with an "OP."

A word on the categories: Many of these titles defy neat categorization, though I have tried! Take a look through the entire list to get familiar with the kinds of books that are here.

For the most complete listing of books and videos on pottery and ceramics available anywhere, contact The Potters Shop, 31 Thorpe Rd., Needham, MA 02194, (781) 449-7687, fax: (781) 449-9098.

## Aesthetics and Philosophy

Personal writings, perspectives, cultural views, aesthetics, design, creativity, and more.

Bachelard, Gaston. *The Poetics of Space.* Boston: Beacon Press, 1994

Bayles, David & Orland, Ted. *Art & Fear: Observations on the Perils (and Rewards) of Artmaking.* Santa Barbara: Capra Press, 1993

Beittel, Kenneth R. *Zen and the Art of Pottery.* New York: Weatherhill Inc., 1989

Bender, Sue. *Everyday Sacred.* New York: Harper Collins Publishers,1995

Caiger-Smith, Alan. *Pottery, People and Time.* Somerset: Richard Dennis 1995

Clark, Garth. *Ceramic Art: Comment and Review 1882-1977.* New York: E. P. Dutton, 1978 OP

Coatts, Margot. *Pioneers of Modern Craft.* New York: St. Martin's Press Inc., 1997

Dissanayake, Ellen. *What Is Art For?* Seattle: University of Washington Press, 1990

Dissanayake, Ellen. *Homo Aestheticus: Where Art Comes From and Why.* Seattle: University of Washington Press, 1995

Dooling, D. M. *A Way of Working.* New York: Parabola Books, 1986

Dormer, Peter. *The Art of the Maker: Skill and its Meaning in Art, Craft and Design.* London: Thames and Hudson, 1994

Dormer, Peter. *The Culture of Craft.* New York: St. Martin's Press Inc., 1997

Fritz, Robert. *Creating: A Guide to the Creative Process.* New York: Fawcett Columbine, 1991

Fritz, Robert. *The Path of Least Resistance.* New York: Fawcett Columbine, 1989

Henri, Robert. *The Art Spirit.* Philadelphia: J. B. Lippincott Co., 1960

Jeffri, Joan. *The Craftsperson Speaks: Artists in Varied Media Discuss Their Crafts.* Westport: Greenwood Press, 1992

Kingery, W. David. *Learning from Things.* Smithsonian Institution Press, Washington, DC, 1996

Koren, Leonard. *Wabi-Sabi: For Artists, Designers, Poets & Philosophers.* Berkeley: Stone Bridge Press, 1994

Larsen, Ronald. *A Potter's Companion: Imagination, Originality, and Craft.* Rochester: Park Street Press, 1993

Lord, James. *A Giacometti Portrait.* New York: Farrar, Straus & Giroux, 1980. A reprint of the original from 1965. This is a riveting account of the artist's state of mind and creative spirit.

Lubar, Steven & Kingery, W. David. *History from Things: Essays on Material Culture.*

Washington, DC: Smithsonian Institution Press, 1993

Lucie-Smith, Edward. *The Story of Craft: The Craftsman's Role in Society*. New York: Van Nostrand Reinhold Co., 1984 OP

Murray, Rona & Dexter, Walter. *The Art of Earth*. Victoria: Sono Nis Press, 1979 OP

Nance, John. *The Mud-Pie Dilemma*. Forest Grove: Timber Press, 1978 OP. An outstanding account of a potter's struggle to survive. Must reading.

Needleman, Carla. *The Work of Craft*. New York: Kodansha, 1993

Piepenburg, Robert. *Treasures of the Creative Spirit, An Artist's Understanding of Human Creativity*. Farmington Hills: Pebble Press, 1998. Very personal reflections and insights of creativity, its origins, and its power.

Pye, David. *The Nature & Aesthetics of Design*. Bethel: Cambium Press, 1982

Pye, David. *The Nature and Art of Workmanship*. Bethel: Cambium Press, 1995

Rawson, Philip. *Ceramics: The Appreciation of the Arts*. New York: Oxford University Press, 1971

Richards, M. C. *Centering*. Middletown: Wesleyan University Press, 1989

Richards, M. C. *The Crossing Point*. Middletown: Wesleyan University Press, 1973

Wildenhain, Marguerite. *The Invisible Core: A Potter's Life and Thoughts*. Palo Alto: Pacific Books, 1973

Yanagi, Soetsu. *The Unknown Craftsman*. New York: Kodansha International Ltd., 1992. A vital study of aesthetics and the human creative drive.

## Business Guides

A variety of approaches towards art and craft business, law, bookkeeping, accounting, marketing, organization, research, and promotion.

Borrus, K.; Herman, L.; Wilson, J. *The Business of Crafts: The Complete Directory of Resources for Artisans*. New York: The Crafts Center, 1996. This book is an addendum in and of itself. A well-done section on crafts business and listings of craft shops, galleries, craft shows, museum shops, catalogs, and much more. You should have this.

Crawford, Tad. *Business and Legal Forms for Crafts*. New York: Allworth Press, 1998

Crawford, Tad. *Business and Legal Forms for Fine Artists*. New York: Allworth Press, 1995

Crawford, Tad. *Legal Guide for the Visual Artist*. New York: Allworth Press, 1995

Dillehay, James. *The Basic Guide to Pricing Your Craftwork*. Torrean: Warm Snow Publishers, 1997

Dillehay, James. *The Basic Guide to Selling Arts & Crafts*. Torreon: Warm Snow Publishers, 1995

DuBoff, Leonard. *The Art Business Encyclopedia*. New York: Allworth Press, 1994

Duboff, Leonard D. *The Law for Art and Craft Galleries*. Loveland: Interweave Press, 1993

Franklin-Smith, Constance. *Art Marketing Handbook for the Fine Artist*. Renaissance: ArtNetwork Press, 1992

Gerhards, Paul. *How to Sell What You Make*. Mechanicsburg: Stackpole Books, 1996

Grant, Daniel. *How to Start and Succeed as an Artist*. New York: Allworth Press, 1997

Grant, Daniel. *The Artist's Resource Handbook*. New York: Allworth Press, 1996

Jefferson, Brian T. *Profitable Crafts Marketing*. Beaverton: Timber Press, 1985 OP. Try to find this book. It is a bit dated but it is one of the best.

Kunitz, Stanley. *Artists Communities*. New York: Lyons Press, 1994

Krakowski, Lilli. *The $1200 Studio*. Ceramics Monthly Magazine, May 1995

Lehmkul, Dorothy & Laming, Dolores Cotter. *Organizing for the Creative Person*. New York: Crown, 1993

McMahon, Kathleen. *In Search of Arts and Crafts on the Internet*. San Francisco: Opportunity Network, 1995

Michels, Caroll. *How to Survive & Prosper As An Artist*. New York: Henry Holt & Co., 1997

Pinson, Linda & Jinnett, Jerry. *Keeping the Books*. Dover: Upstart Publishing Co., Inc., 1993

Pinson, Linda & Jinnett, Jerry. *The Home-Based Entrepreneur*. Dover: Upstart Publishing Co., Inc., 1993

Price, Barclay. *Running a Workshop: Basic Business for Craftspeople*. London: Crafts Council, 1997

Radeschi, Loretta, *The Business Guide Series for Artists and Craftspeople*. Doylestown: Loretta Radeschi, 1997. A series of five small hand books: *Developing a Marketing Plan, Generating Publicity, Pricing Your Work, Retail & Wholesale Shows, Designing a Booth*. Very brief summaries designed to get you thinking in the right direction.

Rosen, Wendy. *Crafting As a Business*. Iola, WI: Krause Publications, 1994

Shaw Associates. *The Guide to Arts & Crafts Workshops*. Coral Gables: Shaw Associates, 1990. A treasure trove of listings of workshops and residencies throughout the world. A wonderful resource.

Shiva, V. A. *Arts and the Internet*. New York: Allworth Press, 1996

Vitali, Julius. *The Fine Artist's Guide to Marketing and Self-Promotion*. New York: Allworth Press, 1996

West, Janice. *Marketing Your Arts & Crafts*. Fort Worth: The Summit Group, 1994

Wettlaufer, George & Nancy. *The Craftsman's Survival Manual: Making a Full or Part-time Living From Your Craft*. Englewood Cliffs: Prentice-Hall, 1974 OP

Williams, Gerry. *Apprenticeship in Craft*. Goffstown: Daniel Clark Books, 1981

## Construction/Home Improvement

You want to get into construction, electrical work, plumbing, and the like? These are the books for you!

Allen, Benjamin W. *Better Homes & Gardens New Complete Guide to Home Repair and Improvement*. Des Moines: Meredith Books, 1997

Editors of Time Life Books. *Complete Book of Old Home Repair and Renovation*. Alexandria: Time Life Books, 1998

Hamilton, Gene and Katie. *Rules of Thumb for Home Building, Improvement, and Repair*. New York: John Wiley and Sons, 1997. In plain English, this book gives you specifications and standards for materials, fasteners, adhesives, painting, wiring, plumbing, exteriors, concrete and more. Plus tips, shortcuts and loads of advice!

Pope, John A. *Readers Digest New Complete Do It Yourself Manual*. Pleasantville: Readers Digest Association Inc., 1997

Wing, Charlie. *The Visual Handbook of Building and Remodeling*. Professional Edition. Emmaus: Rodale Press, 1998. A very complete handbook with building codes, and all aspects of serious construction.

## General Potter's Handbooks

Books that serve as the basis for any library covering history, culture, clay forming, materials, and other areas of general potter's knowledge.

Birks, Tony. *The Complete Potters Companion*. Boston: Little Brown, 1998

Casson, Michael. *The Craft of the Potter*. Woodbury: Barron's Educational Series, 1977

Clark, Kenneth. *The Potters Manual*. Edison: Chartwell Books, 1997

Leach, Bernard. *A Potters Book*. London: Faber and Faber,1976. Unquestionably the single book all potters must have.

Nelson, Glenn C. *Ceramics: A Potter's Handbook*. New York: HBJ, 1984

Peterson, Susan. *The Craft and Art of Clay*. Woodstock: The Overlook Press, 1996

Piepenburg, Robert. *The Spirit of Clay*. Farming ton Hills: Pebble Press, 1996

Speight, Charlotte F. & Toki, John. *Hands in*

*Clay.* Mountain View: Mayfield Publishing Co., 1995

Zakin, Richard. *Ceramics: Mastering the Craft.* Iola, WI: Krause Publications, 1990

## Health and Safety

Although there is no chapter or significant references in this book to health and safety issues, that does not diminish its importance. It is simply a matter of theme and space. Every action you take as a studio potter must be governed by sensible health and safety practices. Many of the general handbooks listed have sections on or make reference to health and safety. The titles listed below are excellent books on the subject and should be consulted on a regular basis.

Clark, Nancy. *Ventilation: A Practical Guide for Artists.* New York: Lyons Press, 1984

McCann, Michael. *Artist Beware.* New York: Watson-Guptill, 1979

McCann, Michael. *Health Hazards Manual for the Artist.* New York: Lyons Press, 1994

Qualley, Charles. *Safety in the Art Room.* Worcester: Davis Publications, 1986

Rossol, Monona. *Keeping Claywork Safe and Legal.* Bandon: NCECA, 1996

## Technical Studio Manuals

Books of a more specific technical nature for more advanced studio reference including information on building your own equipment.

Brain, Charles-Lewton. *Small Scale Photography.* Calgary: Brain Press, 1996

Cardew, Michael. *Pioneer Pottery.* New York: St. Martin's Press, 1969 OP

Chappell, James. *The Potter's Complete Book of Clay and Glazes.* New York: Watson-Guptill Publications, 1991

Conrad, John W. *Advanced Ceramic Manual: Technical Data for the Studio Potter.* San Diego: Falcon Co. Publishers, 1994

Davis, Harry. *The Potter's Alternative.* North Ryde: Methuen, 1987 OP

Fournier, Robert. *Electric Kiln Construction for Potters.* New York: Van Nostrand Reinhold Co. Inc., 1977 OP

Fournier, Robert. *Illustrated Dictionary of Practical Pottery.* New York: Van Nostrand Rein hold Co., Inc., 1977 OP

Fraser, Harry. *The Electric Kiln.* London: A&C Black, 1995

Hamer, Frank. *The Potter's Dictionary of Materials and Techniques.* London: A&C Black, 1997

Harvey, Roger et. al. *Building Pottery Equipment.* New York: Watson-Guptill, 1975 OP

Holden, Andrew. *The Self-Reliant Potter.* New York: Van Nostrand Reinhold Co. Inc., 1984 OP

Olsen, Frederic L. *The Kiln Book.* Iola, WI: Krause Publications, 1983

Rhodes, Daniel. *Clay and Glazes for the Potter.* Iola, WI: Krause Publications, 1973

Wettlaufer, George & Nancy, *Getting Into Pots.* Englewood Cliffs, 1976 OP

White, John. *Artists Handbook for Photographing Their Own Artwork.* New York: Crown, 1994

Williams, Gerry et. al. *Studio Potter Book.* New York: Van Nostrand Reinhold Co. Inc., 1978 OP

Zakin, Richard. *Electric Kiln Ceramics: A Potter's Guide to Clays and Glazes.* Iola, WI: Krause Publications, 1994

# Pottery and Crafts Magazines and Journals

Magazines and journals are my favorite way to keep in touch with what's happening in the clay world. While this is a pretty comprehensive list, there are many others. Look also in the list of Professional Resources, Supplies, and Materials for magazines devoted specifically to marketing and business.

## United States

*American Ceramics*
9 East 45 St.
New York, NY 10017
(212) 661-4397
Fax (212) 661-2389

*American Craft Magazine*
American Crafts Council
72 Spring St.
New York, NY 10012

*Ceramics Monthly*
735 Ceramic Place
PO Box 6102
Westerville, OH 43086
(614) 523-1660
Fax (614) 891-8960

*Clay Times*
PO Box 365
Waterford, VA 20197
(800) 356-2529
e-mail: pbeach1052@aol.com

*Studio Potter*
PO Box 70
Goffstown, NH 03045
(603) 774-3542

*Studio Potter Network Newsletter*
PO Box 70
Goffstown, NH 03045
(603) 774-3542

## Australia

*Ceramics Art and Perception*
35 William St.
Paddington, Sydney
NSW Australia 2021

*Ceramics Technical*
35 William St.
Paddington, Sydney
NSW Australia 2021

*Pottery in Australia*
PO Box 937
Crows Nest, Sydney
NSW Australia 2065
(02) 9901-3353
Fax (02) 436-1681
e-mail: potinaus@ozemail.com.au

## Canada

*Contact*
8601 Warden Ave. Box 56599
Makham, Ontario L3R 0M6
(800) 315-0857

## France

*L'Atelier Societe Nouvelle des Editions
    Creativite*
41 rue Barrault
75013 Paris

*La Ceramique Moderne*
22 rue Le Brun
75013 Paris

## Germany

*Keramik Magazin*
Steinfelder Strasse
10 W-8770 Lohr am Main

*New Ceramics*
Unter den Eichen 90 D-12205
Berlin, Germany
30 8312953
Fax 30 8316281

## Great Britain

*Ceramic Review*
21 Carnaby St
London W1V 1PH
0171 439 3377
Fax 0171 287 9954


*Crafts Council*
44a Pentonville Rd
London N1 9BY


*Studio Pottery*
15 Magdalene Rd.
Exeter, Devon EX2 4TA

## Greece

*Keramik Techni*
PO Box 80653
185 10 Piraeus

## Italy

*Ceramica Italiana*
Nell 'Edilizia Via Firenze
276 48018 Faenza

## Netherlands

*Foundation COSA*
PO Box 2413
3000 CK Rotterdam


*Glas en Keramiek*
Antwoordnummer 1516
5729 ZX Asten
The Netherlands


*Kerameik*
Kintgenskswn
3512 GX Ultrecht

## New Zealand

*New Zealand Potter*
PO Box 881
Auckland New Zealand
(09) 415-9817
Fax (09) 309-3247

## Spain

*Bulleti Informatiu de Ceramica*
Sant Honorat 7
Barcelona 08002

## Taiwan

*Ceramic Art*
PO Box 47-74
Taiwan

# Computer and Internet Resources

The computer and Internet have become a great boon to the potter. The Internet and World Wide Web are powerful information tools as well as a viable means of self promotion and marketing. The computer and its applications have also become important tools for the potter.

## Computer Applications

Computer programs for glaze calculation, inventory control, graphics, catalog and brochure design, and other applications abound. There are so many general database, address book, accounting, and page layout programs that it would be impractical to list them here. Consult your local computer store, ask other craftspeople for their recommendations, and read reviews in computer magazines.

Glaze calculation applications attempt to address three basic aspects: electronic notebook, recipe analysis, and predicting final results. The list below of the most popular glaze applications used by potters as of this date was researched and compiled by Rick Malmgren, e-mail: RMalmgren@aol.com

Ceramis (Windows and Mac)
Needs Filemaker Pro V 3.0 to work
Steve Hunter
8 Main Dr.
Brookfield, CT 06804
http://members.tripod.com/~Ceramis
e-mail: stevehunter@rocketmail.com


Glaze Calculation Workbook (Windows)
David Hewitt
7 Fairfield Rd.
Caerleon, Newport
South Wales NP6 1DQ
http://digitalfire.com/education/people/
    hewitt.htm
e-mail: david@dhpot.co.uk


Glaze Calculator (Windows)
Christopher Green
Seegreen Software
PO Box 115
Westbury on Trym, Bristol BS9 3ND
England
www.seegree.co./glazcalc/
e-mail: supportglz@seegreen.com


GlazeChem 1.2 (Windows)
Robert Wilt
92 Bay State Ave #2
Somerville MA 02144
http://www.mdc.net/~rjwilt/
e-mail: rjw@studiopotter.org


Glaze Simulator (Windows)
Fraser Forsythe, FS Anada Inc.
PO Box 24006
Bullfrog Postal Outlet
Guelph, Ontario, N1E 6V8
Canada
www.golden.net/~fraserf
e-mail: fraserf@golden.net

HyperGlazeII (Mac)
Richard Burkett
6354 Lorca Dr.
San Diego, CA 92115
http://members.aol.com/hyperglaze/


Insight (Windows and Mac)
IMC, 134 Upland Dr.
Medicine Hat, Alberta T1A 3 N7
Canada
www.ceramicsoftware.com
e-mail: sales@digitalfire.com
(403) 527-2826.


Matrix (Windows and Mac)
Lawrence Ewing
21 Slant St. Careys Bay
Dunedin, New Zealand
e-mail: lewing@clear.net.nz

## Internet Resources

Open up any search engine, type in pottery or ceramics, and the universe will be at your fingertips. However, to make a search more productive you'll need to be more specific. The following list of web sites, and other Internet resources for pottery information was compiled and is presented here courtesy of Michelle Lowe (mishlowe@indirect.com). It is divided into types of collections that are available on the Internet. You will need to consult your own Internet software regarding how you access these resources. By the way, my e-mail address is sbranfpots@aol.com

Usenet groups
bit.listserv.clayart
rec.crafts.pottery

## Mailing list

CLAYART is a computer conference that serves as a means of communication for those interested in the ceramic arts. It is open to anyone wishing to participate, but will be particularly useful for those in ceramic-related areas of academia, private studios, galleries, etc. Once you are a subscriber, you will receive e-mail messages daily in the form of questions, answers, general statements of information, and more. As a subscriber, you can interact at your own discretion or simply sit back and observe the activity of the other subscribers. There are different ways to receive the list each day and these options are explained after you subscribe. I read my CLAYART mail every day and have found it to be useful, fun, and a great way to keep in touch with others in clay.

To join CLAYART, send the following e-mail message to: listserv@lsv.uky.edu with this in the message body: SUBSCRIBE CLAYART YourFirstName YourLastName

## Live Pottery Chat

IRC channel- #pottery at aspen.co.us.starlink.org (or any starlink server). It is a registered channel for potters to chat about clay stuff. For more information about IRC and the potter's channels try this url: http://apple.sdsu.edu/ceramicsweb/ircpotters.html

## World Wide Web Resources for Pottery Materials, Information, or Equipment

Aardvark Clay
http://www.ceramics.com/aardvark/

American Art Clay Co.
http://www.amaco.com/

American Craft Malls
http://www.fastlane.net/homepages/procraft

A.R.T. Studio Clay Co.
http://www.artclay.com/

Axner Pottery Supply
http://www.axner.com/

Burkett's, Richard Ceramics Web
http://apple.sdsu.edu/ceramicsweb/ceramicsweb.html

Castable soda kiln project
http://www.mpgallery.com/kiln/kiln.htm

Clayart postings archived
http://www.potters.org/categories

Duncan
http://www.duncan-enterprises.com/

Feldspar Corporation
http://www.ceramics.com/~ceramics/feldspar/

Geil kilns
http://www.kilns.com

Georgie's, Portland Oregon
http://www.georgies.com

Glaze Simulator and Rapid Fire Kiln Design
http://www.golden.net/~fraserf

Hansen, Tony-Insight and Magic of Fire
http://www.digitalfire.com/

Interglaze
http://psfa.sdsu.edu/interglaze/interglaze.html

Kaplan's, Jonathan miscellaneous ceramic links and books
http://www.craftweb.com/org/jkaplan/cdg.shtml

Kilnman
http://www.kilnman.com/

Kilnsite—kiln design
http://homepage.macomb.com/~gstengel/

Laguna Clay
http://www.lagunaclay.com

Minnesota Clay Company
http://www.mm.com/mnclayus/

Moore's, Faith—getting started in ceramics
http://miavx1.acs.muohio.edu/~moorefe/
    Index.html

NCECA—National Council for Education in the
    Ceramic Arts
http://www.arts.ufl.edu/nceca/

Paperclay
http://www.paperclayart.com/

Plainsman Clays
http://www.memlane.com/business/imc/pla/
    products.htm

Potters for Peace
http://www.cc.cc.ca.us/pfp/index.htm

Pottery supplier links and addresses
http://www.amug.org/~mishlowe/FAQs/
    claysuppliers.html

Skutt Ceramic Products
http://www.skutt.com/

Studio Gora—used gear for sale
http://www3.sympatico.ca/gora.art/products.htm

Talbott's, Marshall pottery and art bulletin boards
http://www.potteryinfo.com/

Used Equipment for Sale
http://www.kilnray.com

## Individual Artists

Earl Brunner
http://members.aol.com/brunnerec/

Edouard Bastarache
http://sorel-tracy.qc.ca/~edouardb/

Jeroen Bechtold
http://www.euronet.nl/users/bbvbbv/index.html

Paul Benford
http://onlinerage.com/minipots/

Bill Buckner
http://billtom.home.mindspring.com/

Bill Geisinger
http://kilnman.fhda.edu/geisinger.html

Joe Gora
http://www3.sympatico.ca/gora.art

Karen Greene
http://www.halcyon.com/cjlew/kgreene/kg.html

Phyllis Michele Greenhouse
http://www.accesspro.net/rapture/

Peggy Heer
http://www.ffa.ucalgary.ca/artists/pheer/

Don Jones
http://www.highfiber.com/~claysky/

Krueger Pottery
http://www.iwc.com/krueger/

Michelle Lowe
http://www.amug.org/~mishlowe/pottery.html

Kathy McDonald, Willow Tree Pottery
http://members.tripod.com/~kmcd3/

Rhonda Reed
http://www.gva.net/rreed/

Gary Shaffer
http://www.weir.net/~gshaffer

Andrew Werby
http://users.lanminds.com/~drewid

Kenneth Westfall
http://www.ruralnet.org/pinehillpottery/

Robert Wilt
http://www.mdc.net/~rjwilt/

Rusty Wiltjer, Wiltjer Pottery
http://www.maine.com/shops/wiltjer/

## Group and/or Changing Exhibitions

Arizona Clay Club
http://www.amug.org/~mishlowe/azclay/
   AzClay.html

Artscape
http://www.artscape.com/ceramics.html

Clay Arts House (TOUGEI-KAN)
Japanese ceramics
http://www.coara.or.jp/coara/silicon/my.html

Craft Web
http://www.craftweb.com

Goshen College Art Gallery
http://www.goshen.edu/

Kutani Ware.
http://www.njk.co.jp/kutani/

London Potters Guild
http://www.coraltech.com/londonpotters/

National Museum of American Art
http://www.nmaa.si.edu

Manchester Craftsmen's Guild
http://artsnet.heinz.cmu.edu/mcg/

Oregon Potters Association
http://www.oregonpotters.org/

Philadelphia Museum of Art Craft Show
http://www.libertynet.org/~pmacraft

Strictly Functional Show
http://www.art-craftpa.com

Virtual Ceramics Exhibition
http://www.uky.edu/Artsource/vce/
   VCEhome.html

## Historical Pottery and Philosophy

The Arts & Crafts Society
http://www.arts-crafts.com

The Stahl's Pottery Preservation Society
http://www.ot.com/stahls

# Professional Resources, Supplies, and Materials

Sources for supplies and materials are often taken for granted by those in the know. However, except for obvious ceramics supplies and whatever else may be listed in the catalog of your local pottery supply, much of the equipment and paraphernalia useful and even critical to the potter can be difficult to locate.

Always exhaust all local sources for supplies and materials before you search out of your area. Don't assume that because a particular supplier is larger or more well known they can serve you better than a small local store. Likewise, think beyond the obvious source for a particular item and you may find a wider selection and possibly save some money. For example, compressors and airbrushes can be purchased at pottery suppliers, art supply stores, auto supply stores, paint stores and automobile painting equipment and supply stores.

Often I browse hardware stores taking written or mental notes about their inventory. Fasteners, electrical hardware, and all sorts of items designed and sold for one purpose can, with a little bit of imagination, be just the thing you were looking for. Browsing through a commercial restaurant supply, I came across large, heavy-duty spatulas perfect for glaze mixing and better than ones sold at a pottery supply for that purpose. There were also inexpensive plastic containers with firm fitting lids for glaze and slip storage, and large, round, stainless steel bowls that were perfect for draping slabs over and pressing them into. I could go on but I'm sure you get the idea.

I have done the best I could to put these listings into categories, though some defy accurate categorization or have products that span more than one category. Read through the listings to become familiarized as much as possible.

## Professional Resources

Books and magazines are a great resource. Be sure to look at the addendum on magazines and journals. In addition there are specific resource-type publications designed to aid the craftsperson in the area of marketing and promotion.

*AmericanStyle Magazine*
3000 Chestnut Ave.
Suite 304
Baltimore, MD 21211
(800) 642-4314
www.americanstyle.com
Produced by the Rosen Group, contains articles aimed at the craft collector with contact information for the craftspeople whose work appears in the issue.

*Art Calendar*
PO Box 199
Upper Fairmont, MD 21867
(410) 651-9150
Monthly magazine of art and craft business guidance and advice. Also comprehensive listings of shows, grants, residencies, apprenticeships, internships, and other professional opportunities.

*Choices for Craftsmen & Artists:*
*The Yellow Page Directory of Crafts Show Information*
PO Box 484
Rhinebeck, NY 12572
(914) 876-2995
e-mail: smartfrogs@aol.com
Very comprehensive directory of craft shows covering Connecticut, Massachusetts, Vermont, New Jersey, New York, and Pennsylvania. Detailed listings including type of show, entry requirements, and everything you need to know to make informed decisions.

*Crafts Report*
PO Box 1992
Wilmington, DE 19899
(800) 777-7098
Fax (302) 656-4894
The most popular business publication for the craftsperson. Articles about all aspects of marketing, promotion, and business practices. Extensive classified sections and lots of advertisements from galleries, craftspeople, and companies offering marketing tools and materials.

*The Guild*
931 E. Main St. #106
Madison, WI 53703
(800) 969-1556
www.guild.com
Publishers of several art and fine craft source books *including The Architects Sourcebook, The Designers Sourcebook*, and *The Hand Book*. Participating artists are juried and then pay for their listings. Very high quality publications distributed free to the design and gallery trade. Excellent marketing tools.

## Pottery Supplies

Open up a copy of *Clay Times* or *Ceramics Monthly* and you'll find page after page of pottery supply companies, so there's no need for me to rewrite the list here. The ones listed here are ones I have had personal contact with over the years and, at least in my experience, have been reliable, honest, and comfortable to do business with. There are many others just as reliable. Get a copy of *Potters Guide* published by The American Ceramic Society, 735 Ceramic Place, Westerville, OH 43086. It is an annual buyers guide for materials, equipment, and services.

Amherst Potters Supply
47 East St.
Hadley, MA 01035
(413) 586-4507
Full-service potters supply. Carries their own
    moist clays.

Brackers Good Earth Clays
1831 E 1450 Rd.
Lawrence, KS 66044
(888) 822-1982
Friendly, knowledgeable, and helpful full-service
    pottery supply.

Davens
5076 Peachtree Rd.
Atlanta, GA 30341
(800) 695-4805
Full-service potters supply carrying many of the
    well known brands of equipment and supplies.
    Moist clay and materials as well.

Dedell Gas Burner and Equipment Co.
RR1, Box 2135
Newfane, VT 05434
(802) 365-4575
Harry Dedell is the guru of combustion and he
    will be able to help you! Complete line of
    equipment for all gas kilns.

Duralight
School St.
Riverton, CT 06065
(203) 379-3113
Coils for electric kilns. Hundreds in stock. They
    can also duplicate your unique coil if you send
    the broken pieces or furnish electrical
    specifications. Custom designed coils as well.
    Very reliable.

Georgies Ceramic and Clay Co.
756 NE Lombard
Portland, OR 97211
(503) 283 1353
Full-service potter's supply.

Highwater Clays
PO Box 18284
238 Clingman Ave.
Asheville, NC 28814
(704) 252 6033
Full-service potters supply and manufacturers of
    very high quality moist clays. I have often used
    their clays when I'm on the road doing
    workshops and have always been pleased.

Sheffield Pottery Inc.
US Rt. 7, Box 399
Sheffield, MA 01257
(800) SPI CLAY (413) 229-7700
Full-service pottery supply including moist clay,
    materials, equipment, supplies.

Standard Ceramic Supply Co.
PO Box 4435
Pittsburgh, PA 15205
(412) 276-6333
Moist clays, materials, chemicals, and a range of
    supplies.

Trinity Ceramic Supply
9016 Diplomacy Row
Dallas, TX 75247
(214) 631-0540
Full-service potter's supply with wonderful
    people to deal with!

Ward Burner Systems
PO Box 333
Dandridge, TN 37725
(423) 397-2914
Designers and suppliers of combustion systems, ceramic fiber, high temperature wire, brick, assembled raku kilns, industrial vacuum cleaners, and more. Knowledgeable, friendly, and willing to go the extra step for customers.

## Business Tools and Supplies

Some of these companies in the section on office and packing supplies also have products in this category. Be sure to check out your local Staples, Office Depot, or similar store.

Mitchell Graphics Inc.
2363 Mitchell Park Dr.
Petosky, MI 49770
(800) 841-6793
Color cards of all kinds, catalog sheets, brochures, posters, and more. Quantities vary according to the kind of job it is. I have used them with satisfaction.

Modern Postcard
1675 Faraday Ave.
Carlsbad, CA 92008
(800) 959-8365
This is the place to go for full color cards and other color promotional pieces. They target the arts and crafts market. Small quantities are welcome. I've used them numerous times and have never been disappointed.

My Card
division of Amalgamated Technologies Inc.
267 Elm St.
PO Box 354
Somerville MA 02144
(617) 628-4025
Color business cards, postcards, announcements, etc. Caters to the arts and crafts trade. Small quantities are a specialty.

New England Business Services
500 Main St.
Groton, MA 01471
(800) 225-6380
The source for business forms and papers including letterhead, business cards, invoices, sales slips, purchase orders, check writing systems, and much more.

Pate' Poste Adcards
43 Charles St.
Boston MA 02114
(617) 720-2855
All kinds of high quality color cards. 1000 piece runs are the minimum.

ReadyMade: Factory Direct
480 Fillmore Ave.
Tonowanda, NY 14150
(800) 544-2440
Generic signage, labels, tags, and more.

## Industrial Supplies

Including commercial tool suppliers, industrial shelving and storage systems, hardware, and other items too numerous to list or categorize.

American Science & Surplus
3605 Howard St.
Skokie, IL 60076
(847) 982-0870
This catalog truly defies categorization. All kinds of stuff is the best way to describe this. You simply have to have this for at least the entertainment value.

Arrow Safety: Safety Products for School & Industry
1007 Monitor St.
La Crosse, WI 54603
(800) 284-2147
Goggles, face shields, respirators, first aid supplies, back supports.

Arrow Star
3-1 Park Plaza, Dept. 93
Glen Head, NY 11545
(800) 645-2833
Storage systems, shelving, barrels, dollies, packaging, rubber matting, material handling equipment.


Direct Line
6401 West 106th St.
Bloomington, MN 55438
(800) 241-2197
All kinds of industrial and heavy-duty equipment and supplies: heat guns, generators, lawn and garden equipment, tarps, hand tools, air compressors,


Enco: Machinery, Tools & Supplies
5000 W. Bloomingdale
Chicago, IL 60639
(800) 873-3626
Heavy industrial machines and tools. Also hand and power tools. Fun to look at.


Global Industrial Equipment
22 Harbor Park Dr., Dept. 6683
Port Washington, NY 11050
(800) 645-1232
Storage systems, shelving, packaging, carts, work benches, stools, plastic containers, and more.


Lab Safety Supply: Personal & Environmental Safety
PO Box 1368
Manesville, WI 53547-1368
(800) 356-0783
Face protection, gloves, materials handling equipment.

Magid Glove & Safety Manufacturing Co. LLC
2060 North Kolmar Ave.
Chicago, IL 60639
(800) 444-8030
The best source I have found for kevlar gloves, wide selection and good prices. Also other protective equipment including face shields, respirators, and more.


Masune: First Aid & Safety
490 Fillmore Ave.
Tonawanda, NY 14150
(800) 831-0894
Everything in first aid including the usual medical supplies and face protection, back supports, and other supplies.


McMaster-Carr Supply Co.
PO Box 440
New Brunswick, NJ 08903
(201) 329-3200
Also has warehouses in Atlanta, Chicago, and Los Angeles. A very similar concern to W.W. Grainger. A treasure trove of stuff. You should have this catalog in your studio.


McNichols Co.
PO Box 30300
Tampa, FL 33630-3300
(800) 237-3820
All kinds of metal products including wire cloth, perforated metal, grating, expanded metal.


Nilfisk of America
224 Great Valley Parkway
Malvern, PA 19355
(215) 647-6420
Manufacturer of the premier industrial vacuum cleaner. Suitable for fine clay dusts. Several sizes and attachments available. Sold through distributors but also available direct, often at a better price. Onsite service and maintenance contracts available (and recommended). We use this machine at The Potters Shop and it is wonderful.

Northern Professional Equipment & Supply
PO Box 1499
Burnsville, MN 55337-0499
(800) 556-7885
Automotive, air tools, power tools, work gloves, hand tools, hand trucks, materials handling.

Pulmosan Protective Equipment
PO Box 622
Reading, PA 19603
(215) 371-7720
Respirators, kevlar gloves, face protection.

Rand
PO Box 3003
515 Narragansett Park Dr.
Pawtucket, RI 02861-0503
(800) 366-2300
Bags, cartons, tape, shelving, storage bins, packing supplies, scales, matting, stools, workbenches, dollies.

Revere
PO Box 35311
Cleveland, OH 44135
(800) 321-1976
A variety of products including industrial paints, floor marking systems, outdoor furniture and fixtures, asphalt sealers, and other supplies of this type.

Ryerson
PO Box 5376
Chicago, IL 60680
(800) 621-3309
Storage bins and boxes, metal storage cabinets, work benches, hand trucks, and other industrial supplies.

Smith of Galeton
66 Sherman St.
PO Box 215
Galeton, PA 16922
(800) 221-0570
All kinds of work gloves including kevlar and other high heat materials.

Turnkey
500 Fillmore Ave.
Tonawanda, NY 14150
(800) 828-7540
Everything in storage and materials handling: bins, shelving, carts, hand trucks, and more.

W.W Grainger, Inc.
5959 W. Howard St.
Chicago, IL 69648
Branches nationwide This is the catalog to get. From nuts and bolts to fans, barrels, electrical, shelving, flooring, motors, adhesives...I can go on and on. Thousands of pages and thousands of items. Fast service, low prices, they deal only to qualified businesses so be prepared with a business name, letterhead, or other form of substantiating material. Do not be without this catalog. I use them all the time.

## Office and Packaging Supplies

Many of the companies listed under industrial supplies also carry packing and shipping supplies as well as furniture. Local office supply stores and the large chain stores such as Staples and Office Depot are often the best sources for office supplies as well as business forms, packing material, and more.

Associated Bag Co.
400 West Boden St.
Milwaukee, WI 53207
(800) 926-6100
Plastic bags, packing envelopes, boxes, sealing tapes, packing material, strapping.

Consolidated Plastics Co., Inc.
8181 Darrow Road
Twinsburg, OH 44087
(800) 362-1000
Bags, packaging, and shipping supplies, also commercial matting and flooring, plastic containers, and miscellaneous industrial supplies.

DEMCO
PO Box 7488
Madison, WI 53707-7488
(800) 356-1200
Everything for libraries and schools (and for us!).
Office supplies, tape, magazine file cases,
video cases and storage, office furniture, carts,
too many more things to list. Get this catalog.

Modern Office
7545 Golden Triangle Dr.
Eden Prairie, MN 55344
(800) 443-5117
Desks, chairs, tables, shelving, and other office
furnishings.

Paper Direct
100 Plaza Dr.
Secaucus, NJ 07094-3606
(800) 272-7377
Wide variety of decorative and special use papers
for letterhead, brochures, presentations,
certificates, etc.

Premier Packaging
1635 Commons Parkway
Macedon, NY 14502
(800) 203-5558
Retail packaging supplies including gift bags and
boxes, decorative wrap, tags, labels, tissue
paper, and more.

R & M
PO Box 2152
Santa Fe Springs, CA 90670
(800) 231-9600
Invoices, sales slips, tags, security equipment,
packing tape, hand trucks.

Robbins Container Corp.
222 Conover St.
Brooklyn, NY 11231
(718) 875-3204
Cartons, padded bags, bubble wrap, packing
peanuts, tape.

Springfield Corrugated Box, Inc.
74 Moylan Lane
Agawam, MA 01001
(413) 593-5211
New and used cartons, tape, tissue paper, foam,
bubble wrap, miscellaneous materials.

Tape Products
11630 Deerfield Rd.
Cincinnati, OH 45242
(800) 543-4930
All kinds of tapes, packing, and shipping
supplies.

Uline
2200 S. Lakeside Dr.
Waukegan, IL 60085
(800) 295-5510
Shipping supplies of all kinds: wrapping material,
bags, packing supplies, cartons, and more.

# Pottery Workshops, Courses, and Schools

This is a list of pottery schools and studios that
offer workshops during the summer as well as
during the year. For more listings look in the
April issue of *Ceramics Monthly* magazine for
their annual summer workshop directory. Also
consult other magazines on a monthly basis for
workshops and courses. See the suggested reading list for a wonderful and invaluable resource,
*The Guide to Arts & Crafts Workshops*.

Alfred University
Alfred, New York
(607) 871-2412

American Handweaving Museum and Thousand
Island Craft School
314 John St.
Clayton, NY 13624
(315) 686-4123

Ancient Arts
PO Box 27
Masonville, CO 80541
(970) 223-9081
e-mail gwood@psd.k12.co.us

Anderson Ranch Arts Center
PO Box 5598
Snowmass Village, CO 81615
(970) 923-3181
e-mail: artranch@rof.net

Appalachian Center for Crafts
1560 Craft Center Dr.
Smithville, TN 37166
(615) 597-6801

Archie Bray Foundation for the Ceramic Art
2915 Country Club Ave.
Helena, MT 59601
(406) 443-3502
e-mail: archiebray@archiebray.org

Arrowmont School of Arts and Crafts
PO Box 567
Gatlinburg, PA 37738
(423) 436-5860
e-mail: arrowmnt@aol.com
www.smokymtnmall.com/mall/arrowmt.html

Art and Clay Studio
851 W. San Marco #4
Santa Fe, NM 87505
(505) 989-4278

Baltimore Clayworks
5706 Smith Ave.
Baltimore, MD 21209
(410) 578-1919

Banff Centre
Office of the Registrar
Alberta, Canada
(800) 565-9989
e-mail: arts_info@banffcentre.ab.ca
www-nmr.banffcentre.ab.ca

Brookfield Craft Center
PO Box 122, Rte. 25
Brookfield CT 06804
(203) 775-4526

California College of Arts and Crafts
5212 Broadway
Oakland , CA 94610
(510) 594-3710
e-mail: nsadek@CCAC-art.edu

Center for American Archeology
Dept. C, PO Box 366
Kampsville, IL 62053
(618) 653-4316
e-mail: nformationdesk@CAA-archeology.org

Clay Art Center
40 Beech St.
Port Chester, NY 10573
(914) 937-2047

Coyote Arroyo Studios
1753 13th St.
Penrose, CO 81240
(719) 372-6846

Craft Students League
Ceramics Dept.
610 Lexington Ave.
New York, NY 10022
(212) 735-9804

Craft Summer
Miami University
Rowan Hall
Oxford, Ohio 45056
(513) 529-7395
e-mail: Craftsummer@muohio.edu

George Griffin Pottery
1 Suncat Ridge Rd.
Sopchoppy, FL 32358
(850) 962-9311

Great Barrington Pottery
Rte. 41
Housatonic, MA 01236
(413) 274-6259

Greenwich House Pottery
16 Jones St.
New York, NY 10014
(212) 242-4106

Haystack Mountain School of Crafts
PO Box 518
Deer Isle, ME 04627
(207) 348-2306
e-mail: haystack@haystack-mtn.org

Herron School of Art
1701 N. Pennsylvania St.
Indianapolis, IN 46202
(317) 920-2416

Hood College Ceramics Progra
401 Rosemont Ave.
Grederic, MD 21701
(301) 696-3456
web site: www.hood.edu

Horizons
108 N. Main St.
Sunderland, MA 01375
(413) 665-0300
e-mail: horizons@horizons-art.org
web site: www.horizons-art.org

Idyllwild Arts Summer Program
PO Box 38
Idyllwild, CA 92549
(909) 659-2171 ext. 365
e-mail iasumcat@aol.com

Indianapolis Art Center
820 E. 67th St.
Indianapolis, IN 46220
(317) 255-2464
e-mail: inartctr@inetdirect.net
web site: www.indplsartctr.org

Interlaken School of Art
Stockbridge, MA
(413) 298-5252

International Artists in Residence
PO Box 204
703 Wood St. SE
Medicine Hat, Alberta, Canada
(403) 527-8663
e-mail: jjesse@agt.net

John C. Campbell Folk School
1 Folk School Rd.
Brasstown, NC 28902
(800) 365-5724
e-mail: jenjccfs@grove.net
web site: www.grove.net/jccfs

Laloba Ranch Clay Center
PO Box 770226
Steamboat Springs, CO 80477
(970) 870-6423
e-mail: LalobaRanch@compuserve.com

Long Beach Island Foundation of the Arts and
    Sciences
120 Long Beach Blvd.
Loveladies, NJ 08008
(609) 494-1241 ext. 301

Mendocino Art Center
PO Box 765
Mendocino, CA 95460
(707) 937-1764
e-mail: mendoart@mcn.org

Metchosin International School of Art
650 Pearson College
Victoria, BC V9C 4H7 Canada
(250) 391-2420
e-mail: missa@pearson-college.uwc.ca

Montana State University Billings
1500 N. 30 St.
Billings, MT 59101
(406) 657-2303
e-mail: art-selsor@vultur.emcmt.edu

Native Soil
602 Davis St.
Evanston, IL 60201
(847) 733-8006

Nova Scotia College of Art and Design
5163 Duke St.
Halifax, Nova Scotia B3J 3J6
(902) 494-8225
e-mail: nforrest@nscad.ns.ca

Odyssey Center for the Ceramic Arts
236 Clingman Ave.
Asheville, NC 28801
(704) 285-0210
e-mail: odyssey@interpath.com

Oregon College of Art and Craft
8245 S.W. Barnes Rd.
Portland, OR 97225
(503) 297-5544

Penland School of Crafts
Penland, NC 28765
(704) 765-2359

Peter Callas Studio
1 Orchard St.
Belvidere, NJ 07823
(908) 475-8907
e-mail: callas@interpow.net

Peters Valley Craft Education Center
19 Kuhn Rd.
Layton, NJ 07851
(973) 948-5200
e-mail: pv@warwick.net

Pipe Sculpture Workshops
5819 Alder St.
Pittsburgh, PA 15232
(412) 661-0179

River Bend Pottery
22 Riverbend Way
Wilton, NH 03086
(800) 900-1110
e-mail: JBaymore@Compuserve.com

Robert Compton Pottery
3600 Rte. 116
Bristol, VT 05443
(802) 453-3778
e-mail: Robert@RobertComptonPottery.com
www.RobertComptonPottery.com

Rochester Folk Art Guild Pottery
1445 Upper Hill Rd.
Middlesex, NY 14507
(716) 554-3539

Santa Fe Clay
1615 Paseo de Peralta
Santa Fe 87501
(505) 984-1122

School for American Crafts
Rochester Institute of Technology
James E. Booth Bldg.
73 Lomb Memorial Dr.
Rochester, NY 14623-5603
(716) 475-5778
e-mail: RDSFAA@RIT.edu

School of Art, Ceramics
Montana State University-Bozeman
Bozeman, MT 59717
(406) 994-4283
e-mail: zar 7001@montana.edu

Silvermine School of Art
1037 Silvermine Ave.
New Canaan, CT 06840
(203) 866-0411

StoneHaus
2617 N. 12th Ave.
Pensacola, FL 32503
(850) 438-3273

Taos Art School
PO Box 2588
Taos, NM 87571
(505) 758-0350
e-mail: artschol@laplaza.org

Taos Institute of Arts
Box 5280 NDCBU
Taos, NM 87571
(800) 822-7183
e-mail: tia@taosnet.com
web site: www.taosnet.com/tia/

The Ojai Foundation
9739 Ojai Santa Paula Rd.
Ojai, CA 93023
(805) 646-5232

Touchstone Center for Crafts
RD 1, Box 60
Farmington, PA 15437
(724) 329-1370
e-mail: tcc@hhs.net

Truro Center for the Art
Box 756
Truro, MA 02666
(508) 349-7511

Tuscarora School of Pottery
PO Box 7
Tuscarora, NV 89834
(702) 756-5526

Vermont Clay Studio
24 Main St.
Montpelier, VT 05602
(802) 223-4220

Watershed Center for Ceramic Arts
19 Brick Hill Rd.
Newcastle, ME 04553
(207) 882-6075
e-mail: lgipson@saturn.caps.maine.edu

Wesleyan Potters
350 S. Main St.
Middletown, CT 06457
(860) 346-5925

Western Colorado Center for the Arts
1803 N. Seventh St.
Grand Junction, CO 81501
(970) 243-7337

Women's Studio Workshop
PO Box 489
Rosendale, NY 12472
(914) 658-9133

Worcester Center for Crafts
25 Sagamore Rd.
Worcester, MA 01605
(508) 753-8183
e-mail: craftcenter@worcester.org
web site: www.craftcenter.worcester.org

# Index

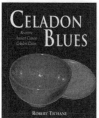

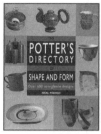

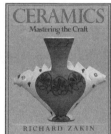